A Jungian Exploration of the Puella Archetype

Girl Unfolding

Susan E. Schwartz

LONDON AND NEW YORK

Designed cover image: Cover Design by Barbara Aliza

First published 2025
by Routledge
4 Park Square, Milton Park, Abingdon, Oxon OX14 4RN

and by Routledge
605 Third Avenue, New York, NY 10158

Routledge is an imprint of the Taylor & Francis Group, an informa business

© 2025 Susan E. Schwartz

The right of Susan E. Schwartz to be identified as author of this work has been asserted in accordance with sections 77 and 78 of the Copyright, Designs and Patents Act 1988.

All rights reserved. No part of this book may be reprinted or reproduced or utilised in any form or by any electronic, mechanical, or other means, now known or hereafter invented, including photocopying and recording, or in any information storage or retrieval system, without permission in writing from the publishers.

Trademark notice: Product or corporate names may be trademarks or registered trademarks, and are used only for identification and explanation without intent to infringe.

British Library Cataloguing-in-Publication Data
A catalogue record for this book is available from the British Library

Library of Congress Cataloging-in-Publication Data
Names: Schwartz, Susan E., 1946– author.
Title: A Jungian exploration of the puella archetype: girl unfolding / Susan E. Schwartz.
Description: Abingdon, Oxon; New York: Routledge, 2025. | Includes bibliographical references and index.
Identifiers: LCCN 2024028011 (print) | LCCN 2024028012 (ebook) | ISBN 9781032582917 (hardback) | ISBN 9781032582887 (paperback) | ISBN 9781003449447 (ebook)
Subjects: LCSH: Archetype (Psychology) | Jung, C. G. (Carl Gustav), 1875–1961. | Women and psychoanalysis.
Classification: LCC BF175.5.A72 S37 2025 (print) | LCC BF175.5.A72 (ebook) | DDC 155.2/644—dc23/eng/20240723
LC record available at https://lccn.loc.gov/2024028011
LC ebook record available at https://lccn.loc.gov/2024028012

ISBN: 978-1-032-58291-7 (hbk)
ISBN: 978-1-032-58288-7 (pbk)
ISBN: 978-1-003-44944-7 (ebk)

DOI: 10.4324/9781003449447

Typeset in Times New Roman
by codeMantra

'Susan Schwartz offers a long-awaited creative incentive to delve into the intricate layers of the puella archetype. What makes this book particularly compelling is its thought-provoking examination of the puella's role in our culture and a re-evaluation of her previous demeaning portrayals. Through a nuanced analysis that draws from diverse disciplines, the author provides a multifaceted view that enriches our understanding of this complex archetype. By intertwining theory with clinical examples and dreams, the author brings the puella archetype to life, making it accessible and relevant to a wide range of readers. This book is an important contribution to the field and a must-read for anyone interested in the complexities of the human psyche.'

Ursula Wirtz, *Jungian analyst, Zürich, Switzerland*

'A study on Puella manifestation in contemporary times, coupled with consideration of its cultural context, is essential for integrating the dualities within the psyche. These dualities include the balancing of feminine and masculine energies, independence and connectedness, vulnerability and strength. The book on Puella is relevant for a deeper understanding of a woman's maturation process and transitions, for revealing sources of feminine potential and creativity.'

Professor Gražina Gudaitė, *Vice President of IAAP*

'In her latest book, *Girl Unfolding – Puella's Emergence: A Jungian Exploration*, Susan Schwartz provides the reader with an astute reappraisal of the puella archetype. Schwartz carefully reveals the positive, creative potential of the puella that has been obscured or lost in traditional interpretations of the puella personality. Weaving together rich clinical vignettes with elements of poetry, philosophy and psychoanalytic thought, Schwartz masterfully creates a much-needed contemporary counterpoint to the familiar, but one-sided conventional interpretations of the puella experience.'

Mark Winborn, *PhD, Jungian psychoanalyst and clinical psychologist. His books include* Interpretation in Jungian Analysis: Art and Technique *and* Jungian Psychoanalysis: A Contemporary Introduction

'Susan Schwartz shares her unique perspective as both a clinical psychologist and a Zürich-trained Jungian analyst as she peels back the layers of the psyche to expose the eternal girl energy in all of us. In this pioneering exploration of the neglected puella archetype, she challenges the notion of preserving youth at all costs, guiding readers to embrace their capacity for symbolisation and trust in the surrender to the as-yet-unknown. By confronting our identification with the father and reclaiming the disregarded and wounded feminine, we can embark on a transformative journey towards a more complete personality.'

Laura London, *creator of* Speaking of Jung *podcast*

A Jungian Exploration of the Puella Archetype

This fascinating new book explores the puella as an archetypal, symbolic and personality figure reaching into the classical foundations of Jungian analytical psychology, focusing on the modern conflicts reverberating personally and culturally to remove the obstacles for accessing our more complete selves.

Puella is youthful, charming and seductive and unfolds the creative, unusual wisdom of the feminine. Postmodern fluidity presents other realities, rethinking and reenacting the truth to oneself. If denigrated, psyche is halted from development, until addressed. The author employs a cross-disciplinary approach and clinical vignettes from narratives of real people from diverse backgrounds reflecting Jungian thought and treatment, along with other psychoanalytical perspectives for the unfolding of puella.

Examining the puella as a key figure in psychological development within a diverse world, this book will be appealing to Jungian analysts, and also to mental health professionals of various paradigms interested in Jungian analytical and philosophical thought.

Susan E. Schwartz is a Jungian analyst and clinical psychologist in Arizona, USA. She has presented at conferences in the USA and worldwide. She has published books with Routledge: *The Absent Father Effect on Daughters: Father Desire, Father Wounds* (2020) and *Imposter Syndrome and the 'As-If' Personality in Analytical Psychology: The Fragility of Self* (2023). Her website is www.susanschwartzphd.com.

To Frederic, a continual and perspicacious critic and support for all my endeavours.

Contents

	Acknowledgements	xi
1	Introduction	1
2	Archetypal girl/woman	4
3	Puella's shadow	17
4	Where is mother?	27
5	The bones of the father	39
6	The empty chair	50
7	The diachrony of dreams	60
8	Beauty – inside the mask	69
9	Performativity	82
10	Bluebeard fairy tale	94
11	Puer quandary	105
12	Unreal to oneself	115
13	Into the void – loss of the symbolic	125

14 A fascist state of mind – the complex	137
15 End notes – gaining joy	149
Index	*153*

Acknowledgements

I want to acknowledge first the many people who I worked with in their analyses.

This book was enhanced by the support of many colleagues, especially Daniela Roher, PhD, who tirelessly read the rough drafts. The book cover reflects the artistic ability and creativity of Barbara Aliza. Katie Randall, editor at Routledge, has continually and enthusiastically supported my ideas and given generously of her time. And I am grateful to the thoughtful and attentive editing of LeeAnn Pickrell.

Chapter 1

Introduction

Follow your passions, we're told. Live according to your values. That's all great, but what if you've lost your way? What if life seems meaningless? Exploring this through the figure of puella as an archetypal, symbolic and personality aspect reaches into the classical foundations of Jungian analytical psychology and forward into future development. The puella is more than youthful, a charmer, appealing and seductive; she represents the energetic, the unusual and the wisdom of the feminine in her many forms. Harkening back while looking forward, the puella figure lives out differently in each of us. She leads to creative and innovative expression, pointing to the future. When distorted and disturbed, however, she halts the development of the psyche until these issues are addressed. As James Hillman wrote in *The Puer Papers*, 'She can be too preoccupied about being unlovable, believing her love could be false' (1989, p. 57).

In this book the narratives of real people, their struggles and accomplishments, combine with Jungian thought along with other psychological and philosophical perspectives to portray the many facets of this aspect of the personality. It entails a journey from the classical Jungian approach to the current day to reconnect parts of the self. There are many aspects puella needs to face and move beyond, especially how narrowly she has been defined. How easily the fictions and true stories could trade places, how quickly the verities of her life could confuse and keep her from being able to think about her realities. Feelings, mourning, grief and acknowledgement of depression can evolve to desire, imagination and access to the symbolic in encounters forging transformation.

I am writing this from my years of experience as a Jungian analyst working with people who do not know how to harness this puella energy creatively or how to access its potential as a part of feminine. The puella has often been demeaned, described as remaining too young, ethereal and unrealistic, unknown and unconscious, even a self-centred narcissist. In extreme cases, the puella person cannot root in life, unable to take themself or the world seriously, and they remain complicit in an intricate series of psychological webs. Jung commented in 'The Psychology of the Child Archetype', 'The "eternal child"… is an indescribable experience, an incongruity, a handicap, and a divine prerogative; an imponderable that determines the ultimate worth or worthlessness of a personality' (1968, CW 9i, para. 300).

This writing aims to rescue the puella aspect of the personality from the past where women have been treated as though being a girl is an indication of stunted growth. They learn to stop growing at the girl level, meaning they can never achieve maturity, which has actually meant some form of mimicry of 'manhood'. Because she is rendered inadequate, the word *girl* has been associated and synonymous with growth interrupted. Here, on the other hand, is a revaluing of the girl – puella – with her trove of talents and creativities marking this aspect of the personality. Women and the puella within us all are special, not as the unfinished masculine or in the likeness of the male, but as solid and clear in our own right (D. Roher, personal communication).

The chapters present different aspects, discontinuities and challenges to the puella type, illustrated with clinical examples, dreams and symbols linking the personal to the collective. The content for her unfolding appears in the images, feelings, somatic manifestations and synchronicities informing life experiences. Each clinical example notes the hindrances and the pathways through them. The knowledge acquired facilitates the unfolding movement in the active process of personality transformation.

Aspects of puella as a symbolic and psychological figure appeared in my previous two books and received much commentary. People, yes mostly women, not only cisgender but also lesbian and heterosexual, all from various ethnic backgrounds, colours and cultural heritages, conveyed relief in being understood and supplied with validating information. Their interior life and its conflicts were finally being recognised, identified and acknowledged rather than put down. Their resonance with puella reaffirmed the significance of this part of their personality. Puella's hunger for life is passionate and fierce. However, many have lost the certainty of what it is they love and what brings ecstasy and joy. They yearn to reclaim their bodies and souls, the passions inspiring creativity, to be fully alive, setting new flexible patterns. Puella embodies the bud opening to potential, youth and new beginnings extant within us all.

Yet, this book is not only for or about beginners or only women but also for the feminine in its many defined and undefined forms living in us all. The 'girl unfolding' promotes exploration and interest in the emerging psychological depths. There are also cultural effects from the process of engagement in analytical work. Although puella is the eternal girl, she is the late bloomer and contains potential that can manifest throughout the life cycle. She appears in the figure of Salome in the Bible, the young daughter of Elijah in Jung's *Red Book*, and was noted in Jung's dream of a young girl in his autobiography *Memories, Dreams, Reflections*. Both can be interpreted as images and symbols of the puella and are apparent in our current era.

This book is meant to educate and provide ideas that readers can apply to their lives. The language is not inordinately technical but clearly presents the terminology of Jungian thought. This material is complex to provoke thoughtful reflection. It also applies to mental-health professionals of various paradigms and those in any form of therapy through the clinical vignettes and therapeutic discussions.

The information is replete with examples of people, their dreams and life backgrounds. These examples are intended for readers to relate to and identify with traits illustrating the inclusivity and breadth of the psyche.

The cross-disciplinary approach highlights connections beyond Jungian borders not only because this is more interesting but also because the singularity of theory and ideas is averse to the expansiveness of the psyche. In this vein I have included material from the American philosopher Judith Butler on valuing our bodies; information on the dead mother complex from French psychoanalyst André Green; and the perspectives of Julia Kristeva, French Lacanian psychoanalyst. They bring focus to the various feminine forms and means of expression, including that of the body.

I include a sampling from various aspects of depth psychology, both theory and clinical, and have tried to be as current as possible. However, I have not found anything specifically devoted to puella in the Jungian literature. There are numerous writings on Kore, Persephone and other maiden goddesses and archetypes but not much material on the girl/child/youth in its puella form. Throughout are quotes from poetry, literature, philosophy and psychoanalytic thought as further expressions of the range of the psyche. Puella needs a more complete portrayal of her role and value in the personality and culture. Conceptually the unfolding of ideas and ways of becoming is inherent in the puella herself.

References

Hillman, J. (1989). *The puer papers.* Spring Publications.
Jung, C. G. (1968). *The collected works of C. G. Jung: Vol. 9i. The archetypes and the collective unconscious.* Princeton University Press.

Chapter 2

Archetypal girl/woman

> We are not provided with wisdom, we must discover it for ourselves, after a journey through the wilderness which no one else can take for us, an effort which no one can spare us.
>
> Marcel Proust, *Within a Budding Grove* (1924)

What does the puella part of the personality and femininity look like? What happens when we decouple femininity from female bodies? We are led to puella with imagination and hope, enchanted and curious about her elusive elements. As Jungian analyst Toni Wolff said years ago, 'What is of practical importance is the awareness of the existence of the problem, and the attempt to resolve the state of inner confusion by attaining greater consciousness' (1956, p. 2). Although the puella character can form within the psyche in various ways, this perspective focuses on the prominent effect of the absent father and the absorption in the mother who is emotionally missing without sufficient connection to her being.

Puella is noticeable with a certain style, a freshness and interest. She can be of any age, energetic with ideas and hope. However, she can also be bogged down with a secret numbness, like carrying a dead weight. The zest is compromised; the strength is as well. She is smart, quick, and the development of personality has yet to unfold. She needs time as something became stunted. It can come from parental lack, neglectful family systems and structures and culturally limiting and prescribed aspects. She is withheld, living behind a wall, taken with destructive complexes and unable to access a more complete self. This exploration is to free her from the shackles and projections into her more natural movement. She is the girl becoming and emerging from what has been into what she can be.

Puella is described through archetypal images and the etymology of the word itself. She is aligned with the maiden of mythology. She is a figure in the life cycle, as Jungian analyst Murray Stein noted, 'The imagos people realize in their individual development are based on archetypal forms which are relatively timeless and unchanging, are shaped by history and culture' (1998, p. 120). We learn about ourselves by examining the puella's roles and enactments, unconscious assumptions and perceptions, acquired consciously and unconsciously.

Puella represents the young feminine on the brink of becoming and at a crossroads. She exists between her individual nature, energy, youth and the innovative, yet can be drawn back to traditional ways. Puella is the creative, unusual, desirous and different. Even so, often infirm in her position, she can become waylaid. Whether women or men, heterosexual, lesbian, gay or nonbinary, puella remains a concept and personality aspect to be understood and made conscious in all people.

Puella stands on a historical, mythological, cultural and personal continuum, symbolising one form of the category called feminine. She works the female voice out of its conformity and repression into creative spaces with her rebellious nature. Her challenging of traditional patterns takes courage, dedication and devotion. This emerges through the process of individuation and by exploring the many facets of the psyche to find what it means to be true to herself.

For example, at the core of Jungian psychology is an understanding that we are a mixture of male and female, masculine and feminine. Notions of woman, man and the feminine are altering dramatically, and more shifts are on the horizon. This presents challenges, not for pathologising but for psyche transforming. The Jungian perspective presents ways of understanding what this means in our current era. Thinking about the feminine has changed with cultural attitudes and awareness of the varieties of conscious and unconscious identifications.

These variations enlarge our understanding while also creating misperceptions. Gender stereotypes indicate the need to rethink gender assumptions influenced by traditional hegemonic codes shaping many of the current adaptations. The fundamental tensions for navigating gender represent radical and widespread changes in the sociocultural environment. As Jung commented, 'It has always seemed to me that I had to answer questions which fate had posed to my forefathers, and which had not yet been answered … things which previous ages had left unfinished' (Jung, 1989 p. 233). The portrayal here is the unfolding of puella through addressing some of these questions, difficulties, challenges and promises.

Puella is fluid; she is the feminine emerging in ways different from previous generations when denied and repressed. This puella exploration marks an era of gender fluidity with open-ended descriptions of feminine aspects. It puts us in an unprecedented land, with self-definitions changing, a moving kaleidoscope of the imaginal, the unknown. Yet, this is not a list of traits and clear markings. We are not one way or another; we are a spectrum, a changing combination, a synthesis creating new forms, the self made of disparate parts based on unconscious energies and forms (Stein, 2022, p. 33). This self is a plurality of new forms, contradictions and challenges without cookie-cutter application.

Puella grapples with various limitations as this aspect also represents the scared and confused, seeking to erase an internal misery. In the series of personal composite vignettes an intriguing and poignant portrait emerges. New attitudes usher in new times, revealing the truths and struggles about what it means to be human. Puella is tender, perceptive and intelligent, yet can resist embracing the shadow with its unknown qualities and the possibility of seeing herself in a new expanded light. As Jung said,

> The shadow is a tight passage, a narrow door, whose painful constriction no one is spared who goes down to the deep well. But one must learn to know oneself to know who one is. For what comes after the door is, surprisingly enough, a boundless expanse of unprecedented uncertainty.
>
> (1968a, CW 9i, para. 45)

Archetype described

The archetype's relevance alters with the times and ideology. There is currently debate and many disputations about what the Jungian concept of the archetype means. I reference Jung's description of the archetypes as general pathways to be filled differently by each of us, 'representations that vary a great deal without losing their basic pattern' (1954, CW 18, para. 523). This is a term generally used to denote something well known and recognised, and it is even part of the general vernacular. The archetype unfolds in its metaphorical nature. Ambivalence and ambiguity lay within the notion of the archetype with its differentiation and complexity oscillating in a dynamic continuum. The archetype and its psychological implications along with the writings of Jung and other Jungian analysts support this viewpoint.

About this controversial subject Jung himself noted in 'General Aspects of Dream Psychology':

> Archetypes, so far as we can observe and explain them at all, manifest themselves only through their ability to organize images and ideas, and this is always an unconscious process which cannot be detected until afterwards. By assimilating material whose provenance in the phenomenal world is not to be contested they become visible and psychic.
>
> (Jung, 1969, CW 8, para. 440)

I use the archetype 'not as reified but what it means to be human and what the psyche needs for healing and wholeness ... with a collectively shared sphere which is unconscious and can impact groups and processes' (Roesler, 2024, p. 245).

The archetype appears through symbols, motifs and themes portraying universal human experiences, punctuated with an emotional range from ecstasy to melancholy. 'We could characterize analytical psychology as a poetic science – concerned with finding, and even creating, meaning' (Roesler, 2024, p. 244). Contained within the archetype are the paradoxes of opposites, a spectrum of possibilities connected through feelings, thoughts, emotions, ideas. In 'Psychology of the Child Archetype', Jung said in one of his numerous descriptions of the archetype: 'Not for a moment dare we succumb to the illusion that an archetype can be finally explained and disposed of ... The most we can do is to dream the myth onwards and give it a modern dress' (1968a, CW 9i, para. 271).

To add to the classical approach to the archetype, its definition and controversy, Jung called the anima an archetype. Therefore, in classical Jungian thought, puella is a form of the anima archetype, or the feminine within us all. Moreover, Jung called the anima soul. He commented, 'In a man the soul, i.e., or inner attitude, is represented in the unconscious by definite persons with the corresponding qualities. Such an image is called a "soul image". Sometimes these images are of quite unknown or mythological figures' (1971, CW 6, para. 808). Here the anima is attributed to the male psyche but updating this concept leads to a fuller definition. As Jung said in a letter dated 8 June 1959, 'The androgyny of the anima may appear in the anima herself' (Jung, 1976; Hillman, 1985, p. 65). The anima has also been described as 'inward ... virginal, closed, generative yet reserved ... an interiority of movement deepening downward ... She is also a reflective factor with "soul-stirring" emotions' (Hillman, 1985, p. 23).

The anima is described as providing a sense of being, and when absent and inaccessible, a person feels the void and emptiness, as the relationship to an essential part of themselves is unavailable. Without relationship to the anima, they feel depersonalised, as Hillman noted (1985, p. 105), due to the loss of personal involvement, a certain interior reflection and introspection, not caring and not believing in their value or purpose. Meaning has disappeared. Here Jung suggested meaning can be restored by accessing the image and imagination (1968b, CW 13, para. 75). Reviving the images leads to accessing a form of self-definition and aliveness. Hillman reminds us of Jung's dream of the girl and the dove, and in this, how Jung became himself through imagination (Hillman, 1985, p. 113). This girl might be representative of puella; as such, by following the image, we find her associated with the spirit in the form of the dove. She seems a significant figure leading we do not know where, but embodying mystery, hope and possibility.

Both Jung and Hillman recognised the value of all forms of the feminine as residing not only in women and men but also in the psyche where she exists in myriad aspects expressed through each person's individual path. As puella comes alive within, the images she inhabits become more creative and fuller with meaning. Puella becomes a valuable part of what enlivens us, restores life balance and supplies energy.

Puella, as an archetype humanly lived in each of us, represents movement in time, revealing patterns and tendencies of psychological development. Jung suggested this archetypal predisposition, this orientating structure, is filled out and given content by the external world. It is experienced and taken in, linked with the archetypal predispositions and rendered meaningful by them. Jung also said, 'It [the archetype] persists throughout the ages and requires interpreting anew. The archetypes are imperishable elements of the unconscious, but they change their shape continually' (1968a, CW 9i, para. 301). The process of interpreting anew is what this expose aims to do. This includes the large and small incremental processes of rebirth, transformation and renewal occurring through the developmental stages involving separation, differentiation, dismemberment and unification.

The universe of the archetypes and their symbolic representations appear in world mythologies. They enact a continuum through history in a psychological and cultural way, widening our personal psyche and connecting us to others. Jung said to Freud in a letter dated 1909, 'We shall not solve the ultimate secrets of neurosis and psychosis without mythology and the history of civilization' (McGuire, 1974, p. 279). We need myth in our lives to gain meaning because we easily think in story form. Stories are how we best remember the important events in our own lives and the lives of those around us, including world events. Myth outlines the natural and often challenging cycles depicting life's rites of passage.

The mythology of puella

The myths here relate to Western consciousness, yet there are similar figures in other cultures emphasising similar and different personality traits. Exploring the tradition of the Greek myths whose symbols and characters have influenced Western culture illustrates psychological and physical dynamics passed down through the ages concerning the feminine. Examining them helps us understand their influence as we evaluate whether they fit or not. This look back is part of comprehending the present while unfolding into the future.

The goddesses Artemis and Persephone (Kore) link to each other and are the maiden part of the triple goddess cycle. They are associated with the maiden, the girl energy; they represent freedom and learning within the stage prior to adulthood and are foundational to development throughout life. By exploring these archetypal figures, we can understand in a broader way the joyful and the difficult aspects of puella.

Knowing these traits helps us better understand relationship patterns, strengthens our choices and decisions in life and aligns us with our essence. For example, the fluctuations of symbiosis and separation in the myth of Demeter and Persephone reflect the ever-changing relationship between mothers and daughters as a part of the movement towards maturation.

This myth also repeats historically intrusive actions by the male. These represent rough personal and societal treatment that aims to subdue the feminine, the young girl. Persephone is raped by Hades, forced without recourse until she decides to eat one pomegranate seed that he gives her. In this small but significant act, she establishes independence and choice and the return to earth and mother, separate from her life in the underworld and Hades.

Artemis

The mythology of all cultures is replete with jockeying for power relations and gender stereotypes. Too often women have been rendered passive and subservient, relegated to supporting the male protagonist. This leads us to the figure of Artemis who is aligned with puella as she is the guardian of young girls' development. Artemis resists patriarchal control, manipulation and the oppression of women, firmly opposing male authority. She illustrates the emancipatory potential of female resilience, wisdom and agency. She teaches feminine power, respect and equality, authenticating, restoring and empowering the physical strength and fortitude of girls.

Artemis protects and teaches as the goddess of the virginal psyche, the incubating, fresh, interior and imaginal containment of energy (Hillman, 1989, p. 190). The virginal reference denotes the singular, wrapped within itself, gestating and not yet ready to open. As virgin she is self-directed, autonomous, enclosed with her attention focused inwards. Virginity means obedience to what she was created to be and what will be awakened and revealed (Shorter, 1987, p. 128). She is athletic, with a spirit of adventure and swiftness along with restlessness. She has the passion and persistence to go the distance and succeed. The personification of Artemis represents an independent spirit – indomitable, untamed, unsubdued, an activist for new feminine growth in the personality.

Artemis is one of the androgynous goddesses endowed with a seamless integration of masculine energy, and she does not need or want the male. Her self-sufficiency prefers solitude and avoids vulnerability by not expressing emotional needs to others. Artemis tends towards emotional distancing and does not trust or engage in intimate relationships. She rejects culturally prescribed behaviours and traditional portrayals of girls as helpless, charming and compliant pleasers.

She is the patroness of the youthful spirit, protects women in childbirth and mothering and the young. Artemis is not a mother but displays other means for nurturance as a goddess of nature, concerned with the outdoors, animals, environmental protection and women's communities. She symbolises the regenerative earth power. She promotes coming to be, representing the defenceless, not as victims but in recognition of the tenderness and vulnerability of new developments needing careful attention, protection and guidance to grow.

Persephone the maiden

Puella exists as the maiden within the female triad of maiden-mother-crone aspects through the arc of life. Western cultural heritage aligns her with the Greek goddesses Artemis and Persephone (Kore). Persephone and Artemis both represent the virginal, the unwed, and are close to nature. However, in the myth Persephone is violently wrenched from childhood, raped and radically changed. This act of violence by her father Zeus's brother Hades brutally separates Persephone from the past life with her mother. This harsh act represents the overpowering by the male dominant patriarchy. It can be likened to the susceptibility of puella to similar influences. Persephone marries Hades and has a child from the rape. Her eating the pomegranate seed given to her by Hades allows her to return to the earth and her mother a portion of every year. Her role as queen of the lower world of the dead combines with the vegetation goddess or Kore in the actions of both shooting forth and withdrawing into the earth like the seasonal changes.

Kore, the maiden, represents youthful demeanour, the still standard judging of the feminine by outer beauty ideals. However, there are dangerous consequences if this is all she is. Women can learn to restrain their forwards movement by becoming an ideal object and unconsciously subject to manipulation by male or patriarchal and traditional ways of being. Being only Kore can indicate an undeveloped part of the personality, internalising patriarchal ideals in the absence of other modelling. It can lead to disappointments in the second half of life, such as inhibition of interior growth, an inability to continue a full life, frustration, psychological crises and loss of meaning.

I have discovered the following in cultural traditions addressing puella and the treatment of the feminine:

> The African /Xam, Swahili, Sudanese, Senegalese and Zulu folktales illustrate the emancipatory and disruptive potential of female power, resilience, wisdom and agency. These contradict, challenge, or satirize androcentric authority. Some folklore also resists or subverts patriarchal control, manipulation, exclusion, and the oppression of women. Their goal-directed events are empowering and liberating for females.
>
> (Sheik, 2018, p. 47)

For example, in a story referencing education for girls in Togolo, the chief ordered girls to attend school and thus they were forbidden from the arduous task of drawing water from far-off bore holes. The wisdom of folklore, myth, fantasy and social history instigates social change and egalitarian relations while celebrating the women of Africa as key protagonists, appearing profound in their power and their humanity (p. 53). This reinforces feminine power and respect, justice and equality. Such narratives authenticate female agency and are restorative and empowering to the African woman's psyche.

However, without the guidance of female models and cultural sanctions, an unstructured girlhood leaves a young woman emotionally and physically vulnerable. Grounding the archetypal in the present-day personal is the case of Petra. Her father spied on her when she was younger, setting up emotional unease, lack of basic confidence, trust or safety. No one believed how betrayed and insecure she felt. She held the disappointments and apprehensions within and eagerly responded at an early age to any overtures from males to be physically intimate. She was seeking love but fell into the Hades energy. Petra had no model of an Artemis mother, only one who could hardly protect herself. She used Petra as a confidant, a partner but not a girl child. Petra took on a radical look, signalling she did not fit in; she was an independent-appearing person, but she was highly dependent and in need of a foundation of safe love.

As an adult Petra was bewildered, wanted to be saved and felt small and needy. A series of partners were possessive and turned violent, raging, abusive emotionally. She left one after the other, each time feeling more defeated and depressed. Her vibrant energy diminished. She tried various medications to compensate the despair. Finally, she began searching in-depth psychologically, commenting she now realised what it was to reflect and value her thoughts and reactions.

She had repeated dreams of her childhood home, each one a bit different, but the return there brought some inner peace, and then she remembered the discomfort of home: Mother listened to her, but she was preoccupied and always doing something else. Father was playful when she was small, but upon puberty, like puella, she could not trust him and kept away. Whatever was in the house was haunting her through the dreams, calling her back into the recesses she tried to forget but needed now to recall for proceeding in her life. As we journeyed through dream after dream Petra slowly began to emerge from the years of torment and depression held within her psyche. This was externally enacted with the partners she chose who further damaged her with possessive and rough treatment. She had formerly been helpless to protect herself but was now beginning to recognise this was detrimental to the love and security she so desired. A previously unknown strength was blooming within her.

Etymology of puella

There are many nuances to puella and a mixture of seemingly contradictory aspects evident in the etymology of this word. It is a term describing the 'emotional associations of a diminutive applied to female children and older girls viewed as erotic objects; it is also used to denote young married women in the sense of being virgin' (Hallett, 2013, p. 203). The Roman elegiac poet Catullus was credited with the use of *puella*, previously a noun for the female child. The term

> designated an affectionately regarded, erotically desired female who was not the wife or paid sexual partner of the male poet or speaker, implying that the women referred to by this term engaged in sexually transgressive conduct that at times involved payment for their favors.
>
> (p. 206)

Puella denoted the young, attractive and clever woman in poetry, music and dance who was considered charming and accomplished through these achievements.

Moreover, the phrase *docta puella* referred to the learned girl aligned with the poet lover, sharing values and interests in disregard of the conventional (Sharrock, 2003, p. 324). Puella was beloved but not married due to her irregular lifestyle. She was idealised, considered to have sophistication and an exciting nature, but she was not part of the Roman noble class where women were without education and could hold no place in literature. Puella was outside the standards of respectable Roman matron due to her artistic and cultural training; however, she still needed the man to propagate her writing due to the way society was then structured (p. 336).

Modern girl/woman

Puella aeterna is the eternal child, but one who feels a fraud, shameful, small, vulnerable and fearful, often based on not being enough. The hallmark of the puella aeterna is one who lives provisionally, hiding in the shadows of disconnection, self-loathing and disavowal of authentic self-expression, while refusing the unconscious parts in need of integration (Schwartz, 2020). Such feelings may be recognised in persecutory internal figures, harsh self-assessments and critiques and emotionally distant partnerships. Without an accurate inner mirror, she assesses herself with inferiority. She needs to be adored but nothing is enough to compensate for the inner emptiness.

Trapped in fantasy, she lives in a bubble, abdicating to the male mirror, submissive, her individuality halted. The narcissistic wounds coincide with an underdeveloped capacity for empathy and compassion for herself as well as others. She is tough on herself and relentlessly critical. There is a destructive and envious force behind the aggression, feeding a determination to win. An inability to satisfy these internal demands leads to depression and anxiety.

This aspect of puella in the personality reflects the destructive side of Eros who was the Greek god referring to relatedness and love. The ancient Greek language distinguished four ways of love: *érōs*, or to be in love with, to desire passionately or sexually; *philía* to have affection for; *agápē* to have regard for, be contented with; and *storgē*, used especially to refer to the love of parents and children or a ruler and his subjects. All these definitions involve passion and emotions. But these are the areas where puella feels the inadequate self-love fighting with self-hate. The sense of ease with others is often coloured by worry about acceptability. Trust is not easily won or established. The virginal nature, inner isolation and singularity are difficult to give up as they have been her retreat and safe space.

Plurality of psyche

The lens here focuses on the modern personality dealing with conflicts and obstacles that present difficulty in finding entry gates for development, initiative, hope and promise. British Jungian analyst Andrew Samuels has written extensively on recognising the plurality of the psyche: 'Pluralism is an approach to conflict that tries to reconcile differences without imposing a false synthesis on them ... without sight of the truth of each element' (2016, p. xii). Puella is an aspect highlighting the multitudinous nature and truths of the psyche. Puella is not simple, but complex and filled with paradoxes. As we explore her through personal narratives, tales, myths, dreams and analytical treatment, we begin to strip away what distracts from her evolution and discover what can promote her value.

She represents the chance to be conscious, to resolve and to ameliorate the personal pain, conflicts and symptoms compromising her life. She heeds, repels and bargains with her discomfort with incompleteness. Puella as active and accessible throughout life represents the desire, enthusiasm and joy needed, perhaps even more so in the elder years. People of older ages want to understand what has shaped them, especially when the puella aspect has gone unexamined until later life. This is not uncommon, although, as mentioned, cultural and Jungian thought on this figure and her influence on the life cycle has been scanty.

In an example, puella is an aspect motivating a woman in her 70s who is coping with the news of Parkinson's disease. Ageing becomes difficult as more courage is needed, and the threat of breaking down increases. She could fall into unfathomable despair, yet the developmental task is to accept her shock, agency and power consciously and use it creatively and openly. Even as her hope has shaded into sadness, discouragement has also shifted into determination. She realises the psychical and emotional demands looming ahead and faces this with resolve to amass the energy to continue and use her interests as valuable sources for sustenance.

Portrayals of puella have tended to reduce her to a cliche, noncommittal in love life as a mere waiting room. Jung called the child image:

> a symbol which unites the opposites ... capable of the numerous transformations ... it can be expressed by roundness, the circle or sphere, or else by the quaternary as another form of wholeness. I have called this wholeness that transcends consciousness the self.
>
> (1968a, CW 9i, para. 278)

Here, puella is a key figure in psychological development, but she often has been a mystery to herself as well as to others, elusive, desiring to be seen but shying from the intimacy of being known.

In popular usage the archetype is identified as a recognised idea, a pattern we each fill differently. The puella is a psychological descriptor unfolding and exemplifying how to develop and give birth to oneself. Simone de Beauvoir, French author of *The Second Sex* (1972), quite famously said, 'One is not born, but rather becomes, a woman'. Puella becoming and expanding means recognising the unconscious, bringing rewards, joy and hope.

> In a nutshell, the archetypal may also be seen as a gradation of affect, something in the eye and heart of the beholder, not in what he or she beholds or experiences. We can think of the quality of a perception or collection of perception, qualities of preoccupation, fascination, autonomy, awe.
>
> (Samuels, 2016, p. 25)

These descriptors combine with examples from Jungian analytical treatment to integrate the puella figure as she emerges, shaped through the complex interactions between individual and culture. This writing paradoxically occurs amid fraught times of cultural and social upheaval, disasters and experiences that daily accentuate the need for self and other awareness. Especially during so much upheaval, we need the puella of youth, the daring unattached to tradition, the playful and the creative.

Puella is one of our many guides through life, composed of various images and symbols and creating a kaleidoscope of increasing consciousness. She represents a creative spark yet needs intent, focus and shaping to unfold the potential contained within her. When easily drawn to each new and innovative thing, she can represent floundering and lack as youth itself does not have enough ballast. Or she might dwell in the shadows, entrapped by complexes into narrow roles, stripping individuality and preventing self-acceptance. This part can be burdened by childhood developmental residues, psychological pitfalls, ponderous cultural dictates and transgenerational heritage.

As you will discover in these pages, puella faces challenges and psychological limitations within herself, relationally and culturally. Her attempts at consciousness can become a hall of mirrors, the frames constructed from early childhood resulting in her being painfully awake or seemingly and irrevocably dead. On the shadow side, many puella types find themselves caught in a restrictive life, impersonating but not being real. Admittedly there is a harrowing nature to transformation as it does not come easily. It takes awareness to the ways we are programmed and collude in our diminishment. Although the puella, or the eternal girl, has strength, savvy, pleasure and creativity, there are many traumas and emotional terrors to comprehend for psychological integration and conscious awareness of this young, pervasive and influential feminine figure.

The ignored characteristics of puella represent the disregarded and wounded feminine and highlight the cultural influences perpetuating these wounds. Society's patriarchal, normative standards and stereotypes have tended to entangle and derail her mind, body and soul. These structures and predominant psychological assumptions perpetuate and unconsciously govern social, professional and interpersonal spheres. As Toni Morrison commented, 'How can a woman be viewed and respected as a human being without becoming male-like or a male-dominated citizen?' (2019, p. 86). This book, ranging from the personal and relational to the collective in conscious and unconscious aspects, involves shifts and complexities while offering ways to disrupt the negative narratives surrounding the images and symbols of puella.

Unfortunately, puella learns early to fit into a box susceptible to parental and cultural conceptions, expectations and limitations. Personal and cultural history, including covert and overt influences, cause many to denigrate their mind and body shape, stifle desires and make themself less than. Especially when subtle, this continues the destructive norms and warped ideals projected onto the feminine.

Although representing enchantment, glitter, wanderlust and curiosity, puella has been downplayed as inadequate and unaware. The qualities of energy, courage and brilliance as well as development and insight are often minimised. Awareness of her as an aspect of the personality – psychologically, physically, emotionally – offers a different dimension. It means we reconsider the circumferences unconsciously placed on the stories we continue to tell ourselves. Postmodern fluidity brings the opportunities of other realities, rethinking and re-enacting how we express ourselves and live true to who we are. Puella, representing new beginnings, also means to listen and value her way of being. The task is to transform the wounds and scars from prior experiences into personality expansion.

We reside in an era with much alienation and destruction to self and others. Within this magnitude of change, uncertainties and transitions, humanity is undergoing another particularly challenging time. Hiding from the terror of falling into a black hole, or the void of nonexistence, exacerbates the threat to psychic survival in the air. It is also disturbingly overlaid with narcissism as a means of turning away in defence against feeling the disappointments and the immensity of the losses. Warren Colman, British Jungian analyst (2006, p. 35), wrote about narcissists tending to assert their imagination of the world as the world. Reality testing then disappears.

Duly noted

Puella as portrayed here is confronted with what is difficult, torn, the shadows and the psyche in conflict. Puella's tragedy takes various forms in an inability to love or feel, affecting mind, body and soul. The ego is fragile, the persona rigid, functioning as façade, with the self abandoned and enthusiasm dulled. Because the psyche also forms from what has been absent, development is possible. A woman cries out that she does not have the right image due to her skin colour, her eyes, her body shape, and she is depressed. She is creative, talented, striking, intelligent, but struggles to manifest confidence and sustain energy. She wonders how to cope with the noise of social media bombarding her, the pieces of herself she cannot bear and seeks to live beyond dominant cultural limitations. This puella woman has the chance to emerge from the mire into herself as she explores the meaning of her suffering in Jungian analytical treatment. In the Terry Lectures, Jung noted the benefits of this work, not only for the woman but also for the world itself:

> Such a [wo]man knows that whatever is wrong in the world is in [herself]himself, and if [s]he only learns to deal with [her]his own shadow [s]he has done something real for the world. [S]he has succeeded in shouldering at least an infinitesimal part of the gigantic, unsolved social problems of our day.
>
> (Jung, 1938, para. 74)

We want to know about puella. The more we recognise the ongoing issues, the more definitive she becomes with personal and collective ramifications. Being conscious of puella, she ceases to be an object and she unfolds into being creative and potent, confident as she discovers her agency, connecting to self and others. Jung wrote, 'It is to be hoped that experience in the years to come will sink deeper shafts into this obscure territory, on which I have been able to shed but a fleeting light' (Jung, 1989, p. 301). She then untangles from the rhetoric of stereotypes, recognises and accesses the freedom to wander in her mind, releasing herself into the full imaginativeness of her being.

References

de Beauvoir, S. (1972). *The second sex*. Penguin.
Colman, W. (2006). Imagination and the imaginary. *Journal of Analytical Psychology*, *51*(1), 21–41.

Hallett, J. 2013. Intersections of gender and genre: Sexualizing the *Puella* in Roman comedy, lyric and elegy. *Revue EuGeStA, 3,* 195–208.
Hillman, J. (1985). *Anima: An anatomy of a personified notion.* Spring Publications.
Hillman, J. (1989). *A blue fire.* Spring Publications.
Jung, C. G. (1938). *Psychology and religion (The Terry Lectures Series).* Yale University Press.
Jung, C. G. (1954). *The collected works of C. G. Jung: Vol. 18. The symbolic life.* Pantheon Books.
Jung, C. G. (1968a). *The collected works of C. G. Jung: Vol. 9i. The archetypes and the collective unconscious.* Pantheon Books.
Jung, C. G. (1968b). *The collected works of C. G. Jung: Vol. 13. Alchemical studies.* Princeton University Press.
Jung, C. G. (1969). *The collected works of C. G. Jung: Vol. 8. The structure and dynamics of the psyche.* Princeton University Press.
Jung, C. G. (1971). *The collected works of C. G. Jung: Vol. 6. Psychological types.* Princeton University Press. (Original work published 1921).
Jung, C. G. (1976). *C. G. Jung letters, Vol. 2: 1951–1961* (G. Adler, Ed.). Princeton University Press.
Jung, C. G. (1989). *Memories, dreams, reflections* (A. Jaffe, Ed.) (R. Winston & C. Winston, Trans.). Vintage. (Original work published 1961).
McGuire, W. (Ed.). (1974). *The Freud/Jung letters.* Princeton University Press.
Morrison, T. (2019). *The source of self-regard.* Alfred Knopf.
Proust, M. (1924). *Within a budding grove [In the shadow of young girls in flower].* (C. K. S. Moncrief, Trans.). The Modern Library. https://www.gutenberg.org/cache/epub/63532/pg63532-images.html
Roesler, C. (2024). *Deconstructing archetype theory: A critical analysis of Jungian ideas.* Routledge.
Samuels, A. (2016). *The plural psyche: Personality, morality, and the father.* Routledge. (Original work published 1989).
Schwartz, S. (2020). *The absent father effect on daughters: Father desire, father wounds.* Routledge.
Sharrock, A. (2003, September 29). [Review of *Learned girls and male persuasion: Gender and reading in Roman love elegy,* by S. L. James]. *Bryn Mawr Classical Review.* https://bmcr.brynmawr.edu/2003/2003.09.29/
Sheik, A. (2018). The more than beautiful woman – African folktales of female agency and emancipation, *Agenda, 32*(4), 45–53.
Shorter, B. (1987). *An image darkly forming: Women and initiation.* Routledge.
Stein, M. (1998). *Transformation: Emergence of the self.* Texas A&M University Press.
Stein, M. (2022). *Four pillars of Jungian analysis.* Chiron.
Wolff, T. (1956). *Structural forms of the feminine psyche.* Jung Institut.

Chapter 3

Puella's shadow

> Thy various works, imperial queen, we see,
> How bright their forms! How deck'd with pomp by thee!
> Thy wond'rous acts in beauteous order stand.
> And all attest how potent is thine hand.
>
> Phyllis Wheatley, "On Imagination," 1773

The dream is recurrent. *The dreamer is young, age five or six, in the family car alone, and the car begins to slide backwards. Mother is maybe around but not seen.* Upon awaking the dreamer is shaken and fearful.

This dream by a man reveals the chaos of the soul, a chaos many can recognise and feel, a shaken moment to an extent shaping life. Looking back is necessary for moving forwards, bringing awareness of the impetus for individuation, for becoming oneself. This dream brings forth the questions, gaps, absences and the space for unfolding new energy.

This man has been breaking the threads to his self over and over in big and small ways for years and, to date, cannot gather his personality by his efforts alone. *In the dream the self is isolated, helpless. The mother position is vaguely present and there is no father figure.* The word *analysis* means to loosen something that has been tied. It reaches into the chaos underneath and brings back meaning into our lives. Analysis will attempt to put the pieces of the personality together, to mend the self torn apart. Part of exploring the psyche is taking a leap into the vastness of the unknown where there is little idea what will emerge.

When a person enters Jungian analysis, the new energy, surprises and the unusual can be shaped by accessing figures like puella. She is a liminal figure, taking the space betwixt and between, encouraging the movement for change. There is beauty and fluidity in the becoming nature of puella. As she comes closer and her intricacies are explored, the self is revealed. Puella represents the eternal child and the meaningfulness of keeping alive the child in adult mental life. This ignites the psyche and keeps the new and creative active.

A problem arises when puella can become caught, swallowed in the maze of the collective, reality compromised. The real is what becomes released with inner psychological work. As Jung described in 'Psychological Aspects of the Mother

DOI: 10.4324/9781003449447-3

Archetype', 'She started out in the world with averted face ... and all the while the world and life pass by her like a dream – an annoying source of illusions, disappointments, and irritations' (1968a, CW 9i, para. 185).

Puella as explored here is not only applicable to women or those in the Western world but also refers to an aspect of the psyche applicable to all people. The trials and joys arising during the process of self-discovery occur in the psyche, allowing us to understand and integrate puella characteristics consciously. An interpretation of this part of the psyche expands from the known to the unknown and gives us room for the flexibility inherent in the psyche and our current era. 'A culturally sensitive psychology does not level out all differences in the psyche that stem from politics, ethnicity, religion, nation, social class, gender and sexual orientation. Jung was against the universal imposition of a single system of psychology' (Samuels, 2016, p. 241). Puella is part of the personality charged with creating and re-creating the self. Culture shapes us but can also limit us unless we become conscious of retaining our individuality and listening to who we really are. Yet, in many areas of life this is almost impossible to manifest. Inner realisation is key to moving forward into other ways of being.

The question is whether we have the courage and the opportunity. Jung said in 1947, in the preface to his 'Essays on Contemporary Events', a sentiment that is applicable to our current day:

> We are living in times of great disruption: Political passions are aflame, internal upheavals have brought nations to the brink ... This critical state of things has such a tremendous influence on the psychic life of the individual that ... The psychologist cannot avoid coming to grips with contemporary history.
> (Jung, 1964, CW 10, p. 177)

A person's subjectivity from the perspective of puella provides a frame within which Jungian analysis and thought has the capacity to expand comprehension, advancing from classical theory into future developments.

Becoming present means being inclusive, stretching beyond the known borders, exploring the limits and repressions to freedom of movement and emotion and challenging the status quo. Puella can becloud her portrait, however, mystify the record of who she is and diminish her import. Here I explore her restlessness, conflicts and complexes in a story about how she gains the ability to assert herself, to live with impact, voice and individual solidity.

Puella appears across all economic classes, social strata or gender identifications. The narratives exploring this concept are applicable to those seeking self-knowledge and expression. At issue is how we use those narratives consciously and how to recognise some people are held in cultural restraints. The puella concept was hardly addressed by Jung. He referred much more to the male version of this personality aspect called the *puer*. I decided to explore the puella topic years ago and have amassed more of the background and foreground to the concept, recognising its place in the personality. The puella is not just an immature character, as formerly described, but one with the potential to evolve into a yet unknown future.

Puella can be aligned with the 'as-if' personality, a type who feels inadequate and insecure but cannot access why she feels this way. She hides both her pearls and her stones, appearing other than how she feels inside; she is a confusing mixture of outer confidence and inner distress. The reasons why she does this are deep seated and require delving into the past to bring it forward into awareness. Depression resulting from repressing what is real is a complex process composed of many aspects (Schwartz, 2023, p. 18). The process will link shadow and self. It will take patience and fortitude to explore the inner workings of her being. She has a complex personality structure with conflicting elements, making the road into and out of herself a circuitous journey. This journey is necessary to regain her footing and declare her stance. Problems and distress promote the inner work.

This work involves awareness, willingness and the capability for continued action and exerting choice. Individuation calls for deepening through accessing the shadow and connecting to the larger scope of the personality, called in Jungian psychology the Self. 'Jung postulated the child motif as the central symbol of the unfolding self towards wholeness. From the "abandoned child" and the "invincibility of the child" Jung derives the "divine child" as hero' (Bovensiepen, 2022, p. 999). Puella in our era consists of a confluence of traits. She is a bit fragile seeming but tough, a bit retiring but also showy, a bit weak but resilient, a bit frightened but persistent, young while ageing, flighty while solid. In other words, she is a mix of qualities apparent in the psyche. We find her in our dreams and extant in relationships with self and others. Here she is explored to expand our range of knowledge from various analytical, clinical and philosophical perspectives.

Puella is part of the psyche moving out of narrow gender restrictions into a more valuable appreciation. There is a slow but sure cultural change in which the binary is no longer a biological or absolute truth. This includes binary thinking that is polarising rather than unifying and growing. The struggle and search for expansion benefits everyone exploring the possibilities available to inhabit body and psyche. This includes sorting out what kind of gender performance is required along with examining what expectations we might adhere to unconsciously, but which no longer fit.

Puella embodies the constructive as well as the destructive side of libido or energy for life. Putting a name on her defines, gives shape, links her in the context of past, present and future experiences. Describing her clarifies qualities and ways to use the energy she represents. She has been called a child-woman while embodying the universality of the human condition. The work in Jungian analysis is in sorting and differentiating, finding the symbols and meanings that change throughout life. It is an ongoing evolving and challenging experience.

Jung in his *Red Book* described a form of puella as Salome, the daughter of Philemon. For him she was a guide into the places yet unknown, and he had to trust in what would emerge from following this surprising and young figure. 'The young maiden represented a feeling that could be called Eros ... It is not form-giving but form-filling ... desire, longing, force, exuberance, pleasure, suffering' (Jung, 2009, p. 563). Jung went on to describe the interaction with Philemon, but here I want to keep the focus on the young maiden. Jung commented on childhood in 'On Psychic Energy' saying,

> This is the time when those far-seeing dreams and images appear before the soul of the child shaping the whole destiny as well as those retrospective intuitions reaching back far beyond the range of childhood experience into the life of our ancestors.
>
> (1969a, CW 8, para. 98)

This writing on the puella recognises the concept has also been rarely mentioned in other Jungian work. This contrasts with what Jung called the comparable masculine aspect, the *puer aeternus* referencing the young boy, the creative and high-flying part of the masculine in the psyche. Puer has been a figure who garnered the attention of, most notably, 20th-century Jungian analysts Marie Louise von Franz and James Hillman. Other psychoanalytic and psychological thought and approaches do not define or make note of puella, making this a unique endeavour.

For years I encountered puella in my analytical work where many declare as self-proclaimed puellas. Puella presents a portrait of layers, changing and altering, flexible and alive. She is a figure on the edge, symbolising the becoming nature within all people to expand and grow.

> To remain a child too long is childish, but it is just as childish to move away and then assume that childhood no longer exists because we do not see it. But if we return to the 'children's land' we succumb to the fear of becoming childish, because we do not understand that everything of psychic origin has a double face. One face looks forward, the other back. It is ambivalent and therefore symbolic, like all living reality.
>
> (Jung, 1968b, CW 12, para. 74)

Erasing the child can keep a person from tapping into deeper life resources. On the other hand, preserving youth at all costs can frame ageing as failure. Remaining unconscious of any realm promotes destructiveness of other aspects on personal and collective levels. The pieces and bits of puella are gathered here, emerging into a fluid whole, shapeshifting, with consciousness and potential actualised, claiming her position in the personality.

This interpretation focuses on the generative nature, the changing and growing aspects of puella and what has kept her repressed and submerged. Without secure identity, relationships to self and others become a trail of confusing mishaps and poor choices. She experiences loss of agency, feels without control and her centre without ballast. She becomes like a puppet gripped by something she cannot grasp. Puella must step back to repair the losses, restore meaning and self-agency, conscious of her actions and their impact. The challenge is to re-examine the value of the eternal girl, the child becoming, able to evolve anew. As Jung said, 'In every adult there lurks a child – an eternal child, something that is always becoming, is never completed, and calls for unceasing care, attention, and education. That is the part of the personality which wants to develop and become whole' (Jung, 1954, CW 17, para. 286).

Because largely unexplored, her becoming is intriguing. Puella's development occurs through the dialectics of being and becoming, the conscious and unconscious uniting in the search for truth (Wirtz, 2023, p. 231). This opens an investigation into her contradictions, opinions and various iterations. Puella represents disruption, fluidity and is integral for becoming oneself. Yet this is fraught, as Jung noted in 'Transformation Symbolism in the Mass', because 'human nature has an invincible dread of becoming more conscious of itself' (Jung, 1969b, CW 11, para. 400).

A woman dreamt there were wire hoops through which people were on rings moving. The place was at a carnival and there was a carousel. A girl was moving towards her on an iron pole, steady, balanced, able, about five or six years old. Why she is coming towards her is unknown. The dream girl is the age when she realised both parents lied, were unreliable and she was essentially on her own. This is the place from which the child must grow. Summoned from the unconscious, the image fills the gap of the missing others – the parents, the security, the foundation. Although she is alone, she is also held within the circle of the carousel and can maintain balance. It seems the strength of this girl says to the dreamer, 'I can do it and I am a part of you'.

'Refusal or turning away from the depths and the symbolic leads to loss of reality' (Stein & Arzt, 2022, p. 173). The becoming and integrating of puella involves the innovative, pushing past former norms and expanding beyond restrictive categories. Yet, this aspect of the feminine has too frequently been considered unworthy of attention, frivolous and repressed.

The ambiguity and complexity of puella are composed of historical layers, culture and upbringing in a shifting psychic territory. In a world shaped with much distress, change and shifting boundaries, it becomes even more crucial for people to be inspired and creative. We live in a reciprocity between the personal and cultural as 'each individual stands in compensatory relationship to the community' (Liebscher, 2015, p. 43). The individual, even when hemmed in by culture, can connect to themselves and others, accessing the collective and the unconscious existing within the personal and conscious life.

Personality exploration and integration as part of the process of individuation creates greater universality and multiplicity. Our modes of knowing and being present contain various paradigms and places from which we see the world (Perrin, 2023, p. 6). Yet Jung's ideas were limited by his time, as is everyone's. Therefore, we come up against residues of compatible and incompatible classical and current concepts, theories, attitudes and ways of being. 'It is a vast and shifting psychic territory in which no final, stable foundation can last, but which must constantly be explored and navigated' (p. 7).

The nature of becoming is developmental, active and unbound. Puella represents a new element enabling each person's individual nature to surface. The more they are aware of her qualities, struggles and obstacles, personally and culturally, and how she has shaped their life, the more their existence is enriched. Puella emerges into a satisfying aliveness with the fascination and openness of the eternal child.

Puella is part of what are called *threshold experiences*, an archetype of new beginnings, an initiation into a new phase of existence where the old self dies to be reborn. However, she is a paradox, unknowable often to herself, free-spirited, whimsical with edgy style. But these portrayals can fail to recognise the flattening of her into a trope, noncommittal, a fleeting love interest. She contains an inner emptiness and lives in the fantasy that real life will begin, but always later. She can be confused with childlike unsteadiness and an incapacity for perseverance, lacking tenacity and giving up too soon. She can feel restless, inundated with ennui, bored but also comfortable in the waiting, entitled while languishing in wasting time. She feels disconnected from her body and especially fears being reduced and earthbound while the future remains elusive.

Puella has been referenced as ethereal, hazy, yet remains prominent in the psyche. Unfortunately, many puella types relate to the world through hiding, mimicry and adaptation at the expense of authenticity. The deep longing for connection has been hurt, cut off, damaged. The remnants of this tragedy can lead to changelessness, an inability to move and the presentation of a rigid persona. They feel lost, stagnant. Reality is fraught with anguish, panic, absence, void. To hide this, puella will exude an appealing but elusive facade. She takes flight from reality into unrealistic dreams. Eventually, life is no longer sustainable in an illusionary world solely reliant on the ego and persona.

Too often puella is described as doll-like, objectified, shaped according to the dominant, collective traditional male desires. The resulting internal distress is a signal of being trapped in unconscious personal, cultural and historical wounds, unfinished mourning processes, intergenerational issues and archetypal anxieties exposing emptiness and disillusionments.

Analytic experiences

And how does this translate to analytical and therapeutic work? The analytical or relational perspective, with its emphasis on the patient's subjectivity, provides an optimal frame in which to consider the various impacts the external world has on our respective subjectivities. Toni Wolff, who accompanied Jung on his psychological descent, commented. 'Conscious and unconscious, I and you, personal and impersonal psychic contents remain undifferentiated' (1956, p. 12). It is puella's task to do the sorting, defining and recombining of personality. Exploring her influence personally and collectively promotes meaning making, negotiating shared and distinct concerns and developing beyond the old traditions.

Jung said, 'Individuals can be stunted all their lives by an image from childhood' (1997, p. 424). As an example, Angelijka, self-defined as puella and female, is floaty, enthused, easily elated and indecisive. In so many dreams teenage boys appeared, attractive to her but also snubbing her. She cannot distinguish who to be with or how she feels; she just wants to be noticed. She retains a romantic but often unrealistic concept of intimacy. In fact, she hardly lets anyone close and is used to being internally isolated. She is susceptible and naïve, and finds it hard to access who to trust. The psychological problem is she does not see how easily she relinquishes her position, thoughts and feelings.

She has given herself over to others, living without definition. Perhaps she will move out of the helpless, isolative stance she has resorted to survive. At an analytical session, she judges she was not a good or compliant client, and it was not a good session. She feels bad for me, but this comment reveals how much she stops her energy with negative self-judgements. She feels burdened with responsibility, making work stressful; she wonders whether she is good enough and never knows for sure. She worries and never takes longer than two weeks off work. Life is overwhelming. She expresses harsh self-judgement and disappointment in others.

She developed an auto-immune disease that depleted her energy after taking care of her mother during a fatal illness. She dreamt *of her mother slumped over and without energy*. She feels the need to be alone as she is easily inundated by the feelings of other. Angelijka realises she needs to find her centre and knows it was lost, especially in the stress of taking care of her mother. Then when her mother died, the world collapsed and now needs to be rebuilt. She is discouraged and wonders whether she can ever heal and find love.

She dreams *of women who will help with her school papers. They are going for a doctorate, but she does not want one, lacking the confidence she can do it*. In the next dream *she is with an actress and other women at the nail salon, and they want her to go for dinner at 9 p.m. but that is too late for Angelijka, yet she says nothing*. In both dreams she cannot assert what she wants. She hesitates and feels caught in a cycle of feeling hopeless, helpless and inadequate and becomes mute.

Feeling defeated and unable to help or save her mother left wide open the 'aspects of herself that have never been known and their only image is a radical absence' (Colman, 2006, p. 362). She dreams *of shaking her mother who is in a dive bar drinking at 11 a.m. and then takes pills. Mother did not respond.* The dream reflects Angelijka's depression and absence of an alive mother. Her mother was a dominating figure and, although encouraging, was not nurturing and took all the air from the room, leaving none for Angelijka who learned to melt into the woodwork. Angelijka has felt an oppressive and heavy burden weighing her down since childhood. She performed for her parents and everyone else. Telling no one, Angelijka has been secretly lonely and without much passion – or direction. She has gone along, floating. 'The emptiness she described was not simply of being lonely but ungrounded in anything outside of her mind' (Ogden, 1992, p. 86).

Angelijka has felt loss all her life, and it set up a sense of hopelessness in attaining love, a lack of trust or commitment to herself and others. 'When love fails, the image becomes one of destruction or death, a psychic or physical alteration in the individual image' (Bovensiepen, 2022, p. 1000). She might appear confident and able, but her emotions are precarious and unexplored; her vulnerability and authenticity are blocked. The disconfirmation or denial of aspects of the child self becomes a dismemberment from what is natural to her. Although her emotions remain disremembered and unavailable, they can dominate (Fleischer, 2020, p. 564). Where do these feelings go, especially if denied and unintegrated?

Ironically, the internalisation of the old ways of relating is the basis of the new forms.

> The acceptance of loss in the external world is met with a corresponding recreation of the object in the internal world. We are threatened with being at a loss: about what to do, what to feel, what to think. We need help; and we need help with meaning. The work of the psychoanalyst consists neither of releasing nor repressing, but of elaborating and working through the psyche, to allow a self-renewal at each internal or external challenge.
>
> (Lear, 2014, p. 475)

Depressed, with little enthusiasm, she is easily bored and cannot find creative expression. She is drained of ambition, without goals. During COVID she described the experience of going to the store; she hated the masks, commented there was too little response from the world and felt very alone and isolated.

This puella as the eternal girl lives removed, often behind the glass of her withdrawn pattern, which keeps her defensively elusive. The psyche is unattached, floating and uneasy. She could remain in this state for years. Unable to attain or sustain her idealistic expectations, a latent chronic sadness can be constellated. It is disparaging, accentuating cravings for acceptance and adoration and fuelling internal drives to do more that are stymied because she is cut off from connection to her authentic self.

Yet, she continues searching, stamina waxes and wanes, but she persists. She is beginning to find herself, who she is uniquely, apart from others. The nascent self is emerging through the analytical work and its rhythm, forming and shaping into Angelijka. Here is the strength in the puella, the part that perseveres and blooms late, but she blooms. In the analytic process she begins to find her foundation and belief in herself. The unfolding is gradual but steady and holding.

An ending

This exploration is not to pin her down, make rigid criteria, or fit her into a box. It reflects the challenge of uncovering the versatility in this concept and its vibrancy present through the life cycle. It is to access the joy and inspiration as puella unfolds. 'As we spiral our way closer and closer to the center of its territory, when we hold both the totality and the partiality of each of its ways of knowing and being we move towards the self images' (Perrin, 2023, p. 9). The task is for puella to become conscious within the psyche of all people, no matter their sexual orientation, culture, ethnicity, economic or societal status and class. Additionally, all these factors of puella shape a person, how they view the world, and provide impetus or not to access the total personality forming into its unique shape.

At the end of Memories, Dreams, Reflections Jung made some remarks about himself:

> The older I have become, **the less I have understood or had insight into or known about myself** ... In fact, it seems to me as if that alienation that so long separated me from the world has become transferred into my own inner world, and has revealed to me **an unexpected unfamiliarity with myself**.
> (Jung, 1989, 358, 359)

The enigma of the unconscious opens to the mystery of discovering 'Who is the I, that I am?'

> *My heart leaps up when I behold*
> *A rainbow in the sky:*
> *So was it when my life began;*
> *So is it now I am a man;*
> *So be it when I shall grow old,*
> *Or let me die!*
> *The Child is father of the Man ...*
> William Wordsworth, "My Heart Leaps Up" (1807)

References

Bovensiepen, G. (2022). Destructiveness: a 'neglected child' in the theory of analytical psychology. *Journal of Analytical Psychology*, 67(4), 999–1019.

Colman, W. (2006). Imagination and the imaginary. *Journal of Analytical Psychology*, 5(1), 21–41.

Fleischer, K. (2020). The symbol in the body: The un-doing of a dissociation through embodied active imagination in Jungian analysis. *Journal of Analytical Psychology*, 65(3), 558–583.

Jung, C. G. (1954). *The collected works of C. G. Jung: Vol. 17. The development of personality*. Princeton University Press.

Jung, C. G. (1964). The collected works of C. G. Jung: Vol. 10. *Civilization in transition*. Pantheon Books.

Jung, C. G. (1968a). *The collected works of C. G. Jung: Vol. 9i. The archetypes and the collective unconscious*. Pantheon Books.

Jung, C. G. (1968b). *The collected works of C. G. Jung: Vol. 12. Psychology and alchemy*. Princeton University Press.

Jung, C. G. (1969a). *The collected works of C. G. Jung: Vol. 8. The structure and dynamics of the psyche*. Princeton University Press.

Jung, C. G. (1969b). *The collected works of C. G. Jung: Vol. 11. Psychology and religion: East and West*. Princeton University Press.

Jung, C. G. (1989). *Memories, dreams, reflections* (A. Jaffe, Ed.) (R. Winston & C. Winston, Trans.). Vintage. (Original work published 1961).

Jung, C. G. (1997). *Visions: Notes on the seminar given in 1930–1934* (C. Douglas, Ed.). Princeton University Press.
Jung, C. G. (2009). *The red book: Liber novus* (S. Shamdasani, Trans.) (S. Shamdasani, J. Peck, and M. Kyburz, Trans.). W. W. Norton & Co.
Lear, J. (2014). Mourning and moral psychology. *Psychoanalytic Psychology, 31*(4), 482–488.
Liebscher, M. (Ed.). (2015). *Analytical psychology in exile*. Princeton University Press.
Ogden, T. (1992). *The primitive edge of experience*. Routledge.
Perrin, J. (2023). *The Animum: Queering Jungian and post-Jungian anima/animus theories* [Paper presentation]. International Association of Jungian Studies, Zurich, Switzerland.
Samuels, A. (2016). *The political psyche*. Routledge.
Schwartz, S. (2023). *Imposter syndrome and the 'as-if' personality in analytical psychology: The fragility of self*. Routledge.
Stein, M., & Arzt, T. (Eds.). (2022). *Jung's Red Book for our time*. Chiron Publications.
Wirtz, U. (2023). Traumatic experiences and transformation of consciousness. In S. Carpani (Ed.), *Anthology of contemporary clinical classics in analytical psychology* (pp. 221–236). Routledge.
Wolff, T. (1956). *Structural forms of the feminine psyche*. Jung Institut.
Wordsworth, W. (1807). *My heart leaps up*, first published in 1807 in *Poems, in Two Volumes*.

Chapter 4

Where is mother?

Every woman participates in motherhood, as 'to our amazement, confusion and greater complexity, we are both' (Rich, 1986, p. 253). Cara described her mother as not there, a vacant shell; all Cara could see was her back or her unengaged eyes. Cara learned to defend against the reality of this absence, this loss and the feelings it set up in her. She did not understand what she did to bring this about but knew it meant she was not liked. She tried to avoid mother, get out of her way. The feelings aroused felt intolerable, and she felt wrong when asking for or needing anything. From the outside, mother managed the home tasks, meals and clothes, and although she said she loved her children, she conveyed no feeling towards or emotional connection to Cara.

With a lifeless attachment to her mother, Cara lived in an inertia of self, with a sense of disembodiment and defensive singularity. This dynamic is also detailed by French psychoanalyst André Green with his concepts of absence, emptiness and negation, emotions unmirrored. According to him this 'constitutes a premature disillusionment and … carries in its wake, besides the loss of love, the loss of meaning, there was no explication to account for what has happened' (Kohon, 1999, p. 150).

Because Cara's mother was the image of a good mother to the outer world, it was confusing. For years she could not put her finger on it. Cara hesitated, toned down choices, held herself back, knew her mother did not understand; she tried to make her happy and fulfil her expectations. This left Cara suppressed, empty, dissatisfied. She had a dream. *In it, because her husband was occupied walking the dog, she could buy herself flowers*. There was something off about going alone to buy flowers and not telling him. It was almost as if she had to hide her desire to get something for herself. The situation could be shared but she chose not to. This is a small but important detail illustrating how much she masked her desires and emotions.

Cara's reaction comes in part from her unconscious knowledge that she had to be the perfect child whose needs were to be satisfied alone. Cara picked up sadness in her mother. Was this sadness perhaps masking the mother's own disappointments? Cara never knew. A mother's emotional lack gives a daughter the idea she has an unlovable self, inadequate, that something is missing. When the natural is repressed, performance becomes everything in a rush to operate from the persona and masquerade the real. Puella types often have an unhappy streak and are not easily able to express their emotions. For Cara, expressing them with mother led to rejection or negation or just nothing.

The daughter's body is unseen, taken over by melancholy and sadness. A mother's neglect and deadness, with its emotional distance, contributes to internal vacuity, vulnerability and lack of psychological connection. Mother's melancholy and passivity transfer to the daughter as an avoidance of spirit and general loss of feeling.

> A mother's victimization does not merely humiliate her, it mutilates the daughter who watches her for clues as to what it means to be a woman ... The mother's self-hatred and low expectations are the binding rags for the psyche of the daughter.
>
> (Rich, 1986, p. 243)

This quote eloquently depicts the double binds mothers and daughters live through, influenced in part by the underlying patriarchal strictures of society and tradition.

A male experiencing the blank mother

Forrest assumed he was the one to hold his parents' marriage together. He saw no joy between his parents, no freedom or spark, just work, be serious, do tasks, a rather dry home life. He viewed them as disappointingly average. He felt precarious inside. This became a pervasive worry about whether he could make it: would he be able to function? He was bullied when young but did not tell his parents or mother because he thought they could do nothing but make it worse. He endured everything alone. But at a basic level, his psychological solidity was shaken, and he was embroiled with internal conflict. Moreover, he knew he was different from the rest of the family. As an adult, although well-educated and in a responsible managerial position, he felt something was off and entered Jungian analysis.

Each week he said things were okay. It was always okay without any explanation, but a tone of caution radiated from him, as if his balance could easily tip over. His commentary about himself was that relationships were work. By this he meant they were disappointing; someone was never satisfied, better to keep it distant and light, stay away from the mess. Saying he wanted a relationship did not make it happen as he did nothing to signal interest and he remained guarded and distrusting. No one could know much about him and certainly not about his inner world. The energy for adventure was submerged in his predictable routine.

Forrest described his mother with contempt, yet visited her frequently, especially after his father died. He sarcastically said she was small-minded and called her vacant, empty, a shell. He reported a haunting dream *of him holding a gun on a mother who holds a gun on her darling five-year-old son. It is a standoff. He will shoot the mother, but will it be before or after she shoots the son?* Forrest wrestled with this image for days and then realised the question was not saving the mother but saving the son. The dream threatens death and victimisation at the hands of a mother, and he was suppressed, cornered into immobility. He surmised the attention to mother was going nowhere. He commented the woman with the son was crazy like his mother who could not help it. *The policewoman appearing later in the dream said she did it because she hated men.* He knew that described his mother, and the dream fit his confusing contention of being born for her. However, his birth locked her into being a mother and into a form of womanhood she may not have wanted or known how to do. More mixed messages about his value descended onto Forrest.

He began to realise how this mother killed the life force, inhabited his sexuality, and how he was unable to leave her or be real around her. She affected the development of puella within him, stifling any movement there. The effect carried over to other relationships as he assumed they brought no pleasure; it was just bodies having sex, not sharing life. His talk of mother was tinged with obsequiousness and thinly disguised disdain.

Yet despite all this turmoil within, Forrest appeared social and even charming. However, the life he had was like the dream, and he saw it held in abeyance at the hands of the death-dealing mother. The dreams revealing his inner world and the conflicts plaguing him contained themes of loss, rejection, mourning and grief. They expressed anxiety and lack of security. They described an impenetrability held down by a negative mother complex, destructive to relationships inside and out. He grappled with the ordeals of his male identity, feeling discordance and disunity. Forrest lived a celibate life, emotionally and physically. He hid his sexual preferences, considering them shameful and disallowed. He was stuck in an old system of repression with a stymied libido. His social self was deceptive, and his private self remained shrouded. He had not contacted the puella energy that might enliven or change the picture within. He lived singularly, a son driven by the mother away from his own nature to connect.

Later Forrest dreamt *about a woman who turns into a black man tied to a guard rail at the bottom of the stairs. The people should not let him get a glass of water as he may escape. The woman is the tricky part.* Then he remembered the previous dream and being at a standstill. He realised yet again she was the problem, and he must get past her to ascend the stairs. She was what he internalised, frustrating and stopping him from intimacy; he was stuck, obedient to a staid and dry mother. He remained psychologically untouched and, with this, emotionally undeveloped, fragile, held hostage by the emotionally empty mother.

The dreams illustrate some of the complex and internally deadening spaces transferred from an absent mother to her child. She is absent to herself and therefore is the same to her child, a vortex from which Forrest could not extricate himself. Becoming aware of how mother images live inside is a part of gaining consciousness. Forrest experienced 'the feeling of being sucked into the deadly embrace of the black and powerful mother of our origins towards the non-being of the indistinct' (Civitarese, 2013, p. 125). Repressions from the past pile up to eventually call forth change. This happened to a point with Forrest, as he gained insight and was curious to learn about his personality. His world remained solitary and closed, however, quite like the mother he disdained. He never acquired the life of puella as he turned from her and stayed with the internalised emptiness, the absence unfilled.

The trap

In *Essays on a Science of Mythology*, Jung and Károly Kerényi integrate psychology and mythology in the myth of Demeter and Kore:

> Demeter and Kore, mother and daughter, extend the feminine consciousness both upwards and downwards. They add an 'older and younger', 'stronger and weaker' dimension to it and widen out the narrowly limited conscious mind bound in space and time, giving it intimations of a greater and more comprehensive personality which has a share in the eternal course of things ... every woman extends backwards into her mother and forwards into her daughter.
> (Jung & Kerényi, 2002, p. 189)

Cara exuded a gentle manner, inquisitive but retiring, shy, methodical, careful. Something held her back even though she seemed active, had a career, partner, children and social life. In her own words, her sensuality had stopped, and she feared life or, more accurately, the unknown. She was someone who had to think carefully before going forwards.

She described mother wanting her to comply with a certain image and to some standard Cara never knew. She did know to avoid the wrath when mother was angry, demanding attention, wanting a model child, not Cara. Now in her late 50s Cara felt she must shed the internalised mother who bound her to not express any wildness and stay small. Yet Cara had a different nature from her mother. She was confused when mother slapped her in the face when she was 10, yelled, was impatient. From this and other experiences, Cara repressed her energy over time, and now she was trying to release herself from her hesitation to be her real self. She remained fearful of change, had low confidence and little self-love. She said she had been tethered to her mother, needed to be untethered, but was apprehensive about what that would mean for her.

Cara *dreamt she was at a hiking area, and it was peaceful sitting by herself. A woman came up and started talking. She was interesting and then another woman and another woman came up as well. Soon there were many women, and they all began to walk in a group to the right. Although one kept falling in the water, she and the others were faster walkers than Cara and soon were way down the trail. Cara tried to follow but felt abandoned, alone, uncertain, fearful. She came to a fork in the road and decided to go left on her own. She did not know whether she would get to the end or whether there would she get a ride. She just knew she could not go the same way as the other women.* In her associations she registered worry about the unknown and being possibly abandoned by the women. But she also knew she could not alter her pace to fit theirs – that if she did so, she would not find her way. The dream confirmed Cara had to go on her path, not the collective way her mother wanted. She had the dream as her mother was dying. She sadly realised the hope of closeness with her mother would remain an unmet desire. She wished her mother could reach out to her, understand her as different from herself and thus see Cara.

She recalled the many childhood nightmares *where her mother's eyes changed to be a witch and glowed at her*. She was afraid of these eyes as she did not know what they meant. Was mother kind or scary? It was as if mother did not know how to look at her daughter. Cara did not want to disturb mother, learned to take second place, not reveal her real feelings, and felt invaded by mother's questions about her life. It seemed mother had an agenda Cara could never decipher. The result was Cara toning down her talents, hiding her personality, making sure no one knew what she thought as she did not know what to anticipate from them.

This mother's voice in her head became restrictive, warning her to take few chances, to not succeed in areas mother did not. In other words, do not be Cara. There was no way around this but to remain a puella, stay too young and not challenge mother. At the same time, mother seemed too fragile to handle Cara's truth, so Cara sat back, her assertion stymied. She felt impotence, despair, anger at the failure of mother to make her feel desirable or sexy. To make the situation more complex, the rage might also be against the impotence and weakness of father who failed to connect to the mother. He psychologically turned to Cara as a consolation she both desired and was confused by.

Cara's dreams were filled with anxiety. *In one she was in a room and there was a slim window high up. This was the only way out, and she was not sure she could make it.* From dreams like these she often awoke in panic. The dream showed her alone, needing to get out. It was going to be a task taking effort and concentration. The dream repeated how she felt with her mother, alone, unable to get help, secure reliance or dependency.

Do you know my name?

Cara is like many females with mothers who mirrored a sense of self shrouded by emotional absence and frustration, harsh and cutting whenever their daughters could not meet their needs. The daughter's individual life becomes frittered away as if it is nothing. Vitality was lost years ago, talents curled up inside. Insecurities with mother result in lack of assertion or solidity, a seeking of safety at the sacrifice of personal development. Donald Winnicott, 20th-century British psychoanalyst, said the following:

> The mother's adaptation is not good enough. The process that leads to the capacity for symbol-usage does not get started (or else it becomes broken up, with a corresponding withdrawal on the part of the infant from advantages gained) … in practice the infant lives, but lives falsely. The protest against being forced into a false existence can be detected early.
>
> (1960, p. 146)

An unconscious rage towards the mother can be part of this dynamic and result in inertia, low self-worth and depressive moods. 'She started out in the world with averted face ... and all the while the world and life pass by her like a dream – an annoying source of illusions, disappointments, and irritations' (Jung, 1968, CW 9i, para. 185). Cara struggled to do her art but remained inert for long periods. Similarly, she lacked confidence and assertion in relationships. Forward movement seemed suspended.

Cara experienced the abandonment of a supportive and emotionally loving and confident mother. She described mother as the cold womb, unattached, demanding attention and never satisfied, wanting perfection, attacking the children for minor infractions. It took years to admit the lack of attachment to mother. Cara dreamt *mother was outside on the porch and startled her. How long was she there, and why did she make no indication of her presence?* This outside presence haunted Cara. How present was she in Cara's life without her realising it?

Cara was in conflict, caught in the grip of a mother she must make happy yet could not love. Mother was a hole into which Cara fell. She worried she could not climb free. Through the heaviness of an underlying depression, she dreamt *of a man who executed a spectacular jump in the air and then crashed on landing.* She said she neither learned to land nor jump spectacularly.

Cara said she did not do spectacular anything. Early on she learned mother could not manage her aliveness. Similarly, the mother complex in a puella is manifested in depressive moods, constant dissatisfaction with herself and the whole of reality (von Franz, 2000, p. 126). Mother's sorrows and self-betrayals seeped into Cara, and she felt defeated and became desolate. Still, she wanted a loving mother and feared what would happen when mother died, and this made her sad, lonely, disillusioned. It is not that Cara could not take care of herself, pay bills, work, but she was defined by a shaky trajectory. Cara's narration in therapy underscored a lonely-to-the-bone psychic state, sensitive to rejection, often stuck in a pit of boredom, anxiety and aimlessness. The despair was simply inescapable, pervading her psyche and body, her life passion subsumed.

The dead mother syndrome, originating from the psychoanalyst André Green, describes radical de-objectification and self-mutilating with aggression directed against the self, not the outer world. The experience of an internal world is attacked, the sense of time frozen, investment in self dismantled and a void fills the mind (Green, 2011). There is loss of meaning, prolonged longing and suffering both conscious and unconscious. This emotionally blank and absent mother is described as 'the trauma in the parent functions as a disorganizing force which transforms the parent into an unpredictable adult who cannot think and feel and has no capacity for containment and empathy' (Cavalli, 2021, p. 601). The impact of this mother figure contributes to life response of lack, withdrawal and an inner absence.

The maternal is blocked from its natural flow. The silence and disappointment in mother kept her silent within and withheld her from life. Cara felt abandoned but kept trying, always hoping mother would become warm, helpful, appreciative and see Cara. It never happened. Although Cara mothered her mother, complying and trying to be good, she felt excluded from the mother's psyche, prevented from knowing her and separated from an intimacy she could only imagine.

Cara is an example of puella with her creative energies stilted; she has difficulty amassing focus. It is as if she is folded up within, the bud unopened. She stayed the daughter, kept under wraps, her personality compromised. The situation has spurred her on to find herself and the journey has been dismaying and disappointing, not in terms of self-discovery but in realising the absence of the mother.

Mother's body

The concept of the abject from French Lacanian psychoanalyst Julia Kristeva applies to the feminine body as well as the rejected bodies of those from different cultures, ethnic, racial, political, geographical and religious groupings. *Abjection* is the human reaction to a threatened breakdown; the body is turned from, despised, radically excluded. The abject is conceived as something that betrays, defiles, stigmatises and is associated with what destabilises the sense of certainty. It represents the possibility, significance and incomprehensibility of the realness of our bodies, the chaos, even the monstrosity felt in the face of the real.

Julia Kristeva identifies the maternal as the receptacle for what has been repressed or abject. Kristeva emphasises the maternal function and its importance in the development of subjectivity and for access to culture and language (1982, p. 10). The body language of the mother is associated with basic life rhythms, tones and natural movement. The abject brings one to the boundaries and distinctions between self and other and heightens the realisation of our existence.

Jung noted:

> But if you hate and despise yourself – if you have not accepted your pattern – then there are hungry animals (prowling cats and other beasts and vermin) in your constitution which get at your neighbours like flies in order to satisfy the appetites which you have failed to satisfy.
>
> (1998, p. 502)

Walking this road involves the recognition of loss and the emotion of melancholia, beginning with the original relationships when tinged with loss. These parts call intensely for us to pursue the psychological depths.

French feminist writer Hélène Cixous examined the uses and misuses of language in relation to women. She addressed the woman's bodily encounter with the mother to find identity, autonomy and modes of expression. Discontinuities in development manifest in experiences of inner disintegration. In analysis delving into this lacuna provides the space to emerge into the more complete self.

Etta is highly intelligent, accomplished in her career but insecure about her brains and ability and constantly feels inferior. Mother was emotionally flat, a woman enclosed in her own world to which Etta had no entry. Etta has assumed she is somehow not alright. As part of this self-evaluation, Etta has no mirrors at home. Mother was always dieting, and her weight was never solid or satisfactory, but then nothing was. Now Etta has gained a few pounds, and she is obsessed about it. She feels pushed by the collective image of a thin female body.

Many puellas obsess about their bodies but are not connected to them; they are never the right weight, ten pounds too much, at least. Some are too thin with no relation to food, but all are hounded by an unattainable image of physical perfection. In this sense her body is abject, met with disgust and separation and put aside.

It is as if Etta has reached what marathoners describe as hitting the wall; she is overcome with exhaustion and bewildered by her ageing and changing body. She finds herself running on empty, typical of many who burn out from lack of maternal connection. The consciousness of one's own selfhood is the basic goal of the process Jung termed 'individuation; the development of the capacity to realize and to experience one's separateness, one's wholeness, one's uniqueness' (Jung, 1968, CW 9i, para. 490).

Etta dreams *of a woman looking out at the water. A small girl in a red dress comes to her and then leaves. There is an abandoned red boat.* The colour red appears in many of her dreams, on chairs, dresses, stones, jewels. It is her special colour and denotes her passion and energy for life. She did not fully appreciate it until the colour appeared over and over, as if insisting on its recognition. The women in her dreams have their back to her and their face is unseen. She thinks nothing of the mother/woman not watching out for the girl and thinks because the girl is alright there is no problem in the lack of maternal watchfulness or attention. But where is the care? There were many secrets at home; she was left alone and never told anyone how vacant it was. Etta felt ashamed about feeling this way and thought she was the problem. She used to look at mother but was met without soul or depth, with a vacancy of expression she could not understand.

Deadness

Emotional deadness also has a role in interfering with the analyst's and analysand's freedom to think. 'André Green made a pivotal contribution to the analytic understanding of the experience of deadness as an early internalization of the unconscious state of the depressed mother' (Ogden, 1997, p. 25). Etta says she has no way of being personal and does not want to burden others. Sometimes she seems a blank slate to herself. As she describes in Jungian analysis, this is much like the mother who was empty, denying the father was alcoholic and making reality into something other than what it was. The real was negated.

Consciousness requires a certain psychic mobility, a capacity to shift between negating and affirming, separating and connecting. The ability to use psyche in this flexible way establishes a creative kind of psychic reality, an index of well-being reflecting the depth and quality of our emotional and thinking life. Green (2000, p. 69) stated, 'But we should not forget that an intersubjective experience or an object relationship or being with the other necessarily connects'. However, this was not Etta's experience with her mother. Rather there was nothing, no flow, no wave of response, a blank unconsciousness of mother. She was caught in 'the dragging movement of regression and the fascinating power of fixation' (2003, pp. 2–3).

The traumatisation, loss and melancholic identification with the mother who is emotionally absent negatively impacts the child's experience of life. The child is susceptible to being like her and becoming submerged in the depleted mother. 'No life is possible beyond the boundary of the dead mother and there is no peace of mind within her embrace' (Kohon, 1999, p. 118). The early traumas and losses create insecurity. Body and psyche become dysregulated, and this form of the negative mother complex sets up similar responses in its intrusive and controlling energy. This has led to Etta approaching many current life situations in a defensive way.

A mother's neglect and deadness contribute to internal vacuity, vulnerability and lack of psychological connection. The internal representation of absence left Etta without supportive mirroring. Melancholy and passivity became part of the avoidance of spirit and general lack of feeling. Etta avoided emotional intensity. She only went so far in relationships. She must be in control of others, her schedule, not too emotional and not revealing any real anxieties. Etta could not risk being overwhelmed by feelings or endure the anguish over the possible loss of any bonds.

She appears older looking, a bit bland, does not want to be noticed, needs the protection of anonymity. Singular, her personality is reduced to illusion and cover. This mother is dead within. She also experienced the trans-generational trauma of the sad, depressed, traumatised mother, a holocaust survivor from numerous traumatic events.

Embedded in the body are experiences extending from the past to present time. Our personal and collective story is sequestered in bodily memory as it reminds us again and again about the losses and the events unable to be recalled solely through language and narration. The body discloses openings to these silent, but loudly resonating memories. This includes repressed depression and anxiety, longing and suffering, the current loss of meaning and connection on conscious and unconscious levels.

Any enlivening qualities were countered by deadening ones for Etta. She was internally running from herself, bombarded and harassed by disturbing and unprocessed memories. Too often silence and repression took over. Without an emotional and responsive mother, and although feeling the disturbance, Etta was blocked from expression.

Etta recalls mother had little say about her own life. Mother was tired, needing to lie down daily, with little energy for anything outside the home tasks she dragged herself through. Each moment was gotten through for some elusive tomorrow. Etta says she must keep doing more and being busy to give life value, to know there is meaning, to feel she has done something. Her brain tells her to do, do another activity and so on. Sometimes she can hardly keep up. And then she too is exhausted.

The parent without the capacity to relate to the child's mind and emotions creates a disturbance in body ownership with behavioural or emotional impacts though life (Knox, 2010, p. 132). Etta learned to separate mind from body. She then develops an auto-immune disease where she must rest, moderate activity, and it is now forcing her to examine her inner world. This need was previously negated with misconnections between mind, body and soul, deriving in part from the missed connection with mother.

She experiences doubt or confusion about whether other people and the world are friendly or hostile, accepting or disapproving. The doubt originates usually in 'relation to a parent whose behaviour makes it difficult or impossible for the young child to experience any understandable and reliable pattern of acceptance or rejection [and this] interferes with the development of trust and reasonable certainty' (Schachtel, 1969, p. 72). Etta's inner discourse is critical and dissatisfied while underneath is a pit of emptiness. She learned to ignore feelings, increasingly evident as her life experiences repeated the absence of sufficient attachment. She cannot yet access the ability to repair the lost parental objects or awaken the lost desire. Far underneath she was consumed with sorrow. Masking her thoughts and feelings, a nameless anxiety intercedes, and she wonders why she should even try. She worries about this lack of passion; like her mother, she works to please others but does not know herself.

In a frustrated and suppressed need to be seen and loved, she dreams *of being in a hotel room, sterile, alone, filled with anxiety*. From dreams like these she often awoke in panic. The dream repeated how she felt with her mother, alone, unable to get help or secure reliance and dependency. It is through relation to others that meaning is created but Etta is very alone in the dream.

As time went on, it became apparent the analysis was based on the nameless but empty experiences with mother. There was little imagery, ideas or emotions except the need to avoid mother's dislike and unexplained disregard. Such experiences are threatening to the self and emotionally deadening, obstructing the ability to process otherness. The psychic universe is no longer filled with presences, but with absences. The awareness of absence enables us to imagine a potential space formed by a good enough relationship with another. However, those who live in the gap cannot imagine a potential space. Rather, they experience life within a fragmentary, unindividuated, non-symbolising perspective. Instead of an object representation is a hole in the psyche, a nothing. Even though unseen there are multi-layered forms yet to be discovered.

The analysis

At times in the analytical treatment the space becomes restricted and claustrophobic, and the time of the analytical hour slows to seeming endless (Connolly, 2013, p. 646). The analyst has the sensation the whole process is going nowhere. Any moment of insight or of affective contact gained in one session has already disappeared by the next session, sucked into an unending spiral of immobility and nothingness. Defences of the self ward off the nameless dread of identification with the dead mother. The treatment is to enliven the capacity for transformation by exploring and separating from the internalised neglect.

In analysis Etta, at times, expresses no room for other thoughts or space for interpretations. All seems intrusive and she cannot think; perhaps she is feeling overrun, like she experienced with mother's absence and her dismay. Rather than this being an impediment, it exposes what recedes into the unconscious and forms into the dissociated elements living in her psyche. She often does not realise how much these elements control her freedom of expression, confidence and ease in being.

It takes a long time for Etta to realise her mother had an impact on her life. She thought there was nothing if she just ignored her. Gradually she begins to see the mother who could not give love had affected her confidence in relationships and ability to trust and allow her real self to emerge. Mother had more influence than she presumed. Mother was not weak but effective in cutting off love. By realising all this, Etta begins to recover herself and the dead mother complex diminishes in power. She no longer just dismisses mother but begins to consciously claim herself. The psychic energy shifts to Etta.

The mind and the psyche shape our embodied experiences. 'Disturbances in the sense of body ownership and of the body image are more central to the loss of temporality characteristic of such states' (Connolly, 2013, p. 636). When Puella experiences the self as detached or dissociated from corporeal reality, she becomes disembodied and identified with the mind. Many feel lifeless with a predominant and profound dissociation between the subjective self and the body, which becomes cold, frozen or dead. Disconnection occurs through abuse of substances, food, activity, sex. All these can be connectors, but they can equally separate us from life (p. 637).

The task of analysis occurs through the intersubjective relationship that fills the absence with eventual feeling. It takes a long time for Etta to realise the analytical relationship is real and composed of two people who can be honest. Gradually, she begins to thaw, to trust and to come alive. The intersubjective experience or being with the other connects our two intrapsychic personality structures to create new experiences.

We make meaning of the past hurts, generating links in our experiences, suturing together the disparate and dismembered:

> What do I know now about my mother?
> I live with the myth of her, my indisputable legend of her ... I really know I am not my mother ... Then, sometimes I feel sadly for her because as colorful and colored we were, our world was defined in black and white ... something is awry. I become uncollected.
>
> (Shange, 2023, p. 6)

Our individual histories are marked by desires and losses and the meaning we make retroactively can be even more impactful. This is the constructive analytical work, bringing a psychic mobility and a capacity to shift from negating to affirming, from separation to connection. Broadly speaking, the ability to use the absences and blank dead spaces in a flexible way establishes a new psychic reality and this becomes the index of well-being. Development, although punctuated by loss, now transforms into movement to fill the gaps and blanks that formerly populated time and space.

References

Cavalli, A. (2021). Transgenerational transmission of indigestible facts: From trauma, deadly ghosts and mental voids to meaning-making interpretations. *Journal of Analytical Psychology, 57*(5), 597–614.

Civitarese, G. (2013). *The violence of emotions: Bion and post-Bionian psychoanalysis.* Routledge.

Connolly, A. (2013). Out of the body: Embodiment and its vicissitudes. *Journal of Analytical Psychology, 58*(5), 636–656.

Green, A. (2000). Science and science fiction. In J. Sandler, A.-M. Sandler, & R. Davies (Eds.), *Clinical and observational psychoanalytic research: Roots of a controversy* (pp. 41–72). Karnac.

Green, A. (2003). *Diachrony in psychoanalysis.* Free Association Books.

Green, A. (2011). *The tragic effect: The Oedipus complex in tragedy.* Cambridge University Press.

Jung, C. G. (1968). *The collected works of C. G. Jung: Vol. 9i. The archetypes and the collective unconscious.* Pantheon Books.

Jung, C. G. (1998). *The Zarathustra seminars.* Pantheon Books.

Jung, C. G., & Kerényi, K. (2002). *Essays on a science of mythology.* Princeton University Press.

Knox, J. (2010). Self-agency in psychotherapy. W. W. Norton & Co.

Kohon, G. (Ed). (1999). *The dead mother: The work of André Green.* Routledge.

Kristeva, J. (1982). *Powers of horror.* Columbia University Press.

Ogden, T. (1997). *Reverie and interpretation: Sensing something human.* Jason Aronson.

Rich, A. (1986). *Of woman born: Motherhood as experience and institution.* W. W. Norton.

Shange, N. (2023). *Sing a Black girl's song: The unpublished work of Ntozake Shange.* Grand Central Station.

Schachtel, E. G. (1969). On attention, selective inattention and experience: An inquiry into attention as an attitude. *Bulletin of the Menninger Clinic, 33*(2), 65–91.

von Franz, M.-L. (2000). *The problem of the puer aeternus.* Inner City Books

Winnicott, D. W. (1960). *The maturational processes and the facilitating environment: Studies in the theory of emotional development.* Hogarth Press.

Chapter 5

The bones of the father

> Dream: *I dreamt the husband of my friend, absolute narcissist and self-centred, only thinking of himself, was buying a house for him and me. We must have been together, but the house would be in his name, not mine. As I awoke, I thought he was just like my father, unable to consider anyone else, unable to give and just wore fancy clothes but did not share or care about anyone else.*

The dream of Lyden, a woman in her 50s, highlights the confusion and loneliness that led to an estrangement from her father to whom she could not get close. From the dream Lyden drew a connection between what can be called a negative father complex and how she had accommodated to its upsetting yet controlling energy. In the dream she was unconscious and would live with him but own nothing. It was all his. She called herself a fatherless daughter. She had difficulty being heard, seemed to get walked on and felt weak and invalidated. In many ways she replicated the relational conundrum of puella.

An image by the Spanish artist Remedios Varo is called *Woman Leaving the Psychoanalyst*. The picture shows her carrying the head of her father. She drops the head in a basket illustrating release, discarding. This action portrays freedom to be herself unimpeded by the father. The image tells a story, but in the painting she is veiled, and we do not know what that means.

These depictions of the father figure shed light not only on the symptoms and problems but also on the need for treatment and renewal. Self-realisation is embedded in all psychological processes as the psyche strives to find balance. In therapy we begin to examine what has been there, what was not, what we need and where we learned to just accept and be helpless. This can be assisted by accessing the creative impulse with its attempt to restore the damage to outer and inner objects that became lost (Hillman, 1979, p. 2). Confusing her own unfolding, puella has not been recognised or accepted when paternal imaginings were projected onto her by the father.

The bare bones of the father need to be explored to understand and gain release on the path towards being oneself. With the experience of a good and present father figure, neither too powerful nor too passive, available emotionally and physically, the puella aspect can form into a healthy solidity of self. Because the father

DOI: 10.4324/9781003449447-5

archetype implies qualities residing or possible in all people, the child can develop a beneficial and supportive father with impetus and energy for their well-being (Kast, 1997, p. 123). The restoration of the father position embroiled in negative dynamics and restored to a fuller place enhances development and impacts the father as well as the child. Part of a father's role is to 'recognize the child's otherness, the rivalries, neglect and desires that characterize father-child relations' (Diamond, 2017, p. 298). The hope is that through inner psychological work a way is found into the self.

The missing father is prevalent in Western society, either physically by abandoning partner and children, or emotionally absent by being absorbed in work, devoid of emotions, feelings or interest while also being dictatorial in his control. If the father relationship is insufficient, the girl continues to seek him and his power in convoluted ways often destructive to herself. She usually does not access her own power. The perpetuation of the myth of the compliant daughter/girl/puella subsumed by the father/patriarchy indicates this. The father retains his desired image as the grand leader and the daughter becomes a mere extension, invisible and unknown.

Inside the daughter, an ache remains, accentuating the issues of living without a present father. Puella, overwhelmed by the father, the patriarchy and the masculine in myriad forms, can take on the role as his darling and then enacts the darling to all. She is colloquially called Daddy's Girl. As such, she fades.

The resistance to and traditions against examining father and his roles are the ghosts living in the unconscious, sapping energy and taking psychic space. When the father's mental representation as negative, absent, assaultive is internalised, the child and then the adult cannot trust or find herself in the other (Knox, 2003, p. 156). Too few opportunities for good experiences between a father and child lead to a legacy of non-involvement and personal detachment. Action becomes inhibited, emotional development arrested and adulthood feigned rather than realised. Without sufficient emotional connection, attachment becomes difficult, inhibiting satisfaction in relationships and making love a difficulty, not a pleasure.

A terrifying vulnerability is obscured just enough to be out of immediate vision. Identification with or ignorance of the absent father effect can bring melancholic attachment to the internalised absence (Schwartz, 2020). Desperate and isolated, puella deadens herself by going through the motions, not fully living, always looking for what is missing. The natural longing for personal involvement and empathic understanding signifies the importance of father relatedness.

In other words, the father has remained a presence even though his lack and absence has been an obvious detriment. In fact, the presence of his absence is powerful in its impact, reverberating through a person and culture. Puella remains attached to the unfulfilled emptiness as the father complex continues to haunt the psyche. Afflicted by this inner loss, in addition to the outer, there is an unconscious need to restore the care of the absent paternal. The emphasis is on how to stay conscious of the hurt and use this experience, which requires growing from the absence, filling in the present, recognising the lack, the unrepaired and the missing.

Acknowledgement of being without the father one wanted means embracing loss, rage, longing, wounds, despair as well as an opening for transformation.

It is not so easy to find corroboration for the detrimental effects of absence when the cultural overlay is combined with a 'long history of denial. Looking at the situation from traditional psychoanalytic theory, post-modern theorizing has consigned the father to oblivion by neglecting the paternal function' (Diamond, 2017, p. 305). More recently this has been changing and the father is now recognised as a significant caregiver impacting the psychic reality of the child. Father is no longer in the shadow of the nurturing mother, and these roles in their traditional forms are in flux. The paternal function is one of the most embedded concepts, both in clinical thinking and in extended social functioning (Diamond, 2021, p. 1).

The issues are multifaceted and applicable to all father figures and father surrogates, including those of female gender who inhabit this position. The father is significant, particularly vis-à-vis aspects of tenderness and sensory intimacy or what has, in the past, been considered the feminine realm. This leaves the paternal to be explored, expanded, enlivened with new eyes and experiences.

At issue is also how the child experiences the father with the mother figure and the quality of their engagement. This is influenced by how the mother figure carries the father in her mind, the intergenerational transmission of paternal roles, relationship dynamics and psychological vacancies.

Even as we are at the crossroads of change, we carry the memory and influence of the father/patriarchy, a time denoting the masculine as central and the feminine less so. Obviously, the balance has been off. These are the issues to unravel and the material from which to re-create. Those who lack a father figure have the need, opportunity and responsibility to fill the gap.

When absent, the father can destroy the verve, harm the creative force and diminish the self-agency of puella. 'The alien sense of identity becomes installed in the child's psyche and is experienced as an alien self' (Knox, 2007, p. 556). The child is plagued with doubts, insecurities, fears and depression from the father line. A recurrent theme has been the tyrannical father figures destroying their children, unable to relate in a meaningful way and contributing to the malignant cracks seeping into our culture.

Disappointment and doubt

All this has influenced puella to remain diminutive, subordinate to the father energy, obsequious; this is an old story. A daughter's life can slant towards disappointment, discouragement and expectations sadly unmet, burdened by the memory of father's absence. The psychic void from the father is experienced depressively as an inner void (Kristeva, 1991, p. 82). How can she find the father as an internal good object?

Reba, a composite of many, neither trusts, nor is she open. An emotionally absent father has left her closed, feeling unaccepted and excluded. Her life is solitary and lived alone on a desolate plane. In this world of enclosure, she is trapped in an airless and enclosed space (Solomon, 1998, p. 234). There is no knowledge of being thought about by the father and no father reflecting a sense of self. She did not experience being seen as herself and therefore has trouble finding herself in relation to others. Recently the façade of self-reliance, although to some extent true, has collapsed under career pressures, revealing a lack of confidence or self-connection.

Reba is beginning to realise the energy it has taken to reinstate this father who was lost, emotionally dead, unavailable. Because father was absent, her adoration became more intense. She lived to please him, to share pursuits and meet his standards of perfection. She became caretaker for father, special to him. They had their secrets, ways of being together; she felt she needed to please him, and she did it well. The mother was experienced either as absent or a rival.

Something must change. But Reba doubts her ability to do this and quickly devolves into many forms of self-attack and self-despair. She resorts, like puella, to being overwhelmed and diminished. She often gives up.

To Reba, father was unemotional, did not take notice of her as a talented dancer, singer, performer and scholar. Her career was not what her father wanted. Her ideas, fears and ambitions were large on all counts. But she easily lost her goals; her daily rhythms were off kilter. She gained weight and gradually stopped exercising and then found it difficult to get back on track. She could not hold her own for very long. Men were attracted to her energy and openness. But then they turned on her. Here was the destructive patterning. This daughter's love was split from her sexuality, or she feared it as a power that could destroy her. She tended to fall in love with men who would not marry but she created them as an ideal. She lived separated from her body as if behind glass. She did not know how to protect herself or distinguish between those who would be able to promote her and those who flaked out with empty promises. She was both too open to the world and too closed and disappointed.

She dreamt *of taking a man to Spain so his heart will begin to beat again.* She said Spain was a part of her heritage, specifically Catalonia, the area that wants to secede and has its own distinct heritage. Spain represents her own toughness and perseverance to persist in her own way. Reba feels estranged from her father who she hopes will want to understand her but never reaches out to do so. She has a disturbed body relationship, either exercising madly or eating bags of chips and gaining weight. She lives partially in a state of psychic deadness.

'The trauma in the parent functions as a disorganizing force which transforms the parent into an unpredictable adult who cannot think and feel and has no capacity for containment and empathy' (Cavalli, 2012, p. 601). The psychological trauma constellation feeds an internalised cycle of oppression, beginning from the paternal neglect, abandonment and emotional rigidity, making it difficult to love or care for oneself. It can lead to psychosomatic symptoms, lack in the capacity for symbolisation and limited psychological insight. There is 'inability to contain and reflect upon affective experience, not having internalized a process of containment of affect. Such patients can experience some of their affect but cannot form a representation or develop meaning' (Willemsen, 2014, p. 699). The internal trauma response of shutting down, defensive and fearful, remain. Reba lost herself in self-sabotage, wasting time and not enjoying her world. She has now lost steam and fears she cannot get it back.

From a young age, her continuity of being was interrupted as the family moved a lot. There seemed no stability or security, and their country of origin was always in upheaval and then in such distress they could not return. Father's defensive responses were associated with the need to protect family, including Reba. Reba carried within her generations of oppression in a complex mixture of cultural backgrounds, crossing borders and boundaries, always moving, escaping war and terror, people tortured and killed. She cannot leave the haunting of these ghosts whose ways of knowing carry wisdom waiting to be unlocked and opened. They are the ghosts her father cannot admit.

Reba's father was brilliant but aloof. He did not easily adjust to the various other cultures and moves as she did. He did not have her facility with languages and the transitions made him gruff, insecure, and he felt unrecognised. He was cautious, fearful, uneasy and found it quite difficult to adapt. She was flexible, open, studied hard and worked to fit in to each place. Their cultures clashed – hers of vibrancy and his of retreat, she of youth and he precarious with age.

She had little opportunity to gain solidity, as she felt continually bombarded. In this situation the wounds became the central organising factor in the personality. She apprehended the world as a traumatising place. She spent much emotional time responding to the anticipated intrusions of others while needing to hide any personality fragmentation and vulnerability. In effect, there was paralysis of the self. This cemented Reba's shame, guilt, grief and anxiety while inhibiting and repressing other feelings such as curiosity or aliveness.

Reba gave up her passion as she got easily wounded. Others took advantage. Incidents occurred early in life when the father ignored her, denigrated her qualities, disallowed her means of self-expression. Because she was deemed too showy, Reba assumed a posture of hiding, had little trust, kept herself secret. Reba *dreamt she was giving a performance, a lecture presentation but there were very few attendees. They seemed lacklustre and contributed little. She could barely get their enthusiasm and decided to end early. She was discouraged and disparaging towards herself. This was her usual defeat pattern.* As she awoke, she realised here was the negative father complex, what she felt with her father as he lacked appreciation of her talents. Ambition, creativity and anything unusual threatened his need to be under the radar and average, unseen meant safety, even though he was highly accomplished in his field.

The negative father complex remained because his nurturance, support and aliveness were insufficient, as in the dream. The dream figures were without energy, their interest was muted. Reba easily got off course, doubting her efforts and keeping herself in the shadows, but with analysis she was becoming increasingly aware and more consistent with her own self-care. The negative complex was connected to her overeating, her emotional withdrawal and her sabotage of her energy. The dream, although simple and clear, contained layers of meaning.

In another dream *a man had many neckties, so many he possessively counted them every day to make sure no one took them. She was going to take some but was not sure why. The man spied her in the neckties and exclaimed she was caught. She had not taken them yet, and he had no evidence. She was afraid he would do something to her and remained cool as if nothing happened. He was a bad guy and would stop at nothing. She realised he was jealous and envious of her.* As she awoke, she wondered whether he was her father, this bad guy who took many forms in her dreams and undermined her achievements, sapping her energy.

Initially it was important to Reba to erase her background and fit in with the Western-colonised image by changing her hair and eye colour. Now she has returned to her natural self and feels better but wonders whether she threatens others with her strong energy. Yet, when she tones it down, she becomes destructive, gaining weight and sabotaging her career. She feels unseen by her father, isolated, hidden, desolate and full of grief. She had longed to find a bridge between them, but he needed to preserve the equilibrium of what he knew but what had sadly been destroyed. But the loss caused the emotional turbulence he tried to avoid. He wanted Reba to avoid it as well, but she wanted to confront, challenge and create anew. The bones of this father might fit him, but they did not fit her.

What if people like Reba are resonating with a collective grief as well as their own? What if they have capacities and sensitivities overwhelming them because no one has believed them? What if they feel different from others, not only because of trauma or neuropsychological differences, but also because they are the carriers of the truths and memories from past generational traumas? Maybe puella figures are such change agents.

Together we can sense the betrayal, the provoked feelings of irritation, the weariness caused from the whole scenario of the negative father complex consciously and unconsciously negating Reba. She always sought more emotion from her father, more personal attention, but he lived behind a wall devoid of emotional expression. He loved her; however, he was unable to understand her. She could not be nourished or loved by him enough, and this affected her ability to move into her own life, separate from his.

Freud (1930) stressed the gravity of the importance of paternal protectiveness when he stated, 'I cannot think of any need in childhood as strong as the need for a father's protection' (Diamond, 2021, p. 27). In Jungian psychotherapy Reba is embarking on the painstaking yet rewarding process for fashioning a related, helpful and kindly interior father image. The psychological and physical wounds are being addressed through attention to the unconscious, bringing her reactions into conscious life. She is continually surprised at the dream messages as they help her to compose images of a different interior father, one who is supportive, who guides and believes in her. She is gradually developing her artistic nature as the psyche responds, restoring a life-sustaining inner world of richness and representation. Although her actual father remains emotionally unavailable, his presence is filled by Reba herself. Adam Philips, British Freudian psychoanalyst, said, 'There can be no representation without passion … Passion entails [inner] circulation and exchange' (1999, p. 166).

Father loss

Stronger than the dead father can be the living father who is dead while alive. The psychological wounds can manifest in narcissistic hatred, feeding an internalised cycle of oppression from paternal neglect, abandonment or emotional rigidity. From these early experiences a cloak of invisibility develops. It is lonely. Dependent and feeling vulnerable, a daughter feels different from others in the world and is fraught with anxiety. There is loss of desire, avoidance of the otherness of new experiences.

André Green declared, 'The dead father was dead because, in order to even think of his murder, he must have some kind of existence that one would like to end' (2009, p. 26). The psyche develops a self-encapsulated system and, as such, splits from reality, allowing in nothing new. The daughter remains stuck in concrete thinking and states of breakdown in which understanding ceases and feeling overwhelms, activating anxieties and generating dissociation. She feels shame and worries she will be rejected. Meanwhile, she remains at an impasse, as the unknown seems a venture too frightening, exposing the many facets of a shadow father bond.

When we look at the father before us, we find in general a disappointing vacant figure, living a stereotype as disciplinarian and distant, a recluse, misanthrope, a rigid ruler, heart vacated. This is a dim view and certainly not applicable to all but to many. The early provision of father attention and love is quite impressive with the evidence that children of fathers less involved in the initial phases of life are more likely to incur the detrimental effects of absent or ineffective fathering. This includes what was named *father hunger* (Herzog, 2001), a complex psychodynamic underpinning associated with a rigidly defensive organisation.

> Because the more receptive and serene paternal functions involving holding, containing, waiting, and empathy have long been ignored, presupposed as maternal or feminine traits, or simply treated as insignificant and peripheral, yielding to these faculties can provide an opportunity to challenge the need to repudiate putative femininity, especially for men more organized around phallic masculinity.
>
> (Diamond, 2021, p. 6)

Effective and related fathers have been not present enough. Even as we are at an apex of change, we carry the influence of past fathers and the limiting boundaries of patriarchy. 'The father is an internalized paternal image from fact, fantasy, family, culture' (Diamond, 2021, p. 7). These are issues to unravel and are simultaneously the material from which to create. In the chain of complex interactions are unexplored exchanges of feeling, desires to identify and differentiate.

Father gaze

What comprises the father gaze and what qualities and attributes does it convey? The danger is whether the gaze indicates brutality; will the child be overpowered, rendered helpless, subject to physical and emotional abuse? The personal narrations here illustrate the emotionally confusing looks, the shadow of feelings unaddressed and unmet psychological needs. To be lovable in father's eyes only when his needs are paramount is a masochistic sacrifice of self. This can destroy any aliveness within the daughter, a fight against individuation, which becomes self-torturing (Knox, 2007, p. 545). She can never do it right, feels inadequate and indecisive. This father becomes both overvalued and feared, his standards of perfection creating an ongoing sense of inadequacy.

Early contacts with the father are significant in shaping character, emotional habits and attachment patterns. The desire for father is intentional and reflexive in which the child is both discovered and enhanced (Butler, 1987, p. 25). The father appears in unconscious father complexes, archetypes and symbols in our life and dreams. An overriding and absent father compromises puella in the world, her career, relationships and self-development. Love means succumbing to control by the other, while the badness is internalised so the other is protected rather than oneself (Knox, 2007, p. 545).

The child's life and the father's relationship with the living child have been negated (Kohon, 1999, p. 184) with his dissociation from affects as his inner life has been killed (p. 100). The child becomes the keeper of the father's tomb as she incorporates him to preserve and keep him alive. The child is 'caught between two losses: presence in death, or absence in life' (Green, 1986, p. 164). A child might grow up in a twilight state, non-differentiated or embroiled in an internal tug of war between wanting to come alive and pulling back. Compulsive and negative thoughts and behaviours kill off desires, feelings and bring dissociation from self and others. Subject to self-betrayal, denial of hungers and pleasure distorted as obsessions take over, the child becomes disembodied, with a frantic emphasis on the persona and ego façade to hide inner distress.

Identification with or ignorance of the absent father effect can bring melancholic attachment to the internalised absence. There is a distorted sense of his reality, and this can leave the child hopeless, submissive and masochistic. Self-affirmation is disjointed, and being present in the moment is an emotional trial. Desperate and isolated, the child deadens themself, the longing for personal involvement and empathic understanding unresolved.

If father has a persona larger than life, the physical, instinctual and emotional aspects of his masculinity and relation to femininity sink into the unconscious. The child may become obedient to the father and all he represents as an authoritarian. This perpetuates father as one-sided and unrelated and may cause puella to recoil from life, fearing the assertiveness necessary to move into the world and lacking the courage to be who she is.

Living in the father's shadow, fearing his look, increases his power to invade the personality and become destructive. The ego is left fragile and weak, deprived of the good father image. The failures of father fall onto puella who also fails. Puella could then live out the negative side of the father archetype, transmitted trans-generationally and passing on the unattended wounds. Envious of the child, father keeps the child from surpassing him as the child's own qualities threaten the father. Their discourse becomes frozen.

Puella-father bond or bondage?

The bond of the puella type to the father begins from birth. The bond grows with her identification based on valorisation of the father and then a psychological restriction against the independence of her psyche. He might be critical, brutally argumentative and emotionally unresponsive or rejecting, impenetrable. An unloving figure and unable to attach, he creates insecurity, low self-esteem, shutting down her internal needs, leaving her defensive and fearful. She retains a pervasive feeling of helplessness and emotional isolation and expects little from others.

Abbey dreamt *someone said she had to take care of her father*. The dream clearly states she must not leave her role of caretaker with her father. Is this the actual father or the internal father? Is it meant to restrain her or provide enlightenment? In Jungian analysis Abbey begins to realise the dream message is leading her to contemplate the causes of her psychic numbness, loss of passion, lack of safety or trust with others. Containing the care of her father will keep her from integrating any assertion of self or activating the ability to separate. By examining their bond, she could gain awareness of herself.

Abbey made what sounded like a weak and ineffective father into a powerful figure needing her help but obstructing her advancement. The father position is meant to help cultivate the unique and separate self, ideally setting the child on their course for individuation, self-reflection and self-acceptance. In development, fathers, even those in dreams and fantasies, help guide the child through the vicissitudes of life. As an internalised figure, father is a combination of actions, family and culture unconsciously transmitted through the generations. In a 'dialectic of recognition' and 'desire for the other's desire' (Civitarese, 2013, p. 154), encountered through the unconscious, interpsychic communication becomes one of the building blocks structuring the child's internal world.

A father figure negatively inhabiting a daughter's psyche can prevent her from living in an autonomous and creative way that is possible only when there is separation from the father (Carotenuto, 2015, p. 26). She might avoid exposing any fragility because she had to appear strong and perfect in the presence of her father. However, the arrogance of her father meant Abbey must obey and live by his rules. This paternal parent attitude devoured the aliveness of puella to feel herself. Through internalised persecutory male figures, a hostile inner world of masochism and sadism, rage and numbness, evolved, keeping her repressed. Until comprehended, the daughter might remain in violent protest to all the father represents, locked in a self-perpetuating negative cycle, wasting her energy in anger and defiance of him but not in promotion of herself. Progressively more and more out of touch with her own thoughts, needs and feelings, she develops a pattern of negative male figures submerging her (Schwartz, 2020). This is a form of the negative father complex enacted throughout the generations, gaining power as it is unconscious.

Abbey felt impotent from the failure of the father to hold and make her feel desirable. Her unconscious reactions were also against the father who failed in his relationship with the mother. His disinterest transferred to Abbey, making her his support.

In analysis, I encouraged Abbey's investment in her internal space and psychic productions. This allowed her to find the capacity to revisit and reanimate psychic space, not as empty, but with the potential to be filled. At times, the more I tried to offer observations the more Abbey felt annihilated by the perceived demand to become who she thought I wanted her to be. This replicated the story with her father but gradually her narrative became conscious and began to shift. In the process, the whole self swung from being distorted in trying to be an imagined someone to inhabiting who she really was.

With sensitivity and receptivity, acceptance of her reality and what had been with all its overwhelming affects became clear. The capacity for imagination was strengthened and the non-representable gradually was found and enacted within the analytic dyad. A way emerged to retrieve, metabolise and elaborate a better father figure in her psyche.

Redefining fathers – taking down the walls of loneliness

Franz Kafka in his famous short work called *Letter to My Father* (1966, p. 7) wrote,

> Dearest Father,
> You asked me recently why I maintain that I am afraid of you. As usual, I was unable to think of any answer to your question, partly for the very reason that I am afraid of you, and partly because an explanation of the grounds for this fear would mean going into far more details than I could even approximately keep in mind while talking. And if I now try to give you an answer in writing, it will still be very incomplete.

We remain in search of the loving father. The father's absence stays with us, but within the absence we can develop new ways of being. How we fill the absent space becomes crucial for personal, physical and cultural development. The point is to fill the emptiness that the neglect of the father figure caused as he is impactful and his influence significant. Family constellations are changing. New visions arise, and roles are more fluid and less polarised.

Facing the gaps is at the heart of analytic work. Analysis brings dissolution and unbinding of imprisoning patterns. Therefore, from the lack, we emerge through mourning to acknowledge the issues for transformation. Although initially disorienting, a new reality can come with the journey towards repair. The explication of these dynamics and its effects is underlaid with the hope fathers and puella both emerge into more conscious and fulfilling relationships. In relation to this Jung said,

> We are confronted, at every new stage in the differentiation of consciousness to which civilization attains, with the task of finding a new interpretation appropriate to this stage, in order to connect the life of the past that still exists in us with the life of the present, which threatens to slip away from it.
> (Jung, 1968, CW 9i, para. 267)

References

Butler, J. (1987). *Subjects of desire*. Columbia University Press.
Carotenuto, A. (2015). *To love, to betray*. Chiron Publications.
Cavalli, A. (2012). Transgenerational transmission of indigestible facts: From trauma deadly ghosts and mental voids to meaning-making interpretations. *Journal of Analytical Psychology, 57*(5), 597–614.
Civitarese, G. (2013). *The violence of emotions: Bion and post-Bionian psychoanalysis*. Routledge.
Diamond, M. (2017). Recovering the father in mind and flesh: History, triadic functioning, and developmental implications. *The Psychoanalytic Quarterly, LXXXVI*, 2.
Diamond, M. (2021). *Masculinity and its discontents*. Routledge.
Freud, S. (1930). *The standard edition of the complete psychological works of Sigmund Freud: Vol. 21. Civilization and its discontents*. Hogarth Press.
Green, A. (1986). *On private madness*. Hogarth Press.
Green, A. (2009). The construction of the lost father. In L. Kalinich & S. Taylor (Eds.), *The dead father: A psychoanalytic inquiry* (pp. 23–46). Routledge.
Herzog, J. (2001). *Father hunger: Explorations with adults and children*. Routledge.
Hillman, J. (1979). *Puer papers*. Spring Publications.
Jung, C. G. (1968). *The collected works of C. G. Jung: Vol. 9i. The archetypes and the collective unconscious*. Pantheon Books.
Kafka, F. (1966). *Letter to his father*. Schocken Books.
Kast, V. (1997). *Father, daughter, mother, son*. Element Books.
Knox, J. (2003). *Archetype, attachment, analysis*. Routledge.
Knox, J. (2007). The fear of love: the denial of self in relationship. *Journal of Analytical Psychology, 52*(5), 543–563.
Kohon, G. (Ed). (1999). *The dead mother: The work of André Green*. Routledge.
Kristeva, J. (1991). *Strangers to ourselves* (L. Roudiez, Trans.). Harvester Wheatsheaf.
Phillips, A. (1999). *Taking aims: André Green and the pragmatics of passion*. Routledge
Schwartz, S. (2020). *The absent father effect on daughters: Father desire, father wounds*. Routledge.
Solomon, H. (1998). The self in transformation: The passage from a two- to a three-dimensional internal world. *Journal of Analytical Psychology, 43*(2), 225–238.
Willemsen, H. (2014). Early trauma and affect: The importance of the body for the development of the capacity to symbolize. *Journal of Analytical Psychology, 59*(5), 695–712.

Chapter 6

The empty chair

This chapter explores the personality characterised by emotional absence, a numbness of psyche and body and a deadening of soul. First, I want to begin with two quotes, one by André Aciman from his essay collection *Homo Irrealis* and one by Jung from his essay 'The Meaning of Psychology for Modern Man'.

> Nothing was as it seemed. I was not as I seemed ... I was confronted by the possibility that perhaps the truest thing about me was a coiled identity, my irrealis self, a might-have-been self that never really was but wasn't unreal for not being and might still be real, though I feared it never would.
> (Aciman, 2021, p. 111)

> As a result of some psychic upheaval whole tracts of our being can plunge back into the unconscious and vanish from the surface for years and decades ... disturbances caused by affects are known technically as phenomena of dissociation, and are indicative of a psychic split.
> (Jung, 1964, CW 10, para. 286)

Drawn to the empty chair in my office, Lucien says it represents the desire to be held and supported emotionally. She wonders what the holding means for her, for me, for us? Now emotionally frozen, the narcissistic and emotional wounds of early childhood have been repeated in adulthood, fostering an 'as-if' personality based on façade. As Lucien says, 'I don't know who I am. There is a peculiar feeling of unreality. I feel like a facsimile, although I cannot say why. I was hoping to break through the sense of living behind a mask'. These comments represent a psychic fragility resulting from unintegrated and unbearably painful emotions. Her zest and passion for life is guarded, the self enclosed and shut off, relationships kept at a distance.

Dreams from this composite clinical example are focused on what can fill the emptiness through the symbolism of the chair for exploring the inertia of self. Disembodiment from emotions and narcissistic singularity are also characteristic of this 'as-if' personality. This Jungian perspective parallels French psychoanalyst

DOI: 10.4324/9781003449447-6

André Green's concepts of absence, emptiness and negation, emotions denied but clamouring for attention. The impact of parents, here specifically the father figure, contributes to the disturbances.

The chair symbolically

The analytical transference and countertransference re-enact repressed desires, dissociations and defences. The conscious self denies the authentic self, which is unconsciously suppressed in the depths of the unrecognisable due to the fear of repeating previous injuries inflicted by oneself and the environment. The symbol of the empty chair holds the possibility of understanding the various emotions of shame, destruction, reparation and hope. The analytical relationship gives space to what formerly was absent. This means gathering language from the void and numbed emotions. Formerly arrested, emotional reactions are accessed through the analysis, dreams and symbolisms, and the empty chair is then no longer empty.

'I begin with nothingness. Nothingness is the same as fullness ... That which is endless and eternal has no qualities, since it has all qualities' (Jung, 2009, pp. 509–510). Lucien disguises emotional reactions behind a persona of confidence and self-reliance. However, she has increasingly sensed a rumbling from within herself. She *dreams of a woman in a flowing dress, red shoes, a man at a piano, dressed in a hat and black suit. There is a formal and large painting behind, and an empty chair arrayed in the same material as the painting. As they begin to play the musical instruments, the painting moves in unison.* She comments, 'I feel confused and impatient as to what to do with it all. So much is churning inside, but I don't know how to give it words or practical meaning'. She adds the dream chair is to receive, and she aligns this with the red chair she looks at in my office.

She sits across from this chair and sees it as giving support, holding. She recently found a chair in a dumpster. It turned out to be valuable, originally constructed at the time of her birth. She restored it as it was in pieces. It is now a decorative piece, not to be sat in.

In his *Red Book*, Jung addressed the spirit of the depths and the spirit of the times. Reflecting an increasingly fragmented and precarious world is a feeling of underlying fragility. Many are living with the estrangement, isolation, loneliness and emptiness like that experienced by the 'as-if' person. Exploring this personality with its fractured bits, pretence and façades involves some of the larger and most diverse and complex issues of our times. British Jungian analyst Michael Fordham (1985) explained this as the defence of the core self, keeping at bay contact with overwhelming experiences, defending against the terror of fragmentation.

As Andrew Samuels put it, 'The symbolic process begins with a person feeling "stuck", hung up, forcibly obstructed in the pursuit of his aims and it ends in illumination, "seeing through", and being able to go ahead on a changed course' (1986, p. 145). The therapist provides a place to bear the wounds of the unfolding narrative in which the unthinkable, awesome, empty spaces can be contemplated.

The symbolic attitude develops within the dynamics and embodied interactions of the intersubjective relational and analytical matrix.

> Linking perception to expectation or connecting visual and auditory modalities ... is a fruit of the transcendent function operating at a very basic level. It involves the capacity to be together, in a meaningful rhythm, learning to communicate with each other's basic psychic and somatic functions.
>
> (de Rienzo, 2021, p. 270)

In the search for psychological understanding, emotions erupt as the therapeutic relationship is a 'haunting repetition... of those traumatizing situations that created the original dissociative responses' (Solomon, 2004, p. 642). Neuroscientist Antonio Damasio contends rationality cannot be separated from emotions, which are 'an integral component of the machinery of reason' (1994, p. xii). Emotions can negatively affect our rational thinking, but their absence can be equally adverse. Damasio highlights the centrality of emotions for our being in the world, saying that 'feelings are the expression of human flourishing or human distress, as they occur in mind and body' (2003, p. 6). At every analytical session conscious and unconscious emotions are enacted in the service of unveiling blocked vitality and authenticity.

The role of mirroring, emotional resonance and empathy include the various nonverbal elements that contribute to establishing safety in the therapeutic relationship. 'Our task is not merely that of making the unconscious conscious but rather of restructuring the unconscious itself. To do that requires the transformational power embedded in unconscious affective, human interactions' (Sieff, 2010, p. 347). The therapeutic space includes encountering the vulnerability, the fantasies and tragedies within the tender and fragile hidden parts of the self. Affective emotional engagement in therapy enables emotional learning, which may bring profound change in the inner patterning that determines the way the patient is able to relate (Wilkinson, 2017, p. 539).

These are the emotional states pleading to be collected: discontinuities in the psyche, places fractured or failed bonds manifest in loss and despair, inner disintegration, frozen emotions linked with de-somatised relationships to oneself (Goss, 2006, p. 681). These appear in images, dreams and symbolic messages from the unconscious that help restore the personality and convey knowledge of the body. Jung described 'a process by which a new content forces itself upon consciousness either from without (through the senses) or from within (from the unconscious) and, as it were, compels attention and enforces apprehension' (1971, CW 6, para. 683).

Creativity and imagination arise in analysis, bringing forth meaningful content and thoughtful reflection. Lucian has another *dream of the red chair in my office several months later. Now there are objects on the chair – an old clock, her antique pendant, an apple.* She associates this to reading about Adam and Eve in an analytical book the night before. *In the dream limbs like branches grew over these objects and covered them in red paint to hold or protect them.* She said the dream was one of reassurance because these special things are contained in the red chair with her favourite colour.

The two worlds of analyst and analysand blend in this relational field and give life to the scenarios moving into the unknown material. Jung described this as the transcendent function arising within the analytic discourse and facilitating personality expansion.

> The suitably trained analyst mediates the transcendent function for the patient, i.e., helps bring conscious and unconscious together and arrive at a new attitude … The understanding of the transference is to be sought not in its historical antecedents but in its purpose.
> (Jung, 1969, CW 8, para. 146)

The psychological journey revisits the incomplete emotional places, old issues; it retraces memories. There might be panic, torpor and disorientation. The analyst is the co-creator of the unconscious, helping transform the undigested and weaving new meanings (Ferro & Nicoli, 2017, p. 6). Naming and visualising the obstacles, joys and tragedies can help access the unconscious, enriching conscious life, transforming energy into new combinations. Jung commented, 'Every psychological expression is a symbol if we assume that it states or signifies something more and other than itself which eludes our present knowledge' (Jung, 1971, CW 6, para. 817). The symbol gives form and shape to the emotional, unconscious patterns leading to a sense of self.

Although the psyche seeks equilibrium, the ego consciousness will do much to avoid discomfort, but the rejected, uncomfortable material maintains pressure to counteract this. If the information is not integrated consciously, it manifests in increasingly difficult symptoms so it can be known. This brings about various emotional reactions, as 'there is no change from darkness to light or from inertia to movement without emotion' (Jung, 1968, CW 9i, para. 179). On the one hand, emotion is an alchemical fire and warmth, bringing everything into existence, and the heat burns the superfluities to ashes. On the other hand, emotion is of the moment, a spark and a major source arousing consciousness.

Do you know my name?

The intersubjectiveness of analysis finds ways into the formerly futile and often deceptive wanderings of a person's internal world. According to American relational analyst Jessica Benjamin,

> The need for mutual recognition, the necessity of recognizing as well as being recognized by the other … is crucial to the intersubjective view; it implies that we have a need to recognize the other as a separate person who is like us yet distinct.
> (1988, p. 23)

The interaction of the patient and analyst on the intersubjective and intrapsychic levels is a 'dialectic of consciousness and unconsciousness, of presence and absence, of affirmation and negation upon which the analytic enterprise rests' (Ogden, 1997, p. 22). We feel empathically what the patient is feeling, and this also indicates the quality of the relationship. The personality is transformed by these reflective, conscious and unconscious emotional interactions.

Transference occurs as each projects the unconscious content activated from the other person. Countertransference occurs in reaction and is also personally stirred from within the analyst. Although this is a reciprocal relationship, the analyst must be aware of being an instrument to contain, facilitate and further movement of the process. In opening the psyche, the body phenomena also are part of the awareness. In the room there are not only two souls but also two bodies in a constant and reciprocal interaction and exchange.

In the transference and countertransference both participants recognise the emotional distress, mourn the losses and search for recovery of the personality. Analysis revolves around the conflicts and tensions of uncovering, resolving and reconciling the opposing forces in the individual (Samuels, 1986, p. 83). The alliance between therapist and client secures trust, connection, fluidity of thought and reverie to move the process to wider perspectives.

> Using their own symbolic attitude, the analyst offers a form of meaning to the patient that enables them to take a 'third position' to their own proto-symbolic productions. In other words, the analyst's interpretative activity promotes the patient's imaginal capacity, enabling a conscious attitude to the spontaneous fantasy productions emerging from the unconscious and to find new meaning in them. In this way, the analytic process involves the development of co-constructed meanings.
>
> (Colman, 2007, p. 575)

This intersubjectivity is necessary to escape the solipsism of a separated and often isolated existence that came from the previous absence and lack. The analytical dialogue serves as the container for the experience of confusion and not knowing (Ogden, 2004, p. 2). It is a gradual process of bringing out the damaged pieces, examining and filling them. Jungian analyst Murray Stein referred to 'a sudden shift into a different way of being in the world in which meaning is generated via congruent correspondence rather than logical chains of thought' (cited in Colman, 2008, p. 472). This indicates synchronicity along with the meaning making capacity of the psyche.

The therapist and 'as-if'

I have been intrigued with this personality type since I first read an article by British Jungian analyst Hester Solomon on the 'as-if' personality. It has long roots in analytical thought but originally was dismissed as being only applicable to women and originally to those assumed to be unanalysable. Solomon described the person as shrouded in disguise. These people feel the need to pose, create images and rely on the façade, 'as-if' unable to be totally present, feeling unreal. The tender vulnerability, raw and unexplored potential is hidden, emotions cut-off, deadened. The unformulated question remains 'Who am I?'

The emptiness, longing and needs of the 'as-if' personality are re-enacted through the therapeutic relationship. The non-verbal communications between client and therapist are important in the recognition and treatment of dissociations. The patterns laid down early in life can be altered in the analytical relationship as the person gains the ability to feel, name and reflect on feelings. This facilitates gradually integrating and healing the effects from the emotional wounds for developing a more coherent sense of self. 'Then the past becomes the past, rather than forever being relived in the present' (Wilkinson; cited in Sieff, 2010, p. 341).

Jungian analytical treatment offers a place to dissolve the falsity, face the deprivations and be finally seen. 'The facets of their experience, behaviour and ways of relating ... manifest in the transference-countertransference so the traumatic complex be detoxified and the individual freed to fully embrace and constructively express and develop themselves and their relationships' (West, 2013, p. 74).

Lucian withdraws into fantasy and illusion from lack, emotional deprivation and disappointments, affecting intimacy with herself and others. Existing inside a protective shell, living within an invented reality is a safer place, away from the assumed threats, insecurities and dangers of the outside world. The fragility of the ego is unconsciously defended. There are anxieties about the ability to survive because existence feels always at stake. This manifests as the self in conflict with itself, attacks through harsh inner talk, destructive food habits, disconnect from the body while living a solitary existence in an empty universe.

According to Jung, the 'blocking of libido' as he called it, can lead to feeling life has lost its zest and enjoyment and a person becomes stuck and lost. 'Libido is appetite in its natural state. From the genetic point of view, it is bodily needs like hunger, thirst, sleep, and sex, and emotional states or affects, which constitute the essence of libido' (Jung, 1967, CW 5, para. 194).

Lucien entered analysis for the first time in her 50s. She was intelligent, quick, in a high-ranking position with a large salary. There was an appeal to Lucien, yet she was emotionally removed. I dreamt of her and wondered if this signalled the presence of possible emotional distance. Was distance a way to hide the 'as-if' or the deadened parts within the personality? I pondered what was behind my dreams and how the therapy could possibly remain without disturbance, the cracks patched. Lucien was compliant but emotionally untouched. I surmised the dreams were alerting me to the smoke and mirrors aspect of this 'as-if' personality, but I did not know all that at the beginning. I just sensed there was distress.

In instances like Lucien, partial selves were acting as integral selves, reinforcing the 'as-if' position by relying on persona and image. This helped maintain psychological certainty with her mental mechanisms framed to eliminate any opposition. She was not moved by desire, as the world needed to be smooth and undisturbed, and little could be taken in or upset the self. This type of person is protected by the rigidly constructed organisation of psychic retreat to avoid the chaos inside. All must be ordered, static. Her life focused on work, a singularity of emotional isolation within. She was stagnating without the instability of growth and change.

Lucien aimed to please and assumed this required hiding her authentic self. Not expressing emotion, needs, expecting little, feeling unsafe, she seemed almost dehumanised. There was little trust in others, and it was hard to let herself be alive as she had little idea what that meant but assumed it would be used against her. Beyond the initial charm something was stifled, avoidant, while seeming open. Who she really was remained the mystery.

She mentioned being teary and depressed, emotions not previously acknowledged, and was now apprehensive due to some anticipated change. But what does she want to change? Career and executive positions have kept Lucien busy and away from feelings and emotions she dared not or maybe could not unfold.

Father not there

Lucien distances and avoids in relationships, engages in sexual encounters but is not emotionally intimate. Under a carefully constructed exterior is worry about everything and fears of abandonment that resurface when she gets attached. Unconscious of this and needing safety, she has put rigid defence systems in place to avoid emotions. She does not verbalise needs and now wonders if this attitude derives from the coldness and lack of passion from her father. If anyone becomes mad or disapproving, a nameless anxiety, an old, sick nausea occurs. Needing her parents to approve of her life dulled her nature and the wild and creative had to be hidden. She often dreams of being in a hotel, a place of impersonal sterility where she is alone.

Lucien learned to mask her thoughts and spontaneous reactions. Her parents expressed no empathy, and there was no space for play with them. Over and over, she felt deceived and betrayed by them. There was no way for her to be thought about or carried in the mind of her emotionally absent father, a blank personality who conveyed no expressions of love. Father resided in his psychological cavern, hardly attending to his children and was someone to stay away from. Lucien could not understand until well into the analytical work how much this vacant and absent father affected her. For so long, no one seemed to notice his blankness of emotion, feelings or interest. Father was a patriarch, dictatorial; his rules were to be followed; she was to obey without question. Mother was an icy shell, half-alive, taking pills for her nerves, busy reading travelogues and going nowhere, displaying little pleasure or joy.

Green's concept of the dead father or mother complex apply to this father and his effect on Lucien. 'The [fa]ther is not actually dead but rather psychically dead, that is, transmogrified from a source of vitality into a 'distant figure, toneless, practically inanimate' (Green, 2001, p.170). Lucien says, 'I feel like the fog again'. This phrase has come to mean she is lost and without feeling, a bit dizzy. It often occurs when being spontaneous, having enthusiasm, doing something father would disapprove.

'Without the felt experience of existing (which is at this stage equivalent to existing in the mind of the other), there is no possibility of representing that which is missing since there is no subject to whom it could be represented' (Colman, 2010, p. 277). Lucien's childhood was devoid of a father who was nurturing and empathy. He did not put his heart into her. To surmount dismay at the parental loss, the child develops a compulsion to imagine, to think, to master the traumatic situation and to mask the hole. Lucien's life became emotionally halted. The absent object (father) is a process whereby, in a desperate attempt to thrive, the child splits off and becomes their own parent. From the emotionally dead parent a child experiences detachment, loss of parental love and psychic holes. When the possibility of a real relationship emerges, like the analytical one, the dead parent zooms in and a black hole opens (Green, 1986, p. 162).

An interior symbolic world that is valued needs experiences of optimal connection and separation (Feldman, 2002, p. 399). However, for Lucien, family life revolved around mechanised order masking the emptiness. Yet, she is reluctant to escape the familiar interactions and face the depth of emotions. The analytic work brings moments of emergence from her psychic narcissistic retreat of singularity into a relational and emotionally connected space.

Conscious awareness of the emotional wounds arouses disillusionments, profound disappointments and the means to cope. Facing illusions and emotional reactions becomes restorative as both participants are actively involved in the interplay of the unconscious processes in the consulting room. The psychological process takes patience because the unmasking of reality connotes a threat to the ego or persona front shown to the world. 'Early experiences of internalizing the presence of an absent object, create the sense of an internal void at the core of the Self' (Solomon, 2004, p. 635). The need for unconditional love, anxiety about hostility and an expectation of being refused had been the norm of Lucien's life.

Being real seems impossible and she believes her survival hangs on a fragile thread. Aspects of the self have never been known and 'their only image is a radical absence' (Colman, 2008, p. 362). Lucien presents like a mannequin set for display, with control over body, food, exercise frantic to keep the right image.

The analytical process requires the capacity to recognise and gather multiple, emotionally based personal and collective threads. By entering the problems in a real way, while accepting and untangling projections, analysis can expand the freedom to dream, feel and think creatively.

The 'as-if' person often begins treatment adept at the socialised self, a conformity that hides self-condemnation and loss of vitality and meaning. The private self is not available as it feels too precarious. This person has spent a lifetime in inner deadness, with their emotional needs unmet. Sharn Waldron writes of what is needed to escape the black hole:

> What is necessary is an actual person to absorb the projection, not a two-dimensional flat production that cannot interact ... the undeveloped core of the patient's self [needs to be] allowed it to emit itself from its incarceration inside

the 'black hole' ... to counteract the massive power of the absence at the heart of the abyss.

(Waldron, 2013, p. 106)

This personality type reflects current cultural tendencies for coverup, superficiality, quick happiness and the search for easy fixes, especially as found on the internet. Their psychological and emotional isolation also contains the yearning for body, self and other connections, rather than languishing in the unreal and illusionary. Being real rather than 'as-if' is a process of release and personal emergence from inner emptiness and loss to igniting desire and aliveness.

The process is difficult as it means uncovering the issues, so the aloneness and separation are filled with presence. Lucien *dreams of standing behind a woman in a Chippendale chair and she puts her hands on the woman's shoulders. Then the woman begins yoga breathing and she keeps hold on her shoulders. It is like they breath together and one enlivens the other.*

Emotions unveiled

Lucien had been an elusive, passive version of a total self, yet now she is clawing through. Each of us carry hidden, emotionally charged stories and desires that guide our thoughts and actions. Like a puppet master, they pull the strings in our life and shape who we are and how we see the world. By bringing these narratives to light, we can break free from their limiting emotional beliefs and tap into our potential.

As Swiss Jungian analyst Verena Kast noted,

Emotion is an expression of the self ... If we decide we no longer want to hide behind empty shells, then we will have to allow certain emotions more room. We will have to let ourselves laugh louder, cry louder, and shout for joy.

(2003, p. 38)

Hope activated in the analytical space is a bridge to connect and transition between what was not existent previously into what now emerges. These experiences through their wealth of symbols increase the capacity to manage as analyst and patient are together between what seemed unimaginable and now becomes possible – to be one's real self.

References

Aciman, A. (2021). *Homo irrealis*. Farrar, Straus and Giroux.
Benjamin, J. (1988). *Bonds of love: Psychoanalysis, feminism and the problem of domination*. Pantheon Books.
Colman, W. (2007). Symbolic conceptions: The idea of the third. *Journal of Analytical Psychology, 52*(5), 565–583.

Colman, W. (2008). On being, knowing and having a self. *Journal of Analytical Psychology, 53*(3), 351–366.

Colman, W. (2010). Mourning and the symbolic process. *Journal of Analytical Psychology, 55*(2), 275–297.

Damasio, A. (1994). *Descartes' error: Emotion, reason, and the human brain*. Quill.

Damasio, A. (2003). *Looking for Spinoza: Joy, sorrow, and the feeling brain*. Harcourt.

de Rienzo, A. (2021). The day the clock stopped. Primitive states of unintegration, multidimensional working through and the birth of the analytical subject. *Journal of Analytical Psychology, 66*(2), 260–280.

Feldman, B. (2002). The lost steps if infancy: Symbolization, analytic process and the growth of the self. *Journal of Analytical Psychology, 47*(3), 397–406.

Ferro, A., & Nicoli, L. (2017). *The new analyst's guide to the galaxy*. Routledge.

Fordham, M. (1985). *Explorations into the self*. Academic Press.

Goss, P. (2006). Discontinuities in the male psyche: waiting deadness and disembodiment. Archetypal and clinical approaches. *Journal of Analytical Psychology, 51*(5), 681–699.

Green, A. (1986). *On private madness*. London: Hogarth Press.

Green, A. (2001). *Life narcissism: Death narcissism*. Free Association Books.

Jung, C. G. (1964). *The collected works of C. G. Jung: Vol. 10. Civilization in transition*. Pantheon Books.

Jung, C. G. (1967). *The collected works of C. G. Jung: Vol. 5. The symbols of transformation*. Pantheon Books.

Jung, C. G. (1968). *The collected works of C. G. Jung: Vol. 9i. The archetypes and the collective unconscious*. Pantheon Books.

Jung, C. G. (1969). *The collected works of C. G. Jung: Vol. 8. The structure and dynamics of the psyche*. Princeton University Press.

Jung, C. G. (1971). *The collected works of C. G. Jung: Vol. 6. Psychological types*. Princeton University Press. (Original work published 1921).

Jung, C. G. (2009). *The red book: Liber novus* (S. Shamdasani, Ed.) (S. Shamdasani, J. Peck, & M. Kyburz, Trans.). W. W. Norton & Co.

Kast, V. (2003). *Joy, inspiration and hope*. Texas A&M University Press.

Ogden, T. (1997). *Reverie and interpretation*. Routledge.

Ogden, T. (2004). *The primitive edge of experience*. Karnac Books.

Samuels, A. (Ed.). (1986). *Jung and the post-Jungians*. Routledge.

Sieff, D. (2010). Neurobiology in the consulting room: An interview with Margaret Wilkinson. *Spring Journal, 84*, 327–348.

Solomon, H. (2004). Self creation and the limitless void of dissociation: The 'as if' personality. *Journal of Analytical Psychology, 49*(5), 635–656.

Waldron, S. (2013). Black holes: Escaping the void. *Journal of Analytical Psychology, 58*(1), 99–117.

West, M. (2013). Trauma in the transference-countertransference: Working with the bad object and the wounded self. *Journal of Analytical Psychology, 58*(1), 73–98.

Wilkinson, M. (2017). Mind, brain and body: The way forward. *Journal of Analytical Psychology, 62*(4), 526–543.

Chapter 7

The diachrony of dreams

> There is a stubbornness about me that never can bear to be frightened at the will of others. My courage always rises at every attempt to intimidate me.
>
> Jane Austen, Pride and Prejudice

The word *diachrony*, which depicts the movement of language through time, comes from the Swiss linguist Ferdinand de Saussure. De Saussure employed a metaphor of moving pictures where each is a frame combining into a whole. This parallels the dreams in which each one is static, standing alone yet connected in an evolutionary way to the development of personality. Puella, however, does not perceive life with this movement. She tends to assume time is forever or it stands still. She tends to wait. Is she sleeping? Unconscious of her value? Denying time, death and living? All this is evidenced in the following series of dreams where each is significant and connected to the evolving personality of the dreamer. Nadine is in analysis, and the transferences are well connected and able to contain the onrush of symbolic material feeding her psyche.

Nadine *dreamt she was coiled by a huge snake. It stared at her with bright red eyes. When she could no longer hold its gaze, she looked away and to her left she saw a woman in a cage. She commented on the cage, but the woman said, 'What cage?' The woman in the cage denies she is caged. Her freedom is in her attitude.* This dream, like so many, might seem obvious but there is more information to be gleaned dependent on the dreamer and her associations. The dream raises many questions, and the answers will be influenced by who Nadine is, where she is in her life, what the other woman represents, unknown aspects about her and what seems trapped but is not.

The large, coiled snake with red eyes reminded me of a painting of Lilith. It was typical of our work together that we each researched the images and brought our findings to the following session. This one revealed the myth of Lilith, previously unknown to Nadine, yet connecting her to some deeper layers in her psyche. Lilith is a figure Jewish mythology and is often said to be Adam's first wife. She was banished in some versions of the myth for not obeying Adam. She represents the strength and position of woman to be herself. As Nadine looked up the mythology and found the picture, she began to fit some pieces together. Now she could feel

DOI: 10.4324/9781003449447-7

the tightness of the snake and what had been holding her. Was it comfortable or restrictive? The snake so tightly wound around her body could be compensatory to the previous distance she had emotionally established from her body as she had separated from herself unconsciously, unwilling to feel. As the snake was so tight, however, she began to feel.

Of course, the snake also represented the apple of consciousness presented to Eve, causing the expulsion of she and Adam from the Garden of Eden. Like all symbolic images, the snake holds many meanings and, in this instance, was drawing attention to whatever had confined Nadine. In the myth Lilith complained to God, defied Adam sexually, was neither appreciated nor listened to, and she left them both. Lilith held to her firmness of conviction, defiance, definitiveness and demanded respect.

The dream also represented the cultural cage Nadine had grown up with. She had been caught, like many, in the restrictions of being a woman, with class limitations and rules. The family upheld and believed in these and reinforced them with an iron hand. For a long time, she was unable to see what the other woman knew in the dream – that there was no cage. Many women the world over are perpetually within the cage of culture and yet to find or feel freedom.

The dream indicated the transference-countertransference with its relational involvement. Meaning was co-created in the transferences of both parties. The real analytic object and the experience occurred neither on the patient's nor on the analyst's side, but in the meeting of these two communicating in the potential space between them. From this, life arose from the analytical relationship through bringing the conscious and unconscious into contact. These dynamics were constellated in each participant and between them. The intersubjectivity went in both directions, the analysand experiencing being seen by the analyst, but also seeing the analyst.

The analyst's challenge is to assist the patient in finding her unknown aspects so she can escape the limits she has inhabited. 'In the final analysis, the therapist must always strive to constellate the healing factor in the patient' (Guggenbühl-Craig, 1999, p. 92). The therapist provides a mirror for the patient to perceive what she could not previously due to the arrested images from a numbed psyche.

The personality becomes enlarged as the ego finds relationship to the self. The unconscious material compensates the one-sided conscious attitudes as the pieces and complexes of the personality come together and point towards the yet unknown. Think about the effect of dreaming on mental life, or the experience of emerging from a dreamless sleep into wakeful consciousness. In these transitions, our consciousness undergoes a profound structural shift. For example, the passage of time and the sense of self and identity is malleable in dreams and is often different from waking time. We are not in a different world, but in a different state of consciousness. These are not only sensory experiences but also our conceptions and misconceptions of ourselves, revealing connections and missed connections with reality. Therapy provides the safe container for the self to unfold by accepting these dissociations, confusions and potentials of the personality.

The interpretation of the dream did not stop here. Its import continued through the analysis, referred to over and over. Like many dreams this one conveyed an aliveness ripe with messages. Applying the dream to the concept of puella, the cage had kept growth at bay. Being in a cage meant there was nowhere to go, no progress or movement. Moving out of the cage, connecting the feelings and emotions to the images, could release the psychological impasses. The cage had been a retreat, a place to gather strength, and the dream said she can now emerge.

The cage might also lead to the release of aspects of the personality trapped or held in from childhood. In fact, Nadine had experienced not only emotional lack of attention from her parents but also anything emotional had to be repressed. There was nowhere to go with it. Siblings were rivalrous for the bit of love available, and Nadine was not close to them, especially as they grew older. Family life with emotionally deadened parents was a place of deprivation. Nadine did not realise it, but she was starving for love.

Under it all were fears of falling apart, nonverbal but present. The lack of relation to her body, or orientation to self and the feeling of being ungrounded, was gradually uncovered in the analysis. The dreams helped bring awareness of what was missing and what she had gotten used to not having. She required little of friends or partners, worried she would be too much. The hunger for love and attention had remained unfilled. As she began to recall dreams and experience the reception to her being, they flowered even more, and she became sustained by the information flowing from the unconscious.

Meaning of time

Diachrony means studying things in their coming to be and acknowledging their change over time. It is concerned with origins and development, phantasy, memory and meaning. Jung regarded time as timeless, without borders, *Kairos*, eternal time. These are moments when unconscious eternal time intersects conscious linear time. At such moments the possibility of illumination, meaning and wholeness become apparent. The meaningful and transformational moment is a vitally important and decisive point when some facet of the unconscious psyche makes itself known, often in dreams as well as waking life.

Although Nadine was strongly marked by the dream experience, she did not fully realise how much events of the past could be alive in the present and be determinate of the future. She simply forgot there were any dreams for many, many years until she began analysis. Then the dreams began opening her to the formerly shut-off memories and, although prolific, did not overwhelm. They gradually revealed the inner world with its hurts, pains, sorrows, longings and joys.

As Jung said in 'The Psychology of the Unconscious':

> The unconscious is a sign of a special heaping up of energy in the unconscious, like a charge that may explode. Caution is indicated. Something deeply buried and invisible may thereby be set in motion, very probably something that would

have come to light sooner or later anyway. It is as if one were digging an artesian well and ran the risk of stumbling on a volcano.

(Jung, 1966, CW 7, para. 192)

Dreams help liberate, clarifying the psyche as it reflects personal and collective issues, illustrating the complexes, strengths, values and life trajectories, adding information and guidance. The perspective of Jungian analytical psychology affirms the significance of the unconscious, its symbols and archetypes, and the reality of the psyche as portrayed through the mirror of the dream. The imagery and the symbolic amplify the psychological material. In short, the dream is a natural and meaningful event, generated by the psychically determined activity in the unconscious.

All dream elements are symbolic, and they have private meanings discovered through the dreamer's associations. Every dream is meaningful, no matter how nonsensical or inconsequential it seems or how little of it we remember. Dreaming is a mental activity with its own logic. By identifying the dream mechanisms, Jung shed light on the workings of the unconscious and its powerful role in human life: 'Every psychological expression is a symbol if we assume that it states or signifies something more and other than itself which eludes our present knowledge' (1971, CW 6, para. 817).

In-depth psychological work constellates self and other, patient and analyst, depicting together the movement of the psyche and appearing in the dreams in one form or another. The symbols have personal and often more than personal significance. They help repair the personality as elucidated in the meaning of the word *symbolon*. The Oxford English Dictionary defines symbol as 'that which is thrown or cast together', from the assimilated form of *syn*, 'together', or 'a throwing, a casting, the stroke of a missile, bolt, beam'; and from *bol*, a nominative stem of *ballein*, 'to throw'. It also references a token or sign. From this we infer the symbol brings together and restores. And the dream with its symbols poses both an enigma and consciousness by uniting with the unconscious.

Dreams create meaning, metabolise experience and express something emergent (Winborn, 2016, p. 252). They get the dreamer closer to reality although their images and symbols are doorways into another reality. Dreams enrich the personality, presenting a paradoxical situation compensatory to the conscious attitude. Their images are of oneself and not oneself, as both the observer and observed. Dreams are hard for some people to catch as they do not want to know. Yet, with their connection to reality, dreams are an important source for integrating puella aspects and harmonising elements in the psyche. And they have collective as well as personal significance and applicability.

The symbolic meaning of dreams elucidates by analogy what is yet unknown or is in the process of becoming known consciously. Their symbols have specific meanings for each dreamer, and their messages convey transformative and guiding possibilities. Dreams reveal personal problems, the current situation of the psyche, the past and future, all displayed through their images, characters and storylines.

Dreams as a series of the creative manifestations of the unconscious are natural ways of making sense of experience, thoughts and concepts.

The unconscious psyche takes many subtle avenues we are not necessarily aware of. One of the gifts of depth psychology is the capacity to understand the invisible forces at work in the unconscious and revealed in dreams. In Jung's words,

> In the last analysis every life is the realization of a whole, that is, of a self, for which reason this realization can also be called 'individuation'. All life is bound to individual carriers who realize it, and it is simply inconceivable without them. But every carrier is charged with an individual destiny and destination, and the realization of these alone makes sense of life.
> (Jung, 1968, CW 12, para. 330)

With awareness, we can grasp the context and understanding for our individual life as we begin to pay attention.

The repression we all engage in comes from denying conscious acknowledgement of our desires, needs and wants, although this attitude creates psychological distress. Nadine said she was in an existential crisis. Now in midlife she realised her focus had been only on the 'we' but there was no 'I'. She thought always of others, waited until the last to consider herself and now did not know how to do otherwise. There was no thought of her value besides just doing the same old routine. She never thought or imagined anything else or anything more.

There is an innate restlessness to the psyche seeking more than the complacency of the here and now, for it wants what it is not and pines to redefine itself. 'It is the containing therapeutic relationship which makes it possible to dream the undreamable as a prelude to being able to think the unthinkable' (Sieff, 2010, p. 344). For Nadine, this meant finding her spirit and life-force, embodied and intentional, aimed towards reflective self-conscious awareness. However, the ability to use her personal truth for psychic nourishment had been compromised. Desperate and isolated, Nadine was realising she deadened herself to get by. Worse still, her deadness might also indicate a developmental deficit she believed in, leaving her feeling as if she was invisible, that she did not count and was just average. She described going through the motions of life, not living it. Knowing she was not fully alive or present, she came to analysis looking for what had been absent, a space needing to be filled.

Inspiration

But then Nadine had *a dream of flying and in it she was inspiration, being inspiration*. What does this dream mean? The dream literally said *she was embodying inspiration*; it was within her and now she must find its outlet. Verena Kast wrote on inspiration, describing it as being associated with ecstasy and creativity (2003, p. 110). She went on to note it is a being seized, a spark, a glowing, an emotionally involved spirit. The subjective relation to and relationship with the interior informs the capacity to create meaning, connect to others and engage in life with fulfilment. The relation to the interior evolves over time and persistently demands we analyse our lives in authentic, honest and confessional ways. This includes facing ourselves in the past, present and as we wish to be. This is part of accessing the spirit and life-force in psyche and soma for reflection and gaining self-conscious awareness.

The word *inspiration* originates from the Greek to mean the poet or artist would go into ecstasy or *furor poeticus*, the divine frenzy or poetic madness. They would be transported beyond their own mind and given the gods' or goddesses' own thoughts to embody. The word also derives from the Latin *inspiratus*, 'to breathe into, inspire', which in English means 'the drawing of air into the lungs' since the middle of the 16th century. It indicates the process of being mentally stimulated to do or feel something, especially the creative. Inspiration can be challenging to understand and describe because being inspired is individually felt and manifested. What inspires one person may not have relevance for another. Nadine's dream points to the development of her own self, her individuality, something she thought impossible before. She is being challenged and reminded of herself.

Dreams show what has been lost and needs to be re-found. 'The mind has the capacity to bring something back again which has been related to an object, without the object being there' (Green, 1979, p. 30). Jung observed the psyche is a self-regulating system maintaining its equilibrium just as the body does. A process too far one way or another inevitably calls forth compensation. As a basic law of psychological behaviour, the theory of compensation remains at the heart of the Jungian approach to dream interpretation. One of the key questions raised when confronted by a dream is to find what conscious attitude it compensates. The dream is not an isolated event separate from daily life. By bringing the unconscious into relation with consciousness the dream aims to restore balance.

Dreams bring back memories and emotions and can bring repair to early life experiences. They are timeless and therefore link the past to the present. They re-enact trauma, restore joy, take and give energy. For Nadine, the dreams were a relief. They helped her remember what she had tried to forget. They brought soulful, sombre events into the present day. Those same terrors and fears were centred around being alone without help. The disturbing events happened when she was too young to integrate the shock. Now she could unpack them in the space of the analytical relationship.

During the analysis Nadine brought many dreams; they were detailed, filled with sound, colour, shifting shapes, and her world was rocked with the new information. The symbols compensate the conscious attitude, and like all of nature, the psyche wants balance, and dream interpretation is based on this theory of compensation (Stein, 2022, p. 85). Populated with new insights, characters unfamiliar and out of her world and characters she knew, the dreams revealed her psyche had much to say. It is interesting there was no dream commentary on the family, parental attitudes, the home atmosphere of the repressed as the disregard had been so emphatic, yet her dreams had nothing to say. They were interested in supporting her depths and revealing the wider universe to her.

> Dreams tell what is happening below the level of conscious awareness within ourselves. They indicate possible developments with the repetition or not of themes, characters, scenes. Each dream brings personal associations and interpretations together and collects them to round out the picture while staying close to the dream itself.
>
> (Stein, 2022, p. 80)

The unconscious has a goal and the capability for realising the potential for development of the personality, and this is what it accentuates.

In his biography, *Memories, Dreams, Reflections*, he recounts his dream of a young girl and a white bird indicating to him the land of the dead. What does this mean? In 1912, a year later he explored the process of active imagination in his descent into the unconscious. It paralleled going to the land of the dead, or the underworld in mythology, as part of the process of becoming. This is the journey one takes to find oneself (Stein, 2022, p. 107). Following on this, Jung's imagination led him to the young woman, a daughter named Salome he interacted with in *The Red Book*. Salome accompanied the prophet, her father Philemon, and they both lived together in the land of the dead. This is what Jung called the *unconscious*, where myths come from. There he found his source, and through these characters he found and followed his myth (Stein, 2022, pp. 110–111). These characters appeared as Jung let himself go into the unconscious, undirected and open.

We too are fascinated by what Jung found there, as he illustrated with drawings, colours, the immensity of *The Red Book*, which draws us into our own land of the dead to find life. The land of the dead represents cultural history, part of the collective unconscious, and it is accessible to us all, each in our own way. Linear time does not exist in the unconscious and regular rules no longer apply. Life is renewed. Jung detailed how he underwent profound transformation:

> We are greatly mistaken if we think that the unconscious is something harmless that could be made into an object of entertainment, a parlour game. Certainly, the unconscious is not always and in all circumstances dangerous, but as soon as a neurosis is present it is a sign of a special heaping up of energy in the unconscious, like a charge that may explode. Here caution is indicated. One never knows what one may be releasing when one begins to analyse dreams. Something deeply buried and invisible may thereby be set in motion, very probably something that would have come to light sooner or later anyway – but again, it might not. It is as if one were digging an artesian well and ran the risk of stumbling on a volcano. When neurotic symptoms are present one must proceed very carefully.
>
> (Jung, 1966, CW 7, para. 192)

As Nadine examined the dream with the snake, she realised the character of Lilith was an entry into the unconscious and release from the cage of repressions. Here was her myth, and it was unfolding and clarifying her life.

Later in a dream, a man gave Nadine a box. He was carrying a woman who looked limp. Nadine said the box revealed what was wrong with the woman. She said she would take it to me, and we would discuss the meaning. In the box was an X-ray of the woman showing the tree of life. This referred her back to a significant event at that tree, a place where she was forever changed. At the time many years ago, there was no way to examine the extent of the change or what it meant for her further development. It was stunted at the tree, representing a traumatic event halting her psychological process, leaving indelible scars. Now she was being restored through the dreams and the memories coming alive, not feared. The dream assisted in spanning the time between then and now for regaining consciousness.

In the process of Jungian analysis and through exploring the intricate patterns of many dreams and the symbols contained within them, Nadine was learning to value her inner world. Jung called them 'uniting symbols' (Colman, 2010, p. 91), bringing to consciousness experiences other than known previously. No longer frozen with distrust and fear, Nadine was gaining confidence in the reality of her psyche and beginning the process of trusting herself and others. She *dreamt of a huge bird nest, the size of the large carpet on the floor. She looked in to find several large ostrich-like eggs. They were gold and covered with precious glittering stones. Just then a huge bird/griffin-like creature swooped overhead and landed on the eggs.* Nadine awoke amazed, confused, excited and with a sense of anticipation.

The nature of the unconscious interconnection of the two participants in the analysis is an essential ingredient. As Jung commented in 'A Psychological View of Conscience',

> As soon as the dialogue between two people touches on something fundamental, essential, and numinous, and a certain rapport is felt, it gives rise to ... an unconscious identity into which two individual psychic spheres interpenetrate to such a degree that it is impossible to say what belongs to whom ... For this a special act of reflection is required.
>
> (1964, CW 10, para. 852)

The signs of the emergence of the self into consciousness are the symbols of the focal points for integration, fostering a sense of patterning and meaning.

References

Colman, W. (2010). Mourning and the symbolic process. *Journal of Analytical Psychology,* 55(2), 275–297.
Green, A. (1979). *The tragic effect*. Cambridge University Press.
Guggenbühl-Craig, A. (1999). *Power in the helping professions*. Spring Publications.
Jung, C. G. (1964). *The collected works of C. G. Jung: Vol. 10. Civilization in transition*. Pantheon Books.
Jung, C. G. (1966). *The collected works of C. G. Jung: Vol. 7. Two essays in analytical psychology*. Princeton University Press.

Jung, C. G. (1968). *The collected works of C. G. Jung: Vol. 12. Psychology and alchemy.* Princeton University Press. (Originally published 1944).

Jung, C. G. (1971). *The collected works of C. G. Jung: Vol. 6. Psychological types.* Princeton University Press. (Originally published 1921).

Kast, V. (2003). *Joy, inspiration, and hope.* Texas A&M University.

Sieff, D. (2010). Neurobiology in the consulting room: An interview with Margaret Wilkinson. *Spring, 84,* 327–348.

Stein, M. (2022). *Four pillars of Jungian analysis.* Chiron Publishing.

Winborn, M. (2016). Review of the book *The necessary dream: New theories and techniques of interpretation in psychoanalysis,* by G. Civitarese. *Journal of Analytical Psychology, 61*(2), 251–254.

Chapter 8

Beauty – inside the mask

A woman *dreamt about silence and beauty not as outer images, but as emanating from within.* An affective experience moderating our relation to the world, beauty is intrinsic, a place for joy, a gift of pleasure. To expand this, one Jungian analyst noted, 'Meaning is, in the first instance, the fundamental manifestation of the passions of intimate relationship with the beauty of the world' (Schmidt, 2019, p. 80). Beauty is found within, an awakening as inner appreciation and a connecting point to the world.

This chapter explores the meaning and use of beauty impressed onto puella from the family and culture. It is interpreted and passed on through overt and covert messages, especially impacting puella. Beauty can be constrained into a position that puella has not chosen but is compelled to adopt, promoting an identity not her own. If traditional standards of beauty are the only currency for valuing our physical selves, we could remain stuck in a paradigm preserving old stereotypes and perpetuating an unattainable beauty myth.

For puella 'the recovery of the aesthetic object and the experience of aesthetic conflict is far more abrupt and at times quite explosive' (Riefolo, 2019, p. 149). Beauty is a psychological issue, and even when it seems puella fits the part, she can feel ugly, negatively judged and unacknowledged. Puella can descend into depressive states founded on the compulsive conviction of having lost the opportunity to possess beauty (p. 152).

The concept of beauty coincides with the cultures of narcissism and self-indulgence as they reoccur throughout history, apparent in the natural attempts to beautify germane to all people. These come in many forms of adornments, remedies, during life and after life, and are depicted in the fairy tales and legends of all cultures (Sinkman, 2012, p. 10). They are the visible dramas playing out in life, revealing how susceptible we are to collective beauty standards. Believing in them but not becoming lost in them is what puella must find in the search for her individuality.

Suffering under the pressure of beauty images, the female who succumbs to collective standards rather than her own is enacted in an extreme form by Argentinian poet Alejandra Pizarnik in the mid-20th century. Alejandra Pizarnik depicted the sorrows wracking the psyche of the puella personality. This is not to imply hers is the fate of all puellas but to accentuate the seriousness of the issue and the pressures

DOI: 10.4324/9781003449447-8

they undergo. Anguished and in despair, puellas are 'likely estranged from their true selves and over adapted to harmful environments at the cost of their desire' (Phillips, 2013, p. 185).

Jungian thought links to the symbolism and images that Alejandra Pizarnik brought to life in her poetry. She committed suicide after years of attempts to deaden her emotional pain. She felt she lacked physical beauty or appeal because she did not fit the collective female mould. To inhabit her melancholic world with its abyss of emotional sensitivity, desire and absence, opens us to an engulfing, bottomless sea of emotions.

Alejandra Pizarnik grew up ridden with unresolved complexes. She suffered from acne, she was overweight and her external looks and inner reflections haunted her. She felt an outsider wherever she went in her restless searching and was plagued by images modelled by her older and classically beautiful sister who fit the collective mould.

Her self-judgement was accompanied by symptoms of depersonalisation and derealisation. Overridden by internal conflicts and physical complexes in the various dissociations between mind and body, her self-judgement was based on shame and self-loathing and difficulty finding self-soothing. In her poetry, she depicted in graphic detail the struggle with her inner negative scrutiny, which made reality disappointing and fraught with anticipated rejection. With the fragility of her ego and attempts to both defend against the basic ability to survive and to destroy, on some level, her existence was always at stake. This manifested as the self in conflict with itself, harsh inner talk, destructive food and drug habits, disconnection from the body and a solitary existence.

> Insecurity and harsh scrutiny are the result of impossible standards in a culture demanding perfection, even though it is and was virtually impossible. Puella feels impelled to meet those standards, with her mental and physical health affected when they cannot be met. This is where beauty standards can be toxic. The body becomes a negative complex and, as such, is a drain on the psyche. The toxicity creates a film between puella and the world, a felt flaw, a disadvantage, a problem to correct but nothing to enjoy. Puella obsessed with outer beauty standards will do anything to make the obsessive goal of perfectionism come true. People who are obsessed with this image will not hesitate to take extreme methods to get rid of their assumed flaws while putting their life at risk. This is the all-too-common battle of many puella types, caught in collective standards but not conscious of and negating their individual forms of beauty.
>
> The ideological regime imposed on the female body from culture and society transfers as internalised violence, anger and the perverse desire to transcend the body altogether. The acts of satisfying hungers, taking in, indulging in pleasures become distorted into various obsessions of body and psyche. Puella types are preoccupied, trying to make their appearance beautiful and perfect for hours on end. They strive to make their flaws invisible while trying to fit the expected image. For Alejandra Pizarnik, the real self was trying to find out what that

was, and her writings display intense self-exploration, seeking but unfound. She exemplified how compulsive negative thoughts and behaviours can kill desires, bringing dissociation from self and others.

Alejandra Pizarnik faced unrealistic, toxic beauty standards throughout her life (Pramesti & Purwanto, 2022, p. 2), owing to her unconventional looks and her less than thin body. Her interest in the enigma of herself reveals a terrible sense of emptiness, negation and lost identity. She desperately desired to efface her very being. Her body expressed the fragility of self in several ways. It represented 'disembodied states of psychic deadness impacting one's relationship to the world' (Connolly, 2013, p. 636). Her talents, creativity and unusual perceptions were ever-present, whereas her dedication to life was curtailed by sorrow, loss, disappointments, poor self-regard and perfectionism. When there is disturbance in body image, the body becomes objectified and functions at cross purposes with itself.

The rhetoric of beauty in Western cultures is an ideology purporting a certain look as a necessary asset while its opposite receives the stigma of ugliness. This is where the superficial advertising and beauty industry have a huge impact on women and their self-perceptions. Beauty standards as touted emotionally degrade. Too often societal rules still define attractiveness according to male standards of desirability. Interiorisation of these standards disrupts the interconnection of the psychological system with contradictions and conflict. Self-appreciation is difficult to access. Nothing is enough, and beauty, if ever felt, is fleeting.

As French writer Hélène Cixous commented in her essay 'The Laugh of Medusa', 'Your body must be heard. Only then will the immense resources of the unconscious spring forth ... values that will change the world' (1976, p. 880). Alejandra Pizarnik's poetry and diaries are lamentations poignantly describing her felt lack of physical perfection and the harmful and restrictive projections and introjections of idealised female images. Jung noted,

> But if you hate and despise yourself – if you have not accepted your pattern – then there are hungry animals (prowling cats and other beasts and vermin) in your constitution which get at your neighbours like flies in order to satisfy the appetites which you have failed to satisfy.
>
> (1998, p. 502)

Alejandra Pizarnik was passionate, and her writing catalogued her despair, dark and violent emotions, and obsessions with death. She explored the mental anguish, troubled relationships, unresolved conflicts wrapped around her vision of herself, expressing elemental forces and primal reactions. Haunted by weighty depressive feelings, she was marked by emotional, interpersonal and behavioural instability. Her personal testament to the loneliness and insecurity plaguing her appeared repeatedly in her desolate poetic images.

Art is a survival strategy for many people who feel ostracised and like they do not fit the ideal mould. Pizarnik's poetry portrays her in a tenacious self-absorption with internal material both emotionally and psychologically disturbing. Her words contain statements about the manifestation of inner experiences, unfolding to reflect an individual soul reacting against collective impactful reverberations.

She described the seminal inroads for contacting the deeper psychological strata, the personal issues also mirrored by her collective experiences. Fraught with difficult struggles her descriptors work along circuitous lines, around and about, making imaginal connections, following the psyche in its poetic bent. As Jung put it, 'Personality is the supreme realization of the innate idiosyncrasy of a living being. It is an act of high courage flung in the face of life, the absolute affirmation of all that constitutes the individual' (1954, CW 17, para. 289).

Melancholia

'If the pain of loss is evaded and left unprocessed, one is increasingly melancholic, the ego fragmented. Melancholy names that condition whereby the grief and pain of loss remain unmetabolized and trapped inside the self' (Frankel, 2013, p. 9). Alejandra Pizarnik wrote about the splintering and disintegration of self while trying to exorcise the pain. Deep wounds scar. Wounds understood and integrated can become a resource, refining themes, melding antagonistic elements. These attempts towards self-knowledge and consciousness penetrate the eye of the complex. Alejandra Pizarnik struggled to emerge from the complexities and various emotions as well as her intensity, confusion and sadness. The themes of insecurity, the reality of cold indifference, lovelessness and the inevitability of death and loss preoccupied her.

In 'Paroles du Vent' ('The Words of the Wind'),[1] she writes about a cry for help at the realisation of looking in the mirror and seeing only herself staring back (Ferrari, 2018; Pizarnik, 2018, p. 16): 'How I would have loved to see myself some other night, beyond this madness of being both sides of the mirror'. Longing for another version of herself and to escape these 'ancient wailing nights' she continues to grapple with a plethora of selves. Poignantly she expresses, 'We suffer and crawl, dance, we drag ourselves. Someone has promised. It's of myself I speak. Someone can't take it anymore' (p. 5). In the poem, 'If for once again', she revisits the past 'broken toys' and 'expectation[s]' she set but assesses she has fallen short. Despite this, she still awaits the answers to the themes she brings to her mirror, 'I speak of sullen dust riven with sullen light, / blue eyes patiently marking time. / Who understands me?' (p. 7). As she expresses the suffering, 'my words are keys that lock me into a / mirror, with you, but ever alone', Alejandra Pizarnik expresses the futility of emotions in words serving to expand the distance between her and a companion. Ultimately, to search for wholeness in the other is to be reminded of the painful internal separateness of the personality. From an analytical explication, this is the wholeness of self she sought in poem after poem.

Alejandra Pizarnik's poetics reach into the somatic, the archetypal and impressionistic, the absurd and surreal. In a poem entitled 'Nemo' it is 'the yellow sun that passes through skin, marking its darkened fingerprints'[2] (Pizarnik, 2017, p. 11).

The poem 'Drawing' concludes with an art object undergoing a foreboding renewal: 'the vase is reborn / Beneath the shadow of the catacomb'[3] (p. 19). Her works reveal the genesis, the nascent gem and what is alluring. However, the tragedy is she was always struggling and could not find acceptance. Such verbal images were defined by Jung as, 'a condensed expression of the psychic situation as a whole ... an expression of the unconscious as well as the conscious situation of the moment' (Jung, 1971, CW 6, para. 743).

Pizarnik pushed against the confines of the narrow gender roles shaping her struggles and treatment of her body. Her poems express issues of missed resonance with self and conflicts with familial and societal expectations. Emphasising this, Jung commented, 'the collective unconscious is located in the body' (1998, p. 175). These issues and questioning traditional roles affected her psychology, fuelled her work and ended in her suicide. Her internal state was experienced as life threatening, with its archetypal images, depression and a lack of sufficient connections.

Beauty and body in analysis

Beauty can be invisible yet is present in clinical work through recognising the ability to be creative and the wish to be transformed (Sinkman, 2014, p. 1). How do we think about our bodies and those of our clients? How do we talk about bodies? In analytical or psychological treatment, we register how a person experiences their own body, including the body of the analyst and how the analyst perceives their own body. This is needed to retain awareness of psychic and physical embodiment. These are part of the process for feeling and hearing what is happening between analyst and analysand, grounding them in physical reality and its materiality.

The search for beauty can represent a desire to correct what are considered interior flaws and, for people like puella, surface flaws. A woman named Olivia is striking in an open, unselfconscious way. She is someone you think would recognise her inner and outer loveliness. She does not and instead has spent a life history preoccupied with body issues. She was never thin enough or too thin and unaware of either how she looked or her effect on others.

As a child, Olivia was not recognised by her parents for her athletic abilities. All she recalls is never liking her body. She restricted food for years and now has experienced weight gain in her late 30s. The model woman is her mother whose psychological and physical demise got worse at about the age Olivia is now. Mother was an alcoholic who mistreated her body, and her sister became lost in drugs and body issues of her own. Olivia had to be better than them, different. Olivia was required to fit parental needs and to make the parent happy. She became absorbed in the family's unaddressed mourning and depression. The various layers of parental emotional and physical absence produced the 'absence of memory, absence in the mind, absence of contact, absence of feeling ... [and this becomes] the substratum of what is real' (Kohon, 1999, p. 8). Olivia, like many puellas, grew up feeling inadequate, but needing to achieve, be the best, yet she did not feel real.

She was raised to imagine how life would be but is now facing what happens when it does not turn out that way. She spent years in one form of therapy or another, trying to get beyond the need to garner approval, the continual internal upset she has felt since young. Life has been spent counting calories and trying to be good but has been fraught with much anxiety underneath. This puella has not been able to realise her beauty to herself or feel comfortable in her skin.

She dreams, *I am in front of a mirror but see no one to recognise; the image is blurred*. She comments, 'I know I have a body but not that it is mine or that I care about and for it – maybe it is even a chore'. We experience the world through the body. However, these people 'experience body not as living reality but as an objectified thing, the self detached from corporeal reality' (Connolly, 2013, p. 637). These narcissistic defences can lead to seeking love and admiration and being the sole object of attention, and surrounding herself with people who see her as perfect or ideal. The puella is forever unknown in this scenario. When the body feels disconnected, the self is artificially disembodied, separated and identified only with the mind. These are the unconscious strategies bolstering defences against the internal threat of disintegration.

The body also registers what is ignored in the psyche. Repression of the things we don't like about ourselves gets projected, whereas the wounds themselves can go into the body, contributing to conditions from depression to anxiety, retreat, dissociation, addictions and somatic symptoms. Superiority that attempts to be expressed through the projected image serves to betray the internally felt inferiority. 'The loss of investment in the body leads to disembodiment or depersonalization in which there is an alteration in the perception or experience of the self' (Connolly, 2013, p. 639). The narcissistic defence disallows love of oneself in a way, supporting self-sufficiency but being parasitically dependent on the approval of others. The task is connection to body as part of conscious presence.

The experience of I and feeling real is constructed from a multitude of unconscious mechanisms and processes. Olivia, as many puella types, is caught in a contrived mechanistic and sterile world where self-esteem and self-worth depend on maintaining certain images and superficialities. The mind-body division keeps her locked in internal destruction and a lack of aliveness. The body becomes a place of unease, as she resorts to dire lengths to alter it by 'attack on the spontaneous psychosomatic being of the self in states of self-hatred and self-division' (Colman, 2008, p. 351). This form of depersonalisation is a defence against the underlying chaos and fragmentation buried beneath the cloak of an appealing façade.

Screaming

Alejandra Pizarnik was a model of intensity and passion and her writings expressed conscious and unconscious personal and collective issues in her search to be. 'To scream so much to fill the holes of absence, that's … what I did' (Vila-Matas, 2016). She oscillated between longing for transformation, escape from constriction and the renewal of self through language. Pizarnik compared herself to American singer Janis Joplin, who was addicted to alcohol and drugs and committed suicide at age 27. She wrote,

> She who died of her blue dress is singing. She sings suffused with death and sings to the sun of her drunkenness. Inside her song there is a blue dress, there is a white horse, there is a green heart tattooed with echoes of her own dead heart.[4]
> ('Nocturnal singer', 2016, 45)

In the poem 'Clock' she wrote, 'A tiny lady, so tiny, / who lives in the heart of a bird / goes out at dawn to utter her only syllable / NO' (*Works and Nights,* 2016, 25).[5] She also wrote: 'I gave the surge of myself to the dawn / I left my body joined with the light / while I sang out the sadness of being born' (*Diana's Tree*, 1962/2014, 13).[6] These examples of her writing demonstrate the emotional reactions and perceptions expressed in her idiosyncratic and thematically introspective poetry. Considered one of the more unusual writers in Latin American literature, her themes were the limits of language, silence, the body, night, the nature of intimacy, madness and death.

Alejandra Pizarnik's childhood combined disillusionment, fear and emptiness. Her family of Russian-Jewish origin lost many relatives in the Holocaust. This transgenerational wound was replicated in her own disliked body, which she repeatedly tried to erase. The impoverishment of the self is affected by early traumatising experiences. The melancholic identification with generations of loss and death impacted Alejandra. 'No life is possible beyond the boundary of the dead [parents] and there is no peace of mind within [their] embrace' (Kohon, 1999, p. 118). The lack of attentive parenting was emotionally wounding, exemplified by her mother's preference for her healthy beautiful sister because Alejandra was asthmatic and stuttered. She wrote, 'to write is to rummage through a tumult of burnt bodies, for the arm bone that corresponds to the leg bone. A miserable mixture. I restore, I reconstruct, so surrounded am I by death'[7] (*Extracting the Stone of Madness*, 2016).

The various layers of parental emotional or physical absence produce the 'absence of memory, absence in the mind, absence of contact, absence of feeling ... [and this becomes] the substratum of what is real' (Kohon, 1999, p. 8). The person grows up feeling inadequate, needing to achieve, but feeling unacceptable – the remains from the early creation of a self inundated with environmental failures and distorted early mirroring (Schwartz-Salant, 1982, p. 48). She expressed double movement, a creative being, an unusual nature, curiosity, fluidity and destruction and despair. Alejandra Pizarnik wrote of her feelings of estrangement, her poetry expressing the ravages of psychological distress, depression and insecurity from not feeling beautiful or loved.

'Nothing exerts a stronger psyche effect ... especially upon children, than the life which the parents have not lived' (1975, CW 15, para. 4). The darkness Alejandra experienced at home marked her early years. Childhood later became one of the central elements of her poetry. She wrote, 'Catch the memory of your face with the mask of what you will be and frighten the child you have been' (2016, p. xx). These early traumas and losses affected Alejandra horribly, setting alight severe depressive mood swings. The disturbed self-connection and its precariousness lingered as the early creation of self was marred by failures of parental blankness, depression and not close enough relatedness. These emotional wounds descended into the shadows. Dissociation developed as a survival attempt with Alejandra's many obsessions taking her into the void.

As an adult, Alejandra changed her name from Flora, choosing a different identity. She moved to France for several years where she seemed centred for a time, living true to herself and her ideals. She was drawn to those French writers recording the silence in the mystery, fleeting and intensity of suffering. But in France she also experienced severe depressions and addictions to pills, alcohol and so on. 'The rage is turned against oneself and transforms the ego to being reviled' (Butler, 2006, p. 180). As Alejandra said in her diary on 12 August 1962,

> Recognizing my addictive nature: I must live inebriated. If not from alcohol let it be from tea, coffee, phosphoric acid, very strong tobacco ... only after I can breathe freely, wander the streets without feeling the imperious desire to kill myself.
>
> (2003)

Even in France she could never satisfy the itch to be better or a different form of female and was subject to a fragile inner cohesion (Hillman, 1989, p. 57). She lived provisionally, unsettled, restless, ethereal, on the edge of survival, wandering without attachments. Her sense of self seemed always disturbed (p. 24), disconnected from finding the meaning she sought as her negative destructive impulses became stronger, drawing her towards death.

Alejandra Pizarnik was bisexual, but in much of her work references to relationships with women were self-censored due to the oppressive nature of the Argentinian dictatorship under which she lived. Her meditations on madness were a theme carried across her entire work along with themes of entrapment and her attraction to death.

Cultural influences

Do the cultural ideals of beauty have a psychic function in the constitution of the feminine? The sense of beauty is interactive, intersubjective and influences how we live physically and psychologically. Females often seem manipulated and subject themselves to search repeatedly for the next beauty product or routine. The relentless, insidious ideals of beauty – thin, fair, young, delicate – are taught to women every day in myriad ways.

Beauty enthrals, and female beauty was perceived and, to a certain extent, is still perceived as both enchanting and dangerous. A girl learns early from literature, popular magazines, movies, video images and the internet and social media about the beauty myth. What is viewed as beautiful has changed throughout history, and it's different in different societies, suggesting beauty is judged and based on specific, perhaps unconscious, norms and ideals. What is behind this pursuit of ideal beauty and eternal youth and what lurks in the depths of the human unconscious?

> Face and body image concerns can have a negative impact on mental health. They are associated with body dysmorphia, social anxiety, obsessive-compulsive disorder, panic, depression, eating disorders, psychological distress, low self-esteem, self-harm, suicidal feelings, all experienced by Alejandra Pizarnik over half a century ago. Compulsive negative thoughts and behaviours kill desires, bringing dissociation from self and others. Affecting behaviour and ways of relating, the interiorisation of female beauty standards too often has impeded psychological development, giving rise to deep emotional and psychological wounds.

The myth of beauty enforces normativity and sameness, especially for women, and perpetuates the subjugation of women to what has been male-dominated ideas. It drives women to purchase the prescribed makeup and clothes, to undergo plastic surgery and practice starvation. The myth keeps puella feeling insufficient, needing ever more alterations. For instance, whatever becomes defined as beauty is determined to be inherently good and beneficial, and without that beauty women are unacceptable and rendered invisible. Often women at the top of their professions, even with all their achievements and success, feel the pressure to conform to mass beauty standards. If anything, women with power and status are scrutinised more and the pressure to look beautiful is increasingly intense. Images of perfection in the modern woman's pursuit of beauty have had a huge impact, often detrimental to her physical and psychological health. Femininity is considered an object in need of change. In a systemic culture that subordinates women, they are blamed for their insecurities and encouraged to practice self-regulation and negation.

The pursuit of beauty can be a treacherous path. Enhancements pushed by fashion and physical appearance standards have intensified with profound consequences, particularly when it comes to ageing. Puella types are susceptible to adopting this attitude, becoming cruel, primarily and intrinsically to themselves. The engagement in extreme beautification measures leaves a woman hollow and alienated. Increasingly stringent expectations of beauty placed on women express an unconscious patriarchal backlash to women's increased freedom and rights.

Facing inwards

Alejandra's Pizarnik's poetry and diaries contain various conjuring and exorcisms as she turned her gaze away from the world, facing inwards to focus on the dark voices she channelled there. British writer Jacqueline Rose commented, 'Shattering the carapace of selfhood, she brings to the surface the physical and mental fragments, the bits and pieces that, at the deepest level we truly are, though we resist such knowledge with all our might' (2018, p. 163). Alejandra Pizarnik wrote:

> Where fear neither speaks in stories or poems, nor gives shape to terrors or triumphs.
> My name, my pronoun – a grey void.[8]
>
> ('Primitive Eyes', 2016, p. 103)

She addresses what she called the curse of being a woman, a Jew, an Argentinian as not merely the ability to profoundly feel her situation, but also to turn it to art. Her last years were a gradual withdrawal from family and social life, suicide attempts and hospitalisations. 'The wounds of self-neglect, absence, and derision appear in the repetitive negative complexes arising from affectively charged experiences between self and others' (Smith, 2021, p. 281). Life complexities, paradoxes and ambiguities created the frightening feeling she was no one or nowhere. Nothing filled the hollow spaces, sense of abandonment or incompleteness. In 1972, at age 36, Alejandra Pizarnik died after ingesting sleeping pills. She wrote,

> the speech of that woman I happen to be, bound to this silent creature who is also me. And may nothing remain of me save the happiness of one who knocked and for whom the door was opened.[9]
>
> ('The Promises of Music,' 2016, p. 61)

The ideological regime imposed on the female body from culture and society can transfer as internalised violence, anger or, perversely, the desire to transcend the body altogether. Any adaptation could sacrifice authenticity for a brittle surface existence. The acts of satisfying hungers, taking in, indulging in pleasures become distorted into various obsessions splitting body and psyche. André Green surmised it was 'a destruction of the psychic activity of representation which creates holes in the mind, or feelings of void, emptiness' (Kohon, 1999, p. 290).

Compulsive negative thoughts and behaviours are also complexes bringing dissociation from self and others. Alejandra Pizarnik seemed 'to face the long repressed but often suspected, underlying internal reality, a hauntingly ever-present background' (Solomon, 2004, p. 636). This negative loop is unstoppable and feeds an internalised cycle of oppression, abandonment and emotional vacuity. With libido devitalised a non-nourishing self-absorption causes a vacuum in identification with the interior and the existential emptiness of the intangible and indefinable. Defences and projections inhibit and disrupt the dialogical relationship with self and others. In fact, an inadequately formed secure identity makes relationships to self and others destructive.

Alejandra Pizarnik's poetry revealed the sorrows and despair in the convoluted process of finding herself. Despite the malign thing within, she summoned the courage to articulate truths not easily assuaged. Yet, the discontent, disequilibrium and inner tension she could not quell or satisfy was also her source of artistic energy as she strove to express herself.

Feeling insufficient, defeated and lost, Alejandra Piznarik's diary entry on 10 August 1962, a month before she committed suicide, read: '*But I remember you ... I dare not love you. Fear of annoying you ... My silence is my mask ... I love you and I fear and I will never tell you this with my true voice, this slow and deep and sad voice ... and you will never know of my love*'. With a fragile inner cohesion, she struggled with the defined and undefined sense of self.

(2003)

We are called to consciousness and to invest in building a physical, psychological and cultural environment supporting and reinforcing the wellbeing, safety and power of all women, both as a collective and as individuals. Jung said, 'We would do well, therefore, to think of the creative process as a living thing implanted in the human psyche' (1975, CW 15, p. 75). Alejandra Pizarnik expressed this living thing with her shifting valences of the self in the border between speech and silence.

Through the craft of her writing, she articulated the demons inside that would not allow her to live. Creative expression was a way through the entrapment she felt psychologically as well as culturally. In her words we hear the struggle between the true and false feminine attempting to shed the false shell.

The end without ending

The psyche is many layered, with psychological oppression, desire for release and emotional reactions all central to the life and writing of Alejandra Pizarnik. Her words put a visage on the inner chaos poignantly exposed through her work. Her poetry traces the process of self-examination on some of the hardest issues for establishing a sense of self.

Poetic images arouse feeling and reveal her passion and energy, not concerning the rational but the emotional. Through poetry, she recorded the angst and internal conflicts that interfered with living as her words poignantly detailed her pain. Her originality and the embodiment of her psychological conundrum remain to this day. The images resonate and reflect creativity, contemplation and anguish. Alejandra Pizarnik revealed the sorrows and despair in the blues of depression, self-loathing and self-dissatisfaction, pining after the beauty and inner peace she could not possess.

Concepts of death, emptiness and desire for self in her own uniqueness contained reflections on personal, cultural and women's issues. If traditional standards of beauty are the only currency for valuing our bodies, we remain stuck in a paradigm preserving stereotypes and perpetuating the unappealing beauty myth. Alejandra Pizarnik's story has meaning for the puella types who feel similarly yet do not have to follow the same destructive path. The point is to learn from her words as she bared her soul. Her writings articulate the dance between discontent and creativity, expressing human feelings of internal distress, body disconnect and struggles with self-image and collective beauty standards relevant to this day. Casting off false selves and façades leads to nakedness, unwrapping the layers of personality so we can live in its raw truths.

> my words which are keys locking me into a mirror, with you, but ever alone … The abyss of absence. But who'll say: don't cry at night? Because madness is a lie too. Like night. Like death.[10]
>
> Alejandra Pizarnik, 'Sex, Night' (2018)

Notes

1. Excerpts from THE GALLOPING HOUR by Alejandra Pizarnik, copyright ©2018 by Myriam Pizarnik de Nesis, copyright © 2018 by Patricio Ferrari, copyright © 2018 by Patricio Ferrari and Forrest Gander. Reprinted by permission of New Directions Publishing Corp.
2. Translation Copyright © 2017 by Yvette Siegert, *The Most Foreign Country* (Ugly Duckling Presse). https://uglyducklingpresse.org/publications/the-most-foreign-country/
3. Translation Copyright © 2017 by Yvette Siegert, *The Most Foreign Country* (Ugly Duckling Presse). https://uglyducklingpresse.org/publications/the-most-foreign-country/
4. Translation Copyright © 2014 by Yvette Siegert, *Diana's Tree* (Ugly Duckling Presse). https://uglyducklingpresse.org/publications/dianas-tree/
5. Translation Copyright © 2014 by Yvette Siegert, *Diana's Tree* (Ugly Duckling Presse). https://uglyducklingpresse.org/publications/dianas-tree/
6. Translation Copyright © 2014 by Yvette Siegert, *Diana's Tree* (Ugly Duckling Presse). https://uglyducklingpresse.org/publications/dianas-tree/
7. Excerpts from THE EXTRACTING THE STONE OF MADNESS by Alejandra Pizarnik, translated by Yvette Siegert, copyright © 2000 by Miriam Pizarnik. Translation copyright © 2016 by Yvette Siegert. Reprinted by permission of New Directions Publishing Corp.
8. Excerpts from THE EXTRACTING THE STONE OF MADNESS by Alejandra Pizarnik, translated by Yvette Siegert, copyright © 2000 by Miriam Pizarnik. Translation copyright © 2016 by Yvette Siegert. Reprinted by permission of New Directions Publishing Corp.
9. Excerpts from THE EXTRACTING THE STONE OF MADNESS by Alejandra Pizarnik, translated by Yvette Siegert, copyright © 2000 by Miriam Pizarnik. Translation copyright © 2016 by Yvette Siegert. Reprinted by permission of New Directions Publishing Corp.
10. Excerpts from THE GALLOPING HOUR by Alejandra Pizarnik, copyright ©2018 by Myriam Pizarnik de Nesis, copyright © 2018 by Patricio Ferrari, copyright © 2018 by Patricio Ferrari and Forrest Gander. Reprinted by permission of New Directions Publishing Corp.

References

Butler, J. (2006). *Gender trouble: Feminism and the subversion of identity* (2nd ed.). Routledge.

Cixous, H. (1976). The laugh of Medusa. *Signs, 1*(4), 875–893.

Colman, W. (2008). On being, knowing and having a self. *Journal of Analytical Psychology*, *53*(3), 351–366.
Connolly, A. (2013). Out of the body: Embodiment and its vicissitudes. *Journal of Analytical Psychology*, *58*(5), 636–656.
Diarios de Alejandra Pizarnik. (2003). Lumen Random House.
Ferrari, P. (2018, 25 July). Where the voice of Alejandra Pizarnik was Queen. *Paris Review*. https://www.theparisreview.org/blog/2018/07/25/where-the-voice-of-alejandra-pizarnik-was-queen/
Frankel, R. (2013). Digital melancholy. *Jung Journal: Culture & Psyche*, *7*(4), 9–20.
Hillman, J. (1989). *A blue fire*. Spring Publications.
Jung, C. G. (1954). *The collected works of C. G. Jung: Vol. 17. The development of personality*. Princeton University Press.
Jung, C. G. (1971). *The collected works of C. G. Jung: Vol. 6. Psychological types*. Princeton University Press. (Original work published 1921).
Jung, C. G. (1975). *The collected works of C. G. Jung: Vol. 15. The spirit in man, art, and literature*. Pantheon Books.
Jung, C. G. (1998). *The Zarathustra seminars*. Pantheon Books.
Kohon, G. (Ed). (1999). *The dead mother: The work of André Green*. Routledge.
Phillips, A. (2013). *Missing out*. Farrar, Straus and Giroux.
Pizarnik, A. (2014). *Diana's tree (Árbol de Diana)* (Y. Siegert, Trans.). Ugly Duckling Press. (Original published in 1962).
Pizarnik, A. (2015). *Music & literature No. 6*. https://www.musicandliterature.org/issues/6
Pizarnik, A. (2016). *Extracting the stone of madness: Poems 1962–1972* (Y. Siegert, Trans.). New Directions.
Pizarnik, A. (2017). *The most foreign country* (Y. Siegert, Trans.). Ugly Duckling Press.
Pizarnik, A. (2018). *The galloping hour: French poems* (P. Ferrari and F. Gander, Trans.). New Directions.
Pramesti, C. N., & Purwanto, S. (2022). Toxic beauty standards reflected in Prakasa's Imperfect: A psychoanalysis. *Dinamika Bahasa dan Budaya*, *17*(1). https://doi.org/10.35315/bb.v17i1.8899
Riefolo, G. (2019). The beauty of psychoanalysis. Marginal notes on beauty as a Process. *The Italian Psychoanalytic Annual*, *13*, 143–159.
Rose, J. (2018). *Mothers: An essay on love and cruelty*. Farrar, Straus, Giroux.
Schmidt, M. (2019). Beauty, ugliness and the sublime. *Journal of Analytical Psychology*, *64*(1), 73–93.
Schwartz-Salant, N. (1982). *On narcissism*. Inner City Books.
Sinkman, E. (2014). *Psychology of beauty: Creation of a beautiful self*. Rowman & Littlefield.
Smith, A. (2021). Sitting through the emptiness. *Journal of Analytical Psychology*, *66*(2), 281–300.
Solomon, H. (2004). Self creation and the limitless void of dissociation: The 'as if' personality. *Journal of Analytical Psychology*, *49*(5), 635–656.
Vila-Matas, E. (2016, 17 May). The unstoppable myth of Alejandra Pizarnik. *Literary Hub*. https://lithub.com/the-unstoppable-myth-of-alejandra-pizarnik/ (Original published as 'An overdose of Seconal', *Music & Literature No. 6* [2015]).

Chapter 9

Performativity

This chapter references the concept of performativity, of being 'the self located outside ourselves', derived from American philosopher Judith Butler (2020, p. 24).

> To be a self is to be at a distance from who one is … cast outside oneself, Other to oneself. Again, the falling into the unknown, not the mirror image but more, less, different, perhaps compensatory and also emergent, changing, unfolding.
> (2004, p. 148)

We impact, move into and through the world through self-expression, both psychological and physical. Individual expression is compromised, however, when roles and norms promote performativity solely according to outer norms and standards, such as those imposed on women by men (Butler, 2004). This creates unconsciousness actions and thoughts that are personally and culturally dangerous. Moving beyond outer performativity to true self-expression is in line with the Jungian process of individuation, the journey towards becoming one's real self, and speaks to accessing the pluralistic nature of a flexible psyche.

It is not only the puella's task but also every person's task to become aware of the many aspects of the personality. As Jung commented, 'Every psychological extreme secretly contains its own opposite or stands in some sort of intimate and essential relation to it' (1956, CW 5, para. 81). In other words, there is a process for integration of gender variances. How they are enacted is not just a given but an opportunity for self-examination.

As Judith Butler commented, 'A proliferation of identities will reveal the ontological possibilities too often restricted by foundationalist models of identity. These leave little room for individual expression and exploration as the theories assume identity is simply there, fixed, and final' (quoted in Salih, 2002, p. 59). Although unquestioned conformity is often required, seductive and seemingly easier to just follow, consciousness means breaking away from conventionality or just following the norm without questioning it. The pressure is to do the latter. Butler described 'identification as not the product of a choice, but the forcible citation of norms with a complex historicity indissociable from relations of discipline and regulation, and sometimes resulting in punishment' (2011, p. 232).

Performativity exists within the broader social context and is composed of unnoticed rote actions. The human condition, including the body, is shaped by the historical time and particular society in which we live. Acts of self-presentation happen all the time and determine who we are. Unfortunately, this can turn into a normalising framework that excludes those who do not fit.

Body unlinked

Feeling unlinked to the body is disturbing to our being. The individuals described here feel out of touch with their bodies, whether they look it or not. And those with bodies whose shapes are different from the dominant ideal are often treated as outsiders, abject socially, and this image becomes internalised.

They become isolated and learn to hide metaphorically, under the tables or in the corners. Self-hatred and self-denigration are assumed to be true. The self hesitates, disappears and often does not know how to return. The energy for self, when not ignited early in life, brings with it silent depression, which, although it might hardly be noticeable to others, is evident within. Bullying and destructive figures might populate their dreams and often there is no connection for getting help. They may even stop trying.

The problem is how easily performativity can dupe us and work against owning our uniqueness. Individuation requires consciousness of self and resistance to collective following as well as reflection on what fits and what doesn't. It takes awareness, and its import is noted in the Jungian commentary regarding body and psyche expressed with true personal representation. However, there are many cultures and groups where a person cannot decide their own way without suffering severe ostracism.

Judith Butler asserts in her book *Gender Trouble* (1990b) that 'identity is performatively constituted'. She formulated a postmodernist notion of gender, contradictory to the traditional fixed binary categories. 'Girl! is not a statement of fact but an interpellation that initiates the process of "girling", a process based on perceived and imposed differences between men and women, differences that are far from natural' (Salih, 2002, p. 61).

Identity is assigned and imposed early in life, subjugated to an existing order and instituted before a person can define themselves. When the individual can take part in making themselves, they participate consciously in the process of individuation. However, the social roles performed and enacted by individuals are strongly validated by society, perpetuating their continued performances so the social order continues. It is difficult to establish one's own way, especially when culture strongly supports something else. 'Femininity is thus not the product of a choice, but the forcible citation of a norm with a complex historicity' (Butler, 1993, p. 232). Refusing fixities makes room for the shifting and provisional and supports actions against those oriented to social acceptance while simultaneously eschewing authenticity and self-authority. This brings up questions such as how do we enact the truth of our self, how is the self constructed, including the body-self? The personality could be trapped, impersonating and performing while sacrificing naturalness and originality.

We locate the tendency to perform in relationships. We find this in our dreams. What role are we playing? How do we act? What restricts the full spectrum of communication and action? Where are the complexes limiting growth? Judith Butler's concept of performativity describes repetition, the copy of a copy and gender parody. For example, the classical Jungian anima and animus descriptors can be stultifying and inadequate if stuck in old rigid forms of personality expression. This mindset could subsume a person, narrowed to old definitions, out of step with the current era, personality reduced to a flat screen.

Puella types described here are not in touch with their body and psyche and miss the connection between them. They might be self-destructive and treat their bodies as abject, in the language of Lacanian psychoanalyst Julia Kristeva. What she describes as the *abject* is the unprocessed, rejected elements. This concept parallels Jung's premise of the shadow representing the negated, submerged and denied aspects of physical and emotional life. 'The naturalness of being oneself is repressed and the performance becomes everything, but one's reality is not in the performance' (Woodman, 1993, p. 22). This might mean the worship of the illusionary learned as an idealised version of performance based on what culture and the collective support. 'There remains a terror of the body and reality, and life becomes a mask to deal with the world' (p. 14).

Meanwhile, puellas face the burgeoning complexity and wide range of collective anxieties and fears currently accompanying and limiting self-expression. Part of puella is transforming and becoming, evolving. Yet part of her is compliant, repressed and dutiful. These opposites can clash and create internal turmoil as she grapples with how to integrate herself.

Anima and animus

Anima and *animus* are dualistic terms associated with feminine and masculine, forming a *syzygy* in classical Jungian archetypal formations. The danger is falling into concretism when the more complex task is integration (Douglas, 1990, p. 151). Deeper exploration of these figures takes us into the unconscious so we can release its energy into conscious life. The terms as defined or delineated and understood in Jung's era up to the mid-20th century have altered and now take on new meanings, images, ideas and identities. Gender reconfigurations typify our current era. The fluid, permeable and flexible are useful, and differences, not just opposing but also varying and not incompatible aspects, enhance enthusiasm, vitality and new visions (p. 197).

Jung designated the masculine principle as *logos*, or the tendency to logic and verbal formulations and the feminine principle as *eros*, or the tendency to emotional connections and relatedness (Jung, 1959, CW 9ii, para. 14). Originating from the idea that anima and animus archetypes are a counterpart of gender identity, anima is traditionally considered as feminine for men and animus as masculine for women. If we can bring these qualities into flexible form and interweave them to fit the individual, we find the unconscious psyche is a variation of many forms as well as a mirror counterpart of conscious identity. Lived reality, however, may look and feel very different than imagined.

The healthy balance of these functions in the psyche stimulates growth and enhances consciousness. Each person is comprised not only of outward physical form but also of an intangible, inward otherness. Balance requires being conscious of what qualities fit and what do not. Repression causes negativity, depression, anxiety, emotional numbness, an inability to act and general disconnection from the self. The general point is how these aspects of anima and animus are raised out of unconsciousness to conscious expression without remaining in dualistic, rigid, oppositional and separated modes of functioning. We are challenged to mix them up and create new ways of being without replacing one binary system with another.

Anima and animus can represent inner and archetypal figures conditioned by each person's experiences. Either aspect can inhibit or encourage a person as they step into life experiences. Both anima and animus can be vampiric and destructive as well as nourishing and encouraging. They are complementary and compensatory and exist in a range of possibilities. The interactions among them enhance the creative and promote the individuation urge to become who we really are and all we can be. As Jung commented,

> What is it, in the end, that induces a [person] to go [their] own way and to rise out of unconscious identity with the mass as out of a swathing mist? ... It is what is commonly called *vocation*: an irrational factor that destines a [person] to emancipate [themselves] from the herd and from its well-worn paths.... Anyone with a vocation hears the voice of the inner [person]: [one] is called.
> (Jung 1954, CW 17, paras. 299–300)

Authenticity

Symbolisation of the psyche and its conflicts and pleasures emerge through the body.

> To reflect one's authentic self. To confirm who one is. Patient and analyst follow the unconscious path proposed by symbolic expressions emerging in the body ... When such dialogue is grounded in the body brings easier access to the affects stored in implicit memory can be remembered and other symbolic ways of being expressed and contained in the analytic container.
> (Fleischer, 2020, p. 558)

At issue is puella often cannot easily find her ground of being. She might shapeshift, trying to fit some imagined or required image. Or she might rebelliously adopt some behaviour to stand out. The range of her reactions can be fungible and at times too flexible when her inner position is weakened. Accessing the body-self is part of the work for establishing an individual self.

Destiny *dreams she is in a dark street when she sees a light. As she walks towards it, a man emerges from the shadows and rapes her. Her response is to go mute. The male is aggressive and she passive, accepting and submissive.* The violence coming from the outside in the form of the male implies what threatens her state of mind. The dream is an image of her inner world and reminds her of times when her voice was muffled and she felt no strength or assertion, a young girl who is an adult but abdicates to others. As an inner image the dream is shocking, assaultive, and without help she is alone and in the dark.

The unconscious is mirroring her silence although the dream has a voice. Destiny neither protests nor speaks up. She is a woman with many ideas that quickly fade without being actualised. She remains in a reality determined by others and is helpless at taking hold of her existence. In the dream she wears pastel colours, indicating the girl, naïve and vulnerable to energy that takes advantage and instils harm.

The dream is sobering and brings to her attention the need to deal with these figures and her reaction of helplessness. She performs the traditional female role, complying with the male, sexually just there, ephemeral, compliant, giving in. Her energy is subject to being usurped, going inactive, a crushed innocence, and her self instincts only reappear when she is alone. She is hard to read. Is she present? Her body absorbs tension as she lives on the edge, not at the centre of her experiences. But like in the dream she is stopped, invisible and unsafe. She is a puella, taking no stand, submissive, indefinite, wanting to avoid upset, to smooth things out, pastel but vulnerable to a rapacious energy.

Becoming aware of her real feelings would open Destiny to a whole new world and animate rather than collapse her body. The dream is a gift, telling her what has been and is still happening. She calls the dream image *masochistic*, and she could circumvent the full extent of its damage and meaning by remaining unconsciousness.

As in myth, Persephone is yanked out of being puella, innocently picking flowers, when she is abducted by Hades to the underworld. He overpowers with his forceful energy and ranks as a Greek god. Between Persephone and Hades there is no consent or communication. And here is the problem. Any way we look at the scenario of the dream, there is no relationship: no Eros, no feeling between the characters. It is a flat acquiescence of parts isolated, cleaved and unintegrated. The dream highlights a situation of learned performativity, a traditional role re-enacted in its crudest and most hurtful form. Analytical treatment will explore what is behind this position, inherited from family and culture, and what she must learn to move out of the complex that ties her to being less than to find her strength and resilience.

Fixities

Judith Butler defines gender as a social role performed and enacted by individuals, validated and accepted by society. According to Butler, the meaning of gender depends on the cultural framework within which it is performed. It defines fixities and universalities, a continuous performance acquiring new meaning with each repeated performance (Mambrol, 2016). Refusing fixities, Butler rejects essentialisms, stable identities and meanings, while eschewing notions of authenticity, authority, objectivity. This view allows the fluidity possible between inner figures and reinforces their flexible expression.

After a time in analysis Destiny dreams, *I am about ten years old and with a girlfriend dancing in the hall. My mother is in a white silk flowing dress. She is really a witch blocking the way out. We must leave and go downstairs to the car to get out. My father is in the next room and not helping me. We do not have much time left.* Destiny recounts the dream with little emotion. Mother has been the one pushing her to get in a relationship, but Destiny wants time to develop her career. She is talented and not ready and worries a partner in a relationship would inhibit her career goals. These factors are impingements on her ego and thus arouse anxiety.

But the dream messages contain more. Destiny is ambivalent about leaving her mother and going into the world. She has few maternal aspects and adamantly rejects anything maternal. However, she is not confident she can move past mother and establish her own way; she is uncertain and worried she cannot do it in time. She is in a state of inertia, not moving, growing, leaving. Mother in the diaphanous dress images a woman of not only delicacy but also the strength of the witch. Is she a good witch or bad? To deny the maternal affects Destiny's access to the feminine within, and she is in conflict between satisfying mother or accessing the maternal and integrating it into being herself.

This mother and daughter have a difficult relationship. Mother is pushy, and Destiny is resentful and, although wanting love, disdains mother's ways. Destiny considers mother undeveloped, small in outlook and unsupportive. Like in the dream Destiny is psychologically caught, indecisive. She wants support but does not perform in front of mother due to the expected critique always followed by emotional upset and lack of confidence. She is encouraged by father and is pulled towards him as she wants a life other than her mother's. The question is how Destiny will break from the prescribed roles as she has not found a way yet.

Until the dream Destiny was unaware of her own witch tendencies, and this lack of awareness cut her off from her energy. The dream clarified much for Destiny, as she was both surprised and relieved to realise, she and her mother were more alike than imagined. As she thought about the dream, she was pleased to find their similarities even in the areas she abhorred, and she became strengthened by this. To her it meant finally encountering mother and accepting her.

In addition, the father who enjoys her music treats her like a puella, a young girl, and Destiny likes being special to him. However, the dream reminds her that he is with mother, not her. The reality of the situation is boldly depicted in the dream, and Destiny feels alone, betrayed in a reality she does not want to face. She needs to leave home to know she can survive and be herself. Remaining Daddy's girl will not work. Nor will fearing mother and distancing from herself.

This *Electra complex*, or the daughter attached to father and his ideas, is added to by numerous dreams *of wanting a partner, hesitating at the ceremony, beds ready but she vacillates*. The future, like in the dreams, is calling but she is unsure she can meet it.

The performance

Performativity promotes an unconscious embrace of old values. Destiny is experiencing 'the self but not compensating for the one-sidedness of the ego in the form of the acceptable and functional persona. It is possible to use the analyst to make up for the missed mirroring experiences' (Sidoli, 2000, p. 102). Psychological and analytical work is an optimal frame in which to consider the various impacts the external world brings to bear on our subjectivities. Within the analytical relationship both participants engage in a dialectic between various, often contradictory, influences. This is where we can expand, comprehend and further develop a more progressive stance beyond the rote and traditional.

> Gender is an impersonation … becoming gendered involves impersonating an ideal that nobody actually inhabits … Performativity has to do with repetition, very often the repetition of oppressive and painful gender norms … This is not freedom, but a question of how to work the trap that one is inevitably in.
> (Kotz, 1992)

Gender is instituted 'through the stylization of the body and, hence, must be understood as the mundane way in which bodily gestures, movements, and enactments of various kinds constitute the illusion of an abiding gendered self' (Butler, 1998, p. 519). To say gender is performative is to argue that gender is real only to the extent that it is performed (Butler, 1990a). Butler argues that the act that one does, the act that one performs is, in a sense, an act that's been going on before one arrived on the scene. Specific body actions define the possibilities for the cultural transformation 'of gender differently from one's contemporaries and from one's embodied predecessors and successors as well'. Butler recognises culture as 'marginalizing those failing to perform the illusion of gender essentialism'. She contends 'the truth or falsity of gender is only socially compelled and in no sense ontologically necessitated' (Butler, 1998, p. 528).

For Butler, gender is what you do, not who you are. Rather than viewing gender as something natural or internal, Butler roots gender in outward signs and actions. Gender is performed through ritualised repetition, giving it the illusion of stability from the repeated performances in accordance with social norms. These performative acts do not express an innate gender but create gender itself. The performance of gender produces the identity it claims to reveal (Allen, 2023).

For example, men speak like this, women dress like that, reproduces and reinscribes the norms, making them seem legitimate and fixed. Societal structures reward those who perform gender according to the strict binary. However, the original itself is a failed copy of an ideal gender no one can embody. We become shaped, not with choice, but the forcible citation of a norm with its complex historicity. Legitimating gender norms affects all aspects of our lives in their insistence on certain performances.

Gender refers to how a person expresses their identity as either male or female, based on clothing, behaviours and the use of linguistic structure such as he or she. This performance is something society determines through the way it tells us what constitutes binary male and female behaviours. Gender qualities that are the exception are largely repressed because societal issues are engrained in attitudes towards gender. If outside the accepted norm, a person can become isolated and considered deviant, which in turn makes them feel precarious, escalating anxiety. This discourages the invitation to embrace the proliferation of gender and an array of expression open to change.

The becoming

The thrust of performativity within Butler's work is held in her concern for becoming. Beginning with a consideration of Simone de Beauvoir's claim that 'one is not born, but, rather, becomes a woman', links between personal and social identity form in strict cultural relationships. Judith Butler's book *Gender Trouble* (1990b) proposed the then ground-breaking theory of gender as a constant performance and a series of cues observed, internalised and repeated. These behaviours are reinforced, and they become unconscious and adaptive as we gain approval and acceptance.

Butler wants to show the ways in which reified, reiterated, repeated and naturalised conceptions of gender can be understood as constituted socially and therefore capable of being reconstituted differently. The learned performance of gendered behaviour, or what we commonly associate with femininity and masculinity, is an act of sorts, a performance. All manner of its symbolic and social signs is imposed on us by the overarching of normative heterosexuality. Our subjectivity is not something permanent or stable but represents the mainstream identity clearly separated from marginalised alternatives.

According to Butler, the meaning of gender depends on the cultural framework within which it is performed, and hence it defies fixities and universalities. Its meaning with each repeated performance also depends on the context. This leaves identity as a compelling illusion, really a retroactive construction resulting from our belief in behaviour from both subtle and blatant coercions. Butler understands gender to be 'a corporeal style, an "act", as it were' (Butler, 1990a, p. 272). That style has no relation to essential truths about the body but is strictly ideological.

> Gender cannot be understood as a role which either expresses or disguises an interior "self", whether that "self" is conceived as sexed or not ... gender is an "act", broadly construed, which constructs the social fiction of its own psychological interiority.
>
> (279)

Gender is not just a process, but it is a particular type of process, 'a set of repeated acts within a highly rigid regulatory frame' (Butler, 1990a, pp. 43–44). The subject has a limited number of costumes from which to make a constrained choice of gender style (Salih, 2002, p. 56). Gender is not something one is; it is something one does, an act, or more precisely, a sequence of acts, a verb rather than a noun, a 'doing' rather than a 'being' (Butler, 1990a, p. 25).

Mourning the others within

Analysis is a dialogue and exploration of the range of the others within our identity. It goes beyond learned performances and explores the reality of oneself. Kristeva notes the strangeness in our evolving identities is a metaphor through which we accept what seem like the strangers within (1991, p. 290). In a desire for rebalancing body, mind and soul, this is interpreted as a condition of searching. It leads to realisations of vulnerability, physically and psychologically. The philosophical frame of performativity can mirror attitudes of anxiety and disenfranchisement. Without sufficient predictability, recognition or security, a person experiences a sense of powerlessness and defeat.

Individuals often enter analysis when inner chaos has reached a critical point. This includes internal as well as external constraints. The chaos can accompany many events over which there is felt to be little control, such as physical illness, the breakup of a relationship, loss of a loved one, a change in career or the frustrations of ageing. Each person will bring their story of love and loss, joy and pain, physical and emotional. The suffering in the present is often woven with threads from the past and the many generations stacked behind.

'Ego consciousness needs to be true to itself ... as aware of the shadow elements that keep it from feeling the empathy ... It needs to be mirrored and to continually clean and polish that inner mirror' (Stein, 2022, p. 170). Life goals can seem pointless for the puella, and they feel lost. Often, the chaos expresses itself as a symptom like depression, anxiety, fear or simply the feeling that nothing makes sense anymore. The old order has lost its meaning as the puella revisits the past and evaluates what has changed and what has not. It brings struggle, shifts in image and despair for many.

Undetermined or negated, puella can feel deprived and without import, subsumed with unacknowledged loss and grief. However, 'accepting loss means we are changed, undergoing a transformation from the loss' (2004, p. 21). In analysis or therapy, the healthy reaction of mourning life passing and making room for new growth occurs alongside being emotionally bereft, refuting natural change, growth or creation. Life cannot be realistically mourned because a person is already lost or never were and they seem to live on in a state of deadness (Butler, 2004, p. 33).

> Psychotherapy is at bottom a dialectical relationship between doctor and patient. It is an encounter, a discussion between two psychic wholes, in which ego knowledge is a tool assisting the goal of transformation. This is not one

that is predetermined, but rather an indeterminable change, the only criterion of which is the disappearance of egohood. No efforts on the part of the doctor can compel this experience. The most he can do is to smooth the path for the patient and help him to attain an attitude which offers the least resistance to the decisive experience.

(Jung, 1969, CW 11, para. 904)

We are meant to encounter those others within and open to the timelessness and changing aspects of our psychological and social selves. The unconscious keeps on presenting various characters and situations, demonstrating we are full of difference and constantly encounter those who are other than ourselves.

Actions oriented to social acceptance reveal how we enact the truth of the self, how the self is constructed, including attitudes to the body. Many factors can ostracise puella from the self and suppress the range of qualities. 'Individuation means the more complete fulfillment of the collective qualities of the human being ... is more conducive to a better social performance than when the peculiarity is neglected or suppressed' (1966, CW 7, para. 267).

The actions

Performance is something society determines through the way it tells us what constitutes male and female behaviours. Butler provides for issues in gender performativity, attempting to redefine and relocate aspects as she traces the concealed gender codes in the social system. She formulates a postmodernist notion of gender contradictory to the traditional notion of fixed categories. By enacting the conventional, we make them real to some extent but that does not make them less artificial, even though validated by society, which perpetuates their continuous performance.

This continual re-impersonation depends on the judgement of others and the need to fit in. No complete self is offered or seemingly desired. Instead, the false self and shell of persona houses the identity. A person then picks up an identity for a while, becoming temporarily the face of the imagined one looking back. The façade makes it seem like they are there when they are not. Instead, they become an object, needing to hide their vulnerable and sensitive reactions in the search for self-legitimisation.

Under such pressure, we could misrecognise ourselves, adopting the viewpoints provided for us. The reproductions of the norm reveal its weaknesses. Impingements upon the ego can be felt as anxiety and affect both our experience of external space as well as our own body. The point of all this is challenging the status quo. In *Gender Trouble* Judith Butler presents the idea that being born male or female does not determine behaviour. Instead, what society regards as a person's gender is a performance made to please social expectations and not a true expression of the person's gender identity. 'Gender reality is performative which means, quite simply, that it is real only to the extent that it is performed' (Butler, 1990a, p. 278).

Butler identifies in the recognition of the performative constitution the emancipatory political and personal conscious and unconscious capacity. Her idea is parallel to Jung's conception of the complex and the slavish following of the complex rather than reflecting on what applies to the self. Being caught in the rigid feminine or masculine, or anima or animus, restricts growth and limits the expansion of the personal.

> Gender identity might be reconceived as a personal/cultural history of received meaning subject to a set of imitative practices which refer to other imitations and which, jointly, construct the illusion of a primary and interior gendered self or parody the mechanism of that construction.
>
> (Butler, 1993, p. 138)

As a result of both subtle and blatant coercions, gender differences are compelled by our belief in what natural behaviour is. Our identities are performed so social reality is continually created as an illusion. Butler, therefore, understands gender to be a corporeal style that has no relation to essential truths about the body but is strictly ideological: 'Gender is the repeated stylization of the body, a set of repeated acts within a highly rigid regulatory frame that congeal over time to produce the appearance of substance and a natural way of being' (1990a, pp. 43–44).

The qualities we define as masculine and feminine are shaped by social and cultural forces. The cracks appear when this proves to be a strait jacket defining femininity and masculinity in tight, prescriptive ways.

> It's my obligation to tell about this one girl out of the thousands like her. And my duty, however artlessly to reveal her life. Because there's the right to scream. So I scream … but the person I'm going to talk about scarcely has a body to sell.
>
> (Lispector, 2011, p. 5)

Rather, human experience is framed through the lens of individuation, of becoming, not through the forced adherence to old stories about sex and gender that imply power hierarchy rather than shared and flexible use of self.

References

Allen, P. (2023, 14 Feb.). What is Judith Butler's theory of gender performativity? *Perlego.* https://www.perlego.com/knowledge/study-guides/what-is-judith-butlers-theory-of-gender-performativity/

Butler, J. (1990a). Performative acts and gender constitution: An essay in phenomenology and feminist theory. In S.-E. Case (Ed.), *Performing feminisms: Feminist critical theory and theatre* (pp. 270–282). Johns Hopkins Press.

Butler, J. (1990b). *Gender trouble.* 1st ed. Routledge.

Butler, J. (1993). *Bodies that matter; on the discursive limits of sex.* Routledge.

Butler, J. (1998). Performative acts and gender constitution: An essay in phenomenology and feminist theory. *Theatre Journal, 40*(4), 519–531.

Butler, J. (2004). *Undoing gender*. University of Minnesota Press.
Butler, J. (2011). *Bodies that matter*. Routledge. (Original published 1993).
Butler, J. (2020). *The force of nonviolence*. Verso.
Douglas, C. (1990). *The woman in the mirror: Analytical psychology and the feminine*. Sigo Press.
Fleischer, K. (2020). The symbol in the body: The undoing of a dissociation through embodied active imagination in Jungian analysis. *Journal of Analytical Psychology, 65*(3), 558–583.
Jung, C. G. (1954). *The collected works of C. G. Jung: Vol. 17. The development of personality*. Princeton University Press.
Jung, C. G. (1956). *The collected works of C. G. Jung: Vol. 5. The symbols of transformation*. Pantheon Books.
Jung, C. G. (1959). *The collected works of C. G. Jung: Vol. 9ii. Aion*. Princeton University Press.
Jung, C. G. (1966). *The collected works of C. G. Jung: Vol. 7. Two essays in analytical psychology*. Princeton University Press.
Jung, C. G. (1969). *The collected works of C. G. Jung: Vol. 11. Psychology and religion: East and west*. Princeton University Press.
Kotz, L. (1992, November). Liz Kotz interviews Judith Butler. ArtForum. https://www.artforum.com/features/the-body-you-want-an-inteview-with-judith-butler-203347/
Kristeva, J. (1991). *Strangers to ourselves*. (Leon Roudiez, Trans.). Harvester Wheatsheaf.
Lispector, C. (2011). *Hour of the star*. El Cuenco de Plata.
Mambrol, N. (2016, October 10). Judith Butler's concept of performativity. *Literary Theory and Criticism*. https://literariness.org/2016/10/10/judith-butlers-concept-of-performativity/
Salih, S. (2002). *Judith Butler*. Routledge.
Sidoli, M. (2000). *When the body speaks: The archetypes in the body*. Routledge.
Stein, M. (Ed.). (2022). *Jung's* Red Book *for our Time*. Chiron.
Woodman, M. (1993). *Conscious femininity: Interviews with Marion Woodman*. Inner City Books.

Chapter 10

Bluebeard fairy tale

A wealthy man, wishing to wed, turns his attention to the two beautiful young daughters of his neighbour, a widow. Neither girl wants to marry the man because of his ugly blue beard – until he invites the girls and their mother to a party at his country estate. Seduced by luxurious living, the youngest daughter agrees to accept Bluebeard's hand. The two are promptly wed, and the girl becomes mistress of his great household. Soon after, Bluebeard tells his wife that business calls him to make a long journey. He leaves her behind with all the keys to his house, his strong boxes and his caskets of jewels, telling her she may do as she likes with them and to 'make good cheer'. There is only one key she may not use to a tiny closet at the end of the hall. That alone is forbidden. He tells her, 'If you happen to open it, you may expect my just anger and resentment'.

Once Bluebeard is gone her friends come to admire all the riches and exclaim how fortunate she is to have all this. However, overcome with curiosity, the very first thing the young wife does is to run off to the forbidden door 'with such excessive haste that she nearly fell and broke her neck'. She has promised obedience to her husband, but a combination of greed and curiosity (the text implies) propels her to the fatal door the minute his back is turned. She opens it and finds a shuttered room, its floor awash in blood, containing the murdered corpses of Bluebeard's previous young wives. Horrified, the young wife drops the key into a puddle of blood. Retrieving it, she locks the room and runs back to her own chamber. Now she attempts to wash the key so that her transgression will not be revealed – but no matter how long and hard she scrubs it, the bloodstain will not come off.

That very night, her husband returns – his business has been suddenly concluded. Trembling, she pretends nothing has happened and welcomes him back. In the morning, however, he demands the return of the keys and examines them carefully. 'Why is there blood on the smallest key?' he asks her craftily. Bluebeard's wife protests that she does not know how it came to be there. 'You do not know?' he roars. 'But I know, Madame. You opened the forbidden door. Very well. You must now go back and take your place among my other wives'. Tearfully, she delays her death by asking for time to say her prayers – for her brothers are due to visit that day, her only hope of salvation. She calls three times to her sister Anne to go to the tower room at the top of the house ('Sister Anne, Sister

Anne, do you see anyone coming?'). And, at last, they come, just as Bluebeard raises a sword to chop off her head. The murderous husband is dispatched, his wealth disbursed among the family, and the young wife is married again, Perrault tells us, to 'a very worthy gentleman who made her forget the ill time she had passed with Bluebeard'.

*****

Fairy tales and myths speak in both clear and multifaceted language, revealing the complexities of the personal and collective unconscious and the world of archetypes. They illustrate how to integrate the personality, bring together dissociated elements, such as the persona and the shadow for accessing the self. Through this story the heroine and hero encounter their true and false selves, social status, various familial and class positions as all are aspects of personality differentiation and integration. Self-recovery occurs through the fairy-tale journey that narrates the meaning of life's events in a personal and collective process.

Fairy tales reveal wisdom and natural pathways and provide answers that emerge from the unexpected. The time is eternal, not linear. The voices of the ages reach forwards, reverberating themes common throughout the generations. They give us hope amid overwhelming odds, teach us to listen and not give up, display means to separate from past woes and sorrows and guide us to a more fulfilling future. They tell us much is possible as the stories extend our understanding of life, beckoning us through the riches and tragedies. They illustrate obstacles and encounters with evil, bad guys, witches and magic utensils while illustrating the resilience of the psyche. Fairy tales are a portal for the archetypal themes replicated also in film, literature and current events.

Fairy tales are not just for children but are for the eternal child in us all. They are like dreams, manifestations of the unconscious and can be analysed like dreams, drawing us into the imagination and giving us awareness of our lives. A striking feature of fairy tales is the absence of specific spaces, names and causality. As metaphors for personal guidance, the symbolic patterns and the characters connect to the personal and ordinary while simultaneously reaching beyond the common and collective experience. They illustrate psychological strategies and emotional insights for dealing with personal and collective problems. They are not just a magical world but provide grounding so we can learn about our life paths. Moreover, the tales reflect the therapeutic journey of the psyche.

This tale of Bluebeard warns about the dangers of puella naïveté and what it takes to claim her individual strength and position. The tale is not sweet; there is no father; the mother seems more socially status conscious than protective and educative of her daughters, especially the youngest. These are serious relational lacunae. 'The bond with mother has not been firmly established and there is no father to rely upon, cutting off the threatening aspects of her own maturing to womanhood' (Wright, 2019, p. 478). This leads to her establishing a fragile, socially constructed identity, without finding her own orientation.

The tale brings attention to what is off in the societal realm where power and sole authority personally and culturally are out of balance and now need to be acknowledged. It begins with an absent father. Most fairy-tale fathers are grandiose, narcissistic, having exaggerated self-importance and false fronts. They are portrayed without attachment or are absolutely absent and miss seeing the daughter due to their unconsciousness. This cuts into a daughter's sense of self. Here no one has taken heed; the problem has gotten worse and devolved into a life and death crisis.

The focus on the superficial is synonymous to the material emptiness in our current times, accentuating the need for eros or emotional relatedness. This tale highlights the dismemberment and disappearance of the feminine at the hands of the male protagonist. Fairy tales pose psychological questions and

> metaphorically describe the process of individuation with the incarnation of the Self. Each tale describes a psychic event of complexity, far-reaching and difficult to recognize in all its various aspects ... the theme remains viable and not exhaustive as their teachings transfer through the generations.
> (von Franz, 1970, p. 2)

The tale of Bluebeard depicts the issues of betrayal in family and culture exacerbated to the brink of death. The situation has become this dire. It is often the case that issues escalate to the intolerable before they gain our attention and inspire a change of the status quo:

> The one-sided patriarchally masculine value-canon of [Western] consciousness ... [has] contributed in a major way to the crisis of our time. Hence understanding the Feminine is an urgent necessity not only in order to understand the single individual but also to heal the collective.
> (Neumann, 1994, xi)

Animus questioned

Jung made many comments on the animus. One of the most palatable is recognising 'the creative, to utilize and reach into the unconscious and use its energy, ideas, quirks and unusual answers to solve problems' (1959, CW 9ii, para. 29). The issue is what this concept represents currently due to the continuing debate about its validity. Jung's ideas originated years ago in a different cultural era and milieu. Much about the animus has become outmoded and calcified, applicable to a different world.

Jung recognised we have many characteristics within us, but he presented them definitively. Our era is fluid, and masculine and feminine are on a spectrum and can be adapted flexibly and individually. As the tale points out, the limitations of stereotypes are not only their definitiveness but also their lack of balance, and this creates a rigidity of personality with often deadly consequences. And it creates a situation for rectification.

I purposely deviate from Jung's definition of the animus, preferring that of Emma Jung. Even more I prefer a wider descriptor, separated from the divisive categories limiting the personality, one that considers more expansive attributes. Therefore, updates are needed. The point I want to make here is how destructive, because unconscious and misused, this part of the personality can become. In this fairy tale the animus as male is cold, ruthless, conniving, a killer. This part of the personality and how it is enacted in the culture remains a baffling element, portrayed here in an extreme and negative form. Bluebeard represents the male energy overpowering the female to the point that by now many women have already been killed. Built from traditional attitudes held over many years, he displays a perverse dominance over the feminine. These attitudes remain when unaware of their dastardly power. Reading about these extremes can bring consciousness of the collusion we might still be enacting against ourselves. And the tale highlights the restrictions many face culturally over which they have little control.

Bluebeard points out unhealthy polarised dynamics. In the fairy tale the younger daughter becomes more aware of what she does not initially suspect. She becomes increasingly capable of acting on her beliefs and feelings. Her courage and creativity highlight the dynamic and pluralistic qualities of puella. Now it is up to her to face the social and personal falsehoods, fears and reality.

Puella might tend to follow the male's direction; she might initially feel too weak and not realise her ability or independence. When we are out of touch with the instincts, Bluebeard takes over. Not only does Bluebeard trade in self-deception, lacking heart or eros, but the characters in the tale are naïvely subject to his deception as well. This includes the mother, the fact there is no father and the other female friends. Why are they all so unconscious and unaware? This is also part of the tragedy; messages from the self have been ignored and are now in a serious state of betrayal.

Demon lover

Bluebeard symbolises a predator figure existing within the individual and the collective. Is he innate? Can he be redeemed? After all, his malignant formation is not uncommon. The tale reveals the haunting paradox of human nature containing experiences both sinister and hopeful. If unrecognised and unowned, the psychic energy cannot be transformed.

A demon lover evolves with the absence of the father figure. Without a male role model, he becomes fused with yearning, sadness, frustrated love, anger and rage, oppression and frustrated desire. The girl most vulnerable to the demon lover is the one who adores or fears the father who in his absence has become idealised. The dark side of the father complex is at the heart of the demon lover (Woodman, 1985, p. 132). An absent father oppresses to the extent he was and is not there. Becoming aware of how father images reside in a daughter's psyche is a step towards gaining consciousness of the effects of his absence. When absent, the father figure and all he represents sink into the unconscious (Schwartz, 2020). The father's absence contributes to an inadequate self-image. The daughter becomes dutiful to authority outside herself, especially in its stereotypical male authoritarian form. She might remain ambivalent about committing to life or experience anger and depression, dismembering her body and psyche in various ways.

The puella can be drawn to the superficial and assume expected roles. In the story the youngest daughter decides to marry Bluebeard. No one forces her, but she is drawn as if by an invisible thread, ignoring the danger signals right in front of her, his blue beard, the previous wives who disappeared. This is a sign he is a demon lover, a figure of psychological guile who appears in disguise and is strange. Yet, demon lovers do not always appear as ugly and fearsome, nor armed with knives and guns. Often, they are seductive, eloquent, offering everything we think we need and want. They seem accommodating, even marvellous. Succumbing to a Bluebeard figure means the daughter will lose her soul and individual life in one way or another.

When young, we might be asleep to the fact we might be easy prey (Estes, 1995, p. 43). At the beginning of the fairy tale, the young woman convinces herself that Bluebeard is not so bad. After all, her mother also thought the same, indicating the problem has passed on to the next generation. Self-betrayal is learned from the family, modelled by parents and supported by peers. Although willing to be his prey at the beginning, her initial hesitancy proves to be a guide. The error in judgement leads her astray, indicating a level of nondevelopment. Yet it puts her on the journey into the knowledge of evil and how to escape. In the process the naïve and emotionally immature puella becomes the heroine. Psychologically and culturally, the youngest daughter must meet and vanquish the male deceiver and killer. The youngest daughter's intuition and instinct for growth emerges beyond her initial naïveté into curiosity and then verve.

All this occurs through her encounter with the demonic, destructive figure of Bluebeard. Otherwise, raped from within by the demon lover and from without by the same attitude in the culture, the young wife is hesitant, denies her daring and halts development. She would remain unconscious, and if so, she would surely die.

The demon lover keeps her living in secret, trapped in a false security, isolated and confined in unawareness. Von Franz notes the necessity of this time, difficult though it may be, as an initiation into oneself (von Franz, 2022, p. 178). When in the grip of the negative masculine complex, the journey out entails getting free of the falseness, from the obsessions, the mechanisms of internal distancing to access the healing layers of the psyche. This breaks down the old patterns, peels off the dross of materialism and status to be real and emerge from the former death-in-life state.

The demon lover in the complex is out to possess her, demanding obedience to his rules. As an inner figure he sends negative assessments that she is too fat, not perfect, too old, too lacking in one way or another. One cannot rest with a demon lover as he brings nothing but destruction to her body and psyche.

Bluebeard represents complexes draining the personality while simultaneously spurring the impetus for consciousness. The tale recounts the trap of patriarchy and materialism, the lure of outer riches while disregarding emotional depravity and ruthlessness. The daughters and mother are seduced by Bluebeard's luxurious lifestyle. The blue colour of his beard signals something is wrong; however, the youngest daughter minimises this and accepts Bluebeard's hand in marriage, illustrating the lure of patriarchy and its values. She enters the grip of the negative complex that is a killer. Likewise, the widespread crises and sterility in contemporary cultural and personal life results in emptiness, fosters anxiety, despair and loss of meaning.

Fairy tales mirror our human experience while offering direction towards the new. 'Persistence in an out-of-date attitude creates an impossible situation ... it is just this persistence that brings about dissociation' (von Franz, 1993, p. 42). It is the dissociation the daughter cannot maintain as she moves towards the forbidden, opening the door to the secret room. The need, willingness and capacity to transgress leads to psychological development. This requires refusing the imposed unconscious narrative, and this refusal is at the heart of individuation. James Hillman, archetypal psychologist, wrote an essay (1964) on betrayal. In it he addressed the necessity to break a promise. The young wife's betrayal of Bluebeard's rules was necessary for her to find trust in herself.

The archetypal core

Archetypal patterns give expression to the perennial dilemmas enacted in the psyche. The archetypes spring from what Jung called the collective unconscious, presenting themselves in dreams, imagination and relationships. Cross-cultural folk tales of demon lovers and devilish bridegrooms are not uncommon, and similar themes prevail to the current day in the media, whether fictional or in the true crime shows permeating cable television. Noticeably the demon lover is usually described as a dark, mysterious and dangerously seductive. The heroine is innocent and becomes his victim and can be destroyed by him.

The fairy tale begins with a dilemma and a subsequent journey with conflicts and challenges. The tales depict working with the tensions between the ego-complex and the personal and collective conscious and unconscious spirit of our times. The way forwards in this tale requires facing evil, and there are shocking realisations and uncertainties until clarity and wisdom come into place. The narrative demonstrates the process of individuation evolving through a series of tasks. These processes bring differentiation that gradually strengthens the personality. By examining the figures and actions of the story, we foster reflection on similar character traits and situations in our own lives.

Bluebeard, a French tale originating in 1697 and written by Charles Perrault, presents the dominant totalitarian figure filled with grandiosity and wanton destruction, especially to the feminine. It is centuries old and tells the story of a murderous husband, a demoniacal figure who possesses and kills a series of wives, interring them in his secret room. Bluebeard has thus far remained unstoppable. In general, it contains the 'themes of traumatic organization and overwhelm – the secret room and the heroine whose life has been sacrificed to uphold patriarchal authority' (Wright, 2019, p. 478). The secret room holds the destruction of the feminine, broken promises, identities and hopes, potentials dashed. This deadly reality has been undiscovered, secret and unconscious to the general populace.

The puella's curiosity about what is on the other side of the door gains in energy as the tale proceeds. Her curiosity leads her to the liberating decision to open the door. Using the forbidden key represents attaining and using knowledge as a way out, interrupting the chain of events.

The puella figure, upon opening the door to the secret room, realises she was duped, captured and must find a way out. The key unlocks reality. She sees what was destroyed and her certain demise unless something changes. She must use her knowledge or die. The blood on the key enacts the wounds. She can neither remain ignorant, nor can she deny her new recognition of Bluebeard and his deadliness. To be unconscious in the clutch of this predator means she will die. Psychologically she is compelled to investigate her own deadness and forms of self-murder. Jung commented on the process for accessing the self:

> If you contemplate your lack of fantasy, of inspiration and inner aliveness, which you feel as sheer stagnation and a barren wilderness and impregnate it with the interest born of alarm at your inner death, then something can take shape in you, for your inner emptiness conceals just as great a fullness if only you will allow it to penetrate into you.
>
> (Jung, 1970, CW 14, para. 189)

The collective attitude has been unconscious of Bluebeard's evil ways, and as with many negative, destructive figures in the personality, this has been going on a long time, causing much damage. The secret room with the corpses of dead wives represents the violent brutality enacted towards the innocent feminine for years. It represents a trap, much like the bargain we make with ourselves when we compromise and betray our intuition and well-being. Finally, the youngest daughter, the puella and last wife, is curious enough and has the fortitude to go against the rules instituted by the male. Courage is needed to face the amount of killing Bluebeard directed towards the feminine. The puella defies tradition, betrays the general attitude of refusal to see reality and halts the march of destruction.

She leaves her friends, sneaking up the back stairs, while Bluebeard is absent, with the key to unlock the secret door. Her wilful act is the acquisition of consciousness, an act of hubris against the powers-that-be and a necessary crime leading to liberation from the unconscious malaise. Pain, suffering and death exist prior to the birth of consciousness. Any step towards individuation threatens and is a suffering of sorts. It is experienced as a crime against the collective, challenging identifications with the traditions of family, party, religion or nation.

The tale shows not only the personal but also the cultural complex of Bluebeard as a powerful shadow figure able to dupe everyone. We find a similar theme in books like Emily Bronte's *Withering Heights* and the character of Heathcliff,

Angela Carter's *The Bloody Chamber*, Oscar Wilde's *The Picture of Dorian Grey* and numerous others commenting on violent, sexual male power, predation and destruction. The same stories are enacted in real world as well.

For example, in Dublin a man named Macarthur was convicted of murder. When the case came to trial in 1982 it led to suspicions the government intervened due to his associations. The story itself was opaque, composed as much of urban legend as fact. When Macarthur committed the murders, he was 37 years old, a well-known figure, handsome with an aristocratic look, erudite, refined manner of speech, drinking in the city's sophisticated bars, attending church. He came from a well-off family, having grown up as landed gentry. In his 20s, he came into a large inheritance. But the inheritance dwindled, presenting a threat to his lifestyle. He thought to commit bank robbery, and in the effort to attain a gun and getaway car, he murdered two strangers, both aged 27. Even now, years after the murders, there was much fascination about this man. He embodied a surreal tension between the signs of both aristocracy and criminality, a man in handcuffs, aloof and detached. The meaning of the event remains surrounded with incredulity and a silence at its centre (O'Connell, 2023).

Like the previously mentioned reality, in the fairy tale, Bluebeard, seemingly above others, engages in female dismemberment for no apparent reason. He commits violence without desire for relationship but rather to overpower and destroy what has become distorted within. The story illustrates eros tangled in a deeply entrenched and deadly complex and dissociated aspect of the psyche. And it is a tale enacted in social systems within which many people are trapped. This can be seen in the repressions enacted against women's appearances and restrictions around dress and societal participation.

Demon lovers have a tyrannical, controlling possession over their subjects. The more the inner world remains unconscious, holding attitudes against its discovery, its negativity and destruction takes over. The puella is lost and pleases the male, doing his bidding at her peril (von Franz, 2021, p. 281). In the tale the mother and sister do not notice the danger and follow the collective script, lured by material riches and a lack of consciousness that will bring death. There has been lethargy and a deadly unawareness throughout the land. Patriarchal power is exacerbated in this story of death and dismemberment, evil and the many already killed.

In such pervasive situations, the puella either accepts the current constrained reality or she must rebel to find another way. Such attitudes contribute to hopelessness, a self-image of being inadequate, infantile and dutiful to male authority and power. She might remain ambivalent about committing to life or experience anger and depression turned against herself. The heroine, noted as the youngest daughter or puella, becomes awakened from this torpor over the personal and collective attitudes.

The tale illustrates a situation where she can no longer perform, be demure, passive, lacking aggression. The energy has been one-sided and the knowledge of this leads to liberation from the destructive events. 'The progressive tendency within the pattern of feminine life appears in the collective unconscious in an effort to produce a new form of femininity ... and new form of Eros' (von Franz, 1993, p. 26). The daughter's curiosity breaks the spell, bringing the destructive, unconscious patterns to light.

Bluebeard symbolises the ruthless inner predator. He is a negative figure who takes over, preventing new life and dominating the psyche. He pushes her around, dictates and in-authenticates her initiative (Estes, 1995, p. 309). As a negative force, he hinders her movement out in the world; as a positive force, he encourages and promotes her strength and unusual nature. The heroine, like the puella, signifies innocence encountering the necessity of growing awareness and accessing her strength to survive. She does this by encountering the evil and the truth of what has happened and that could continue unless she intercedes. Bluebeard has become too destructive, overpowering and misaligned psychologically. There is no feeling, no love or desire for relating with his death-dealing energy. These figures, when encountered in the unconscious, allow the puella to realise and restore eros personally and collectively.

Myths, fairy tales and sacred texts are replete with stories of the dismembered and sacrificed females. This speaks to the psychic splitting in the collective unconscious continuing for centuries. From the Greek Medusa to the Handless Maiden and the fairy tale of Bluebeard, from the Greek story of Iphigenia sacrificed for her father to Jephthah's daughter in the Bible, the feet, hands and heads of women and girls have been routinely dismembered. These dismemberments remain alive to this day and are even visible in the appropriation of Medusa's severed head by Gucci, the contemporary haute couture fashion designer of women's clothes.

The exploration of fairy tales in their most gruesome aspects has value because these stories help integrate the real themes on the healing journey. They often begin with hunger in the form of something wanted and lacking, which gives rise to the need to find oneself. When understood, the lacks and losses lead to meaning making. What emerges are the creative aspects of the psyche.

Fairy tales express the psyche through their imagery, story lines and symbolism. Their truths unwrap the complexes, and the developmental processes reveal the psychological answers that expose the puella's destiny. These images and motifs expose the old patterns, the range of archetypal messages and the necessary challenges. As with any psychological development, without failure there would be no story or progress. Along the way and through interdiction and violation the rules must be broken to change the world. The desire for change is simultaneously transformative and transgressive. By the end of the story the initial absence and lack are filled with other figures and personality expansion.

Bluebeard is a tale of trials for the young female through her encounter with the masculine demon lover who is a killer. This energy is a cultural and personal description of the influences by which the young feminine has been threatened and exposed. This energy, when submerged into the unconscious, takes a negative form as portrayed throughout this fairy tale. It is meant to kill anything becoming conscious and rising to awareness. At first, the heroine is helpless but gradually she gains the strength to confront authority and be saved. 'Without this sort of revolt, no matter what she has to suffer as a consequence, she will never be free of the power of the tyrant, never come to find herself' (Jung, 1978, p. 24).

The tale is a horrifying reality of the internalised demon lover. The stark realisation of the number of dead bodies reflects the amount of damage from narrow and socially prescribed gender roles, limiting the personality. The story demonstrates that overweening power and submission undercuts life potential.

Heroine challenges

Bluebeard functions as an inner predator, dismembering, destroying power and self-destiny for anyone other than himself. The tale highlights the misogyny still hiding in plain sight in psychological theory and practice. Remaining in the grip of a dominating complex, trapped in powerlessness, the heroine in the tale will perish unless the self is claimed. This means having the courage to do what it takes to face the challenges change involves. It means being curious, breaking societal rules and listening to inner intuitions. The deadly consequences that come from initially not heeding the signals are changed by taking the uncertain path.

At the beginning and in any number of tales, evil enters when a person is held in unconsciousness. The psychological reality is a descent or a dropping in to access the authentic and total self. Resistance to this brings about the Bluebeard aspect. Bluebeard's distorted masculinity is separated from relating and humanness, lacking a centre of love for the self or others. In this scenario the feminine colludes and is held powerless, retaining a false reality as the actual is too awful and limited by patriarchal power structures. It is a siren song, offering strength in being a handmaiden of oppression while obfuscating the reality there is no equity under the yoke of male supremacy. As the fairy tale illustrates, power in one figure who provides offers no life.

The heroine challenges the status quo. She questions and interrogates the emotions and unconsciousness behind old positions. The initiation begins with the descent into the dark and forbidden. The heroine steps out of the familiar, leaves the places hemming in her energy and escape the confines of traditional ways. In the tale she does what is forbidden by Bluebeard and finds the dead wives. Remember she had to marry him to find the truth. She had to get close to the complex to gain freedom. Her subsequent and frantic panic and resulting inventiveness illustrate tapping into resources far richer than she previously imagined. This moment in the fairy tale puts her up against herself and jolts her out of complacency. Change comes through her surprise at the disconcerting truth she cannot ignore.

If she does not speak, she will die from ignoring the evil. 'The first stage on the right road is the withdrawal of the projection by recognizing it as such' (Jung, 1978, p. 13). As we analyse the tale, we see it as a reflection of the socially prescribed gender roles and how deadly they are when rigid, passively accepted, unexamined and unconscious. It accentuates the imbalance between power and obedience, activity and passivity. The girl's brothers rescuing her at the end, shooting and killing Bluebeard, can be interpreted as strengthened personality aspects now able to answer her call and work for her.

There is more

Passivity turned to activity in this story. However much she has saved herself and others, it is her brothers who represent a helpful but also stronger ability to save her from death at the hands of Bluebeard. They are the ones who kill him. She does not. The young feminine saves the day, not alone, but by the swords of her brothers who are working in her service. She has another step to take to wield her own sword. Or perhaps the brothers are another part of herself, now supported with military power to vanquish Bluebeard. They also represent aggression reclaimed and sexuality restored. There remains more to be done as the damage by the unbalanced, violent and death-dealing aspect was quite severe.

In the end she unites herself with a better partner and her sister does as well. She is spared from dismemberment and disappearance and released from the demonic lover. In the words of Emma Jung, 'When women succeed in maintaining themselves against the animus, instead of allowing themselves to be devoured by it, then it ceases to be only a danger and becomes a creative power' (1978, p. 42). The eventual awareness requires breaking patterns that no longer fit, being real, emerging from the death-like state of unconsciousness. She is freed by this puella who grew into her strength and power through these trials and tribulations and opens a model of the feminine with more to evolve.

References

Estes, C. (1995). *Women who run with the wolves.* Ballantine Books.
Hillman, J. (1964). *Betrayal.* Guild of Pastoral Psychology.
Jung, C. G. (1959). *The collected works of C. G. Jung: Vol. 9ii. Aion.* Princeton University Press.
Jung, C. G. (1970). *The collected works of C. G. Jung: Vol. 14. Mysterium Coniunctionis.* Princeton University Press.
Jung, E. (1978). *Animus and anima.* Spring Publications.
Neumann, E. (1994). *Fear of the feminine and other essays on feminine psychology.* Princeton University Press.
O'Connell, M. (2023). *A thread of violence: A story of truth, invention, and murder.* Doubleday.
Schwartz, S. (2020). *The absent father effect on daughters.* Routledge.
von Franz, M. L. (1970). *Introduction to the interpretation of fairy tales.* Spring Publications.
von Franz, M.-L. (1993). *The feminine in fairy tales.* Shambahla.
von Franz, M. L. (2021). *The collected works of Marie-Louise von Franz: Vol. 1. Archetypal symbols in fairytales.* Chiron.
von Franz, M. L. (2022). *The collected works of Marie-Louise von Franz: Vol. 6. Niklaus von Flue and Saint Perpetua: A psychological interpretation of their visions.* Chiron.
Woodman, M. (1985). *The pregnant virgin.* Inner City Books.
Wright, S. (2019). Confronting *Bluebeard*: Totalitarian regimes in childhood and in the collective psyche. *Journal of Analytical Psychology, 64*(4), 475–484.

Chapter 11

Puer quandary

Puer and puella are differentiated by the fact the puer applies to masculine characteristics and the puella to the feminine ones. They are on a continuum, however, and therefore related to each other. We contain both, their characters and their qualities, within our personality.

The puer represents new psychic contents arising from the unconscious into conscious life, offering release from rote fixations and complexes. This part of the psyche calls us to transcend, to find an opening, a doorway to the imagination. Puer signifies something desired and hoped for, a new theme or movement. Jung said, 'That higher and "complete" (*telios*) man is begotten by the "unknown" father and born from Wisdom, and it is he who, in the figure of the *puer aeternus*—represents our totality, which transcends consciousness' (1969, CW 11, para. 742). Puer represent 'the instinctive, preconscious, original, potentially redemptive and future promise' (Gosling, 2009, p. 147). In their outer appearance, those identified with the puer are often regarded as successful performers and high achievers; however, their inner life remains hidden, its tumult often split from their own consciousness. Puer is a stage in development, but when this is as far as it goes, a person is working against accessing their complete self because development is arrested:

> The conditions of a true critique and a true creation are the same: the destruction of an image of thought which presupposes itself and the genesis of the act of thinking in thought itself. Something in the world forces us to think. This something is an object not of recognition but of a fundamental encounter.
> (Deleuze, 2004, p. 176)

The complete nomenclature of this concept and part of the personality is *puer aeternus*. It originates from the *Metamorphoses*, an epic work by the Roman poet Ovid (43 BCE–c. 17 CE). In the poem, Ovid addresses the child-god Iacchus as *puer aeternus* and praises him for his role in the Eleusinian initiation mysteries for women. Iacchus is later identified with the Greek gods Dionysus and Eros. The *puer* is a god of vegetation and resurrection, the god of divine youth, such as Tammuz in Sumerian mythology, and Attis and Adonis, also in Greek mythology. The figure of a young male god who is slain and resurrected also appears in Egyptian mythology as in the story of Osiris.

Puers can be marked by arrogance, a false front clinging to a façade, black-and-white attitudes; they are rebellious yet also static in their attempt to remain young (Gosling, 2009, p. 139). Puer represents the bravado of the insecure, needing the persona but not knowing how to access the basics of life. They over-identify with the outer and the surface while feeling less than others and hiding any shadow; all this is mixed with what appears to be an abundance of creative and unusual attributes. Puer energy is also about the child, questing, rebelling, adventuresome, high flying, inventive. Like any archetype, the puer psychology also appears in the psyche of women in dreams and relationships to self and others.

Given all this, puers can seem flighty, ready to leave for greener pastures, which is tangentiality reinforced as part of their charm. They can be immature, thoughtless, marked by innocence and free-flowing libido. Their nature is marked with wandering, invention, idealism and fantasy. Although ready to take risks, what seems like an untethered existence is actually a repetitive rendition of the familiar. Changing from place to place and person to person they remain removed and unknown, skimming the surface.

Life is shaped by attempts to evoke the illusion of unity. British psychoanalyst Donald Winnicott (1960, p. 144) wrote about the puer:

> The world may observe academic success of a high degree and may find it hard to believe in the very real distress of the individual concerned, who feels 'phoney' the more he or she is successful. When such individuals destroy themselves in one way or another, instead of fulfilling the promise, this invariably produces a sense of shock in those who have developed high hopes of the individual.

The puer's emotional and relational wounds arise from the early losses, rejections and insufficient holding environments associated with absent or overarching parental figures. These leave the child feeling insufficient. The problem is accentuated as the puer was often the child to support the parents. Childhood was thus left behind as they had to mature too fast, yet their emotional life was arrested.

This aspect of the psyche needs love and attention yet engages in deception of self and others (Solomon, 2004, p. 639). For example, a man says he wants to be the king. The phrase expresses an aloofness and the need to remain untouchable and avoid hurt. An unlinked-up quality, cold and guarded, is distancing and, although off-putting, is based on vulnerability. There is a lack of engagement and restlessness, a brittleness and stiff veneer behind which he exists in a lofty domain, above it all. This means no one sees the dark aspects of the self as they are side-stepped and threatening to the fragile sense of identity (Schwartz-Salant, 1982, p. 22).

Puer is driven by the desire to be seen, to be the best and loved by everyone. The fantasy is of one day making it and becoming someone, yet at the same time they cannot get there when fleeing the present (Hillman, 1989, p. 29). Each situation is for the short term, and relationships are met with similar noncommittal modes.

By living in the fantasy of perpetual youth, the puer avoids the time it takes to nurture their abilities, thus preventing the attainment of dreams. At their core there is a stop, a retreat before it is too hard or too boring. Love remains unknown because it involves sticking with a situation. Puers are known as players, the bad boys, with an inner emptiness behind their charm. This explains their intense cravings for outer acceptance and adoration. No matter what, they are never getting enough.

The adolescent

The puer in the personality represents a new spirit. The puer nature has a virginal quality, signals a deep interiority and freedom from external contamination from others. The puer remains untouched and untouchable. On the one hand, this quality could support the kind of aloneness necessary for self-growth and creative reflection. On the other hand, although open, radical, often daring and outside the social norm, the puer can be radically enclosed leading to inadequate engagement with others, indicating a narcissistic reaction of singularity in which no one and nothing is let in.

This puer embodies a veneration of adolescent qualities, the perpetuation of youth and denial of ageing. The person lives behind glass, removed. The pressure to live 'as-if', bolstered by persona adaptation and a perfect body, belies the emptiness and inability to address narcissistic wounds. The awareness of these wounds reveals limitations, inability, mortality and fragility. Attachment problems, divorce from the body, a distorted and split self-image and difficulty with intimacy and commitment are hidden. They are also combined with energy, passion, great ideas, grand gestures and all are some of the hallmarks of this personality type.

A woman has a dream of the puer figure. *I am at bar-like place. The two guys I am to meet are there. Neither approaches me. A woman comes and I explain nothing is happening. One guy leaves. The guy I like remains, but he is preoccupied. There are no connections made. I do not approach him. I feel badly.* She goes on to say that she realises

> this is the wrong male energy and he no longer wants me. He is a one-night stand, seductive, attractive, aloof but going nowhere. I wonder if one of the guys is the destruction inside that I so often feel, and the other reminds me of my father who was never home to pay attention. The dream shows release from attraction to the parts of myself not paying attention, putting me down. There is no good support or attention from them, and they do not let me achieve or be creative.

This puer figure, although disguised in the persona of appeal and seduction, is associated with masculine rapacious energy. He just takes, lures people in with false promises, attempting to vanquish those weaker. The problem is that when the potentiality of the psyche is not used it becomes perverted (Leonard, 1983, p. 89).

A tension of ambivalent opposites is the structural pre-condition for a dynamic life. However, the puer represents only one end of the archetypal spectrum where the person cannot ground into life or face reality. The aura of knowing and needing nothing, isolating, eliminates the need for relationship and movement. The puer can turn into a tragedy of changelessness, stuck and intractable. Without recognising the span of being, which is the essence of the archetype, there is no movement from here to there.

Therefore, the puer must go back, identify and recover from past wounds to release joy, play and spontaneity. A split from one's roots indicates arrested development more than eternal youth. Distant and cold, impermanent, the puer does not age, and there is no maturing or adapting with flexibility. The risk required to encounter the real self seems daunting. The inner system is not experienced as stabilised or harmoniously ordered but insecure, anxious and overwhelmed. To compensate, the desire is for an enchanting and unattainable magic world of ease and comfort.

Shadow

Puer's inner drive comes not only from the 'oral hunger and omnipotent fantasies but also from the frustration that the world can never satisfy' (Hillman, 1989, p. 27). For years, puers are preoccupied, floating through life with their heads in the clouds. Sex is a performance to gain approval, not a way to express and receive love. There is an ever-present tension that cuts pleasure in both mental and physical activities. Lacking a capacity for realistic self-reflection, adulthood is avoided, the ego narcissistic, hindering the larger self from being known.

The task of puer is to be present. However, they live an ethereal existence, needing immediate satisfaction. Exuding the possible and daring, the puer chases ideals as the eternal child. Time becomes a non-issue because it is just not real. Fantasies abound to avoid the underlying emptiness.

The disembodiment and psychological distancing in a puer can be disarming (Chalquist, 2009, p. 170). An inordinate identification with the persona signals susceptibility to shadow formation and suggests a significant part of the personality lies below the surface. The shadow represents a coming to reality, actualising authenticity and facing natural limits and challenges. The discomfiting but necessary growing awareness of the shadow signals individuation unfolding. However, this person might try to escape the shadow aspects, the depression and anxiety through flights of imagination and grandiosity.

However, they do not deeply partake – be it food, love, emotion or much of anything to do with living or feeling. Drugs and alcohol are appealing because the basic instincts to body and psyche remain dormant. The puer has trouble getting going. The state of perpetual youth is both false and indicates the lack of a stable sense of personal identity. Under it all, the personality is brittle and easily dissembled.

Tending to be unrealistic, they aim high; they will push, wonder and dream to make what seems impossible happen. At the same time the luxury of relaxing into just being is not easy, as this person requires much stimulation and challenge. Patience to move methodically, to listen to the world quietly, to engage with reverie, to contemplate the silence and the self are difficult for this personality type.

Puer is run by romanticised ideals. Sensitivity exists, but then, quite suddenly, the meaning of it all becomes dust (Hillman, 1989, pp. 25–26). The negation of ageing signifies denial of death, resistance to the arc of life and its stages. Sadly, many age without compassion or grace and much sorrow. The puer stares in disbelief at the cruel mirror signalling loss and estrangement, the demand for impossible perfection. They are left disillusioned and disappointed with themselves and others. Existence becomes a search for the elusive moment when real life will begin.

The shadow produces chaos and melancholy and can be felt as the darkest time. Facing the shadow means facing oneself and others without cover and accepting the imperfect. This process can be accompanied by the moments of despair as requisites for self-fruition. The shadowy recesses reveal the parts calling for recognition, accessing the core of the self, resolving the yearning and melancholy to lead to individuality and creativity.

The shadow exerts itself in this person who looks perfect and functions outstandingly according to others, yet when nothing has meaning beyond the moment, life is reduced to nothing (von Franz, 2000, p. 148). The antidote, although difficult, is to descend into the shadows and abandon the false self for the real. The shadow signals the need to reorder the psychological elements. When connected to the shadow, the personality expands with life acceptance.

Persona

An inordinate identification with the persona signals a susceptibility to shadow formation, suggesting a significant part of the personality lies below the surface. The persona for puer represents the outer face turned to the world but not as a true reflection of the personality. The word *persona* derives from the ancient Greek plays and refers to the huge masks behind which the actors spoke. Psychologically, the mask of this person hides the real behind layers of actions and images meant to garner approval and success. The trouble is the insistent and often frantic emphasis on the persona and ego as if these superficial aspects will compensate for perceived lacks. Archetypal psychologist James Hillman (1989, p. 25) described this type of person as unable to find belonging, place or the right niche, as feeling precarious, lacking internal solidity. They are restless.

Focus is on the façade, the fast, yet to be developed, the future with its flight from the present and disconnection from the physical. Our technological world can reflect the same lack of balance with roots in avoidance of the real (Gosling, 2009,

p. 148). A person focused on impossibilities and perfection, as Von Franz noted, is caught in a 'childish state of constant dissatisfaction with themselves and the whole of reality' (2000, p. 87). Although highly creative, the puer is often deficient in their interior support system and without confidence:

> In most cases the patients themselves have no suspicion whatever of the internecine war raging in their unconscious. If we remember that there are many people who understand nothing at all about themselves we shall be less surprised at the realization that there are also people who are utterly unaware of their actual conflicts.
> (Jung, 1966a, CW 7, para. 425)

This person is run by a hungry, empty self. As a man said,

> I am finding that I can no longer garner the energy to keep cycling through the fruitless changes. The anticipation of more years of emptiness is intolerable. The exhaustion with this routine is translating into a deep, abiding urge to simply no longer be.

Animus and anima

Classically the Jungian concepts of the anima and animus symbolise the masculine and feminine elements within. As has been noted, these personality aspects as originally defined are to be scrutinised and given wider meanings. Psychologically, puer remain unaware of the various personality parts circling within themselves. They are vulnerable to differentiation and remain stuck in sameness, quite like Narcissus as he gazed into his own image.

To be a person is to possess otherness, division and difference, promoting links in the polarities and opportunities for unity. It is the otherness and difference the puer rejects and cannot handle. However, this otherness and difference, offering a range of options, a widening of known borders, is psychologically necessary but threatening to the puer. The anima and animus as parts of the self challenge and encourage or can destroy and cause despair because they currently call for change. The question is how each person learns to negotiate them with flexibility and individuality. The psyche seeks balance through internal union, which I likened to a dance between feminine and masculine for accessing passion and life energy. Dynamically this brings life new twists, thoughts and ideas as the masculine relates to the feminine and vice versa, and between them they bring thoughtful reflection, difference and uniqueness.

Anima and animus are concepts leaving in 'suspension the question of "masculine" and "feminine" ... even, and the word is used advisedly, in some confusion' (Samuels, 1989, p. 94). Especially in our current era of flux and change, it cheapens and is simplifying to prescribe a fixed set of properties to the masculine or feminine. The animus and anima as psychological elements and experiences include use of intellect, mind, thought, feelings, emotions and many creative connections applicable to all people. Images are not of women and men per se but 'a metaphor for the richness, potential and mystery of the other' (Samuels, 1993, p. 143). Loneliness and hunger are the result of dormant and unused aptitudes and melancholic passivity comes from avoiding spirit and soul. This individual eventually must go through some sacrifice to access knowledge and relationship and regain feeling.

Every archetype implies another, as James Hillman noted in his book *Anima* (1985, p. 169). There he recounts the tandems and coupling of these elements as inner and outer intertwining and interfusing as Jung commented in *Integration of the Personality* (1940, p. 9). All this means, one archetype implies an other in the many dimensions of pairings.

Ability to love

Needing approval from others and becoming so involved in their own strivings, the puer usually does not see anyone else. Relationship means taking the other in, being seen and vulnerable, but this can be overlaid with shame (Rosenfeld, 1987, p. 274). Puer have trouble giving genuinely and emotionally or responding flexibly and adaptively to another's behaviour. The internal and external worlds are poised between what the person fears in their mind and what they fear in the outside world. Unconscious of this and needing safety, attachment comes through the demands for sameness in a fusion allowing for no differences.

Consequences arise from the original lack of love or correct attachment to parental figures who did not function as adequate positive or receptive mirrors. Much psychic energy is spent denying the early deficient experiences occurring before the child could process the onslaught that was both too high and too low in physical and psychological arousal (Solomon, 2004, p. 646). Without access to joy or pleasure, the person is unable to experience the self as beloved, separate and of value.

Over time it becomes evident these people are stuck in illusions and aloneness, in retreat from life. Holding a feeling of being irreparable damaged, the person cannot experience reality, as they expect it to be devastating and horrifying. No one gets close as this person who appears to be a charmer hides their issues due to deeply felt shame.

The puer attracts others to them, promising engagement. However, they cannot fulfil this promise as they only partially engage, remain emotionally unavailable, mostly to themselves, unable to commit or find fulfilment. The talents are there, but without self-knowledge actualising them often remains a mirage. The centre cannot hold, and distress occurs when the outer accomplishments shoring up the personality are exhausted and the inner reserves collapse.

Jeff has a brief but impactful dream. *In it, much as he tries, he cannot step beyond his boss. He is frozen and unable to move.* Jeff appears as a tightly coiled, small and wiry man in his late 30s. He says the boss in his dream is his father's age and an imposing leader in his field who wields force and threats to keep people in line, like his military father. This brief dream is significant and illustrates the paralysis Jeff has experienced when faced with challenges from any father, authority or parental figure. Jeff is at an emotional impasse – unable to step beyond this internalised father/male image and into his own position.

Jeff's dream reveals a difficult and overbearing father image he must pass beyond. To do this he cannot remain a puer son. When caught in a complex, a person must look for the engendering experiences and turn to the past, to childhood wounds and empathic failures, to understand the causes and reclaim energy. However, Jeff is bewildered, indecisive and internally without potency. The dream heightens his awareness of the situation.

Jeff's situation happens to many puer sons caught in the complex task of internalising good enough fathers. Men often say they could not ask their fathers to show them. He was either not there or emotionally unavailable. They express loneliness, keeping disappointments to themselves and hiding their perceived flaws with a persona of bravado. These adaptations are based on their experiences of father absence or aggression that represses emotion and colours self-defeat. They can feel so frustrated in how to use their potency, they give up expressing autonomy or become overly daring without any caution or awareness. Sometimes there is absence of thought, and the creative is blank. Sometimes there is achievement; sometimes this shining star burns out early.

Effect on the body

This person might experience various forms of depersonalisation or feel unreal in their physical self. In the mildest cases, disembodiment is manifested by a lack of vitality and emptiness, but it is often disguised. The puer constructs a false body-self, an illusionary perfect body. They cling to this obsessively and desperately to keep away any deadening sensations. There is fear that if the body-mask is removed nothing will be there. This suggests feelings of not really being alive, linked to the fact there is has no inner representation of face or body (Connelly, 2013, p. 636). It is like Narcissus who does not see himself seeing himself. Self-hatred, desire to deny the body, disappointment combine with ageing as the looks relied upon alter and bring alienation, anger and rebellion at the natural arc of life.

Meanwhile, the body is objectified, sexualised, drugged while the person feels invisible and disconnected. The search and need for visibility are frustrated in the unease to be close, so distance results instead. No matter how it looks from the outside, the puer is not physically connected or confident. Again, the façade is slick, the charm enchanting, the sexuality seductive, potential and creative possibilities strong. The inner suffering, although not apparent, is destructive.

This person finds fault with everything, and nothing and no one is good enough. The ongoing involvement with self is missing. Partnering is fraught with the itch of something being wrong. Being real includes both the light and dark shadows. But the puer's mirror reflects the singular rather than the multiple subjectivities of the world. Everything narrows to establish safety and eliminate otherness, as anything outside the self feels threatening. 'Relationship to the self is at once relationship to our fellow man, and no one can be related to the latter until he is related to himself' (Jung, 1966b, CW 16, para. 445).

Yet, these people proceed as if they are fine and need nothing from others. They try to ignore the nagging feeling that the centre is shaky as this means recognising the original lacks attachment as part of the maladaptive response to life. Again, psychological dissociation and external distancing develops as a survival attempt and, along with the illusionary setup, compensates the weight of depressive anxiety. Natural body instincts and feelings fall into the unconscious. Frequently uneasy, the person is subsumed with obsessive drives and self-persecutory impulses, the oppressive weight of mindlessness, bingeing on the internet, gaming and television.

Underneath is a tenderness of psyche so raw it does not trust opening to any other. Jeff could not spend the night with anyone as that was too intimate, and he could not tolerate being seen as vulnerable and personal. He lived a form of narcissism in a psychic state of oneness, of life without others, no twoness; his self was divorced from the body and the unconscious from the conscious. A person of this type circles around but does not get into intimacy, feelings or the emotions of love. Often appearing as a desired object, they are adored and idealised, adding to the avoidance of interiority and intimacy. The picture is sustained by projecting uniqueness and grandeur but underneath rumbles a restless, dissatisfied and terrible yearning for something. A puer does not know what it is – it is the self.

As yet undeveloped

Jeff remained searching for love he could not find. He learned more about himself, enough to find comfort from his reading, his choice of activities and his work. He was more at ease with who he was but not enough to reveal much of himself to others. And yet life was more palatable as he understood both his desires and limitations. Life held more satisfactions but still lacked something.

What is unknown and unconscious are the strangers within we do not know. Jung referred to them as the shadow comprised of the parts resisted, the others awaiting integration, the unconscious where empathy for self and other reside. The process of growth into oneself needs time and involves periods of suffering, but by facing the discomfort, we are no longer blindly possessed by unknown and destructive psychological contents.

This requires a psychological turn inwards, to what lies in the depths, and towards what is unconscious and of value but as yet undeveloped. 'The destructive powers were converted into healing forces. This is brought about by the archetypes awaking to independent life and taking over the guidance of the psychic personality, thus supplanting the ego with its futile willing and striving' (Jung, 1969, CW 11, para. 534).

References

Chalquist, G. (2009). Insanity by the numbers, knowings from the ground. In S. Porterfield (Ed.), *Perpetual adolescence* (pp. 169–186). State University of New York Press.

Connelly, A. (2013). Out of the body. *Journal of Analytical Psychology, 58*(5), 636–656.
Deleuze, G. (2004). *Difference and repetition*. Bloomsbury Academic.
Gosling, J. (2009). 'Protracted adolescence': Reflections on forces affecting the American collective. In S. Porterfield (Ed.), *Perpetual adolescence* (pp. 137–154). State University of New York Press.
Hillman, J. (1985). *Anima: An anatomy of a personified notion*. Spring Publications.
Hillman, J. (Ed.) (1989). *Puer papers*. Spring Publications.
Jung, C. G. (1940). *Integration of the personality*. Routledge.
Jung, C. G. (1966a). *The collected works of C. G. Jung: Vol. 7. Two essays in analytical psychology*. Princeton University Press.
Jung, C. G. (1966b). *The collected works of C. G. Jung: Vol. 16. The practice of psychotherapy*. Princeton University Press.
Jung, C. G. (1969). *The collected works of C. G. Jung: Vol. 11. Psychology and religion: East and West*. Princeton University Press.
Leonard, L. S. (1983). *The wounded woman: Healing the father/daughter relationship*. Shambhala.
Rosenfeld, H. (1987). *Impasse and interpretation*. Tavistock.
Samuels, A. (1989). *The plural psyche: Personality, morality, and the father*. Routledge.
Samuels, A. (1993). *The political psyche*. Routledge.
Schwartz-Salant, N. (1982). *On narcissism*. Inner City Books.
Solomon, H. (2004). Self-creation and the limitless void of dissociation: The 'as if' personality. *Journal of Analytical Psychology, 49*(5), 635–656.
Von Franz, M.-L. (2000). *The problem of the puer aeternus*. Inner City Books.
Winnicott, D. W. (1960). Ego distortion in terms of true and false self. In D. W. Winnicott (Ed.), *The maturational process and the facilitating environment: Studies in the theory of emotional development*. International Universities Press, Inc.

Chapter 12

Unreal to oneself

> Knowing does not always allow us to prevent, but at least the things that we know, we hold them, if not in our hands, but at least in our thoughts where we may dispose of them at our whim, which gives us the illusion of power over them.
>
> Marcel Proust, *Swann's Way: Remembrance of Things Past* (2022)

Jung posited that especially in the second half of life we are faced with the challenge and responsibility of a psychological turn inwards. This is when we explore what lies in the depths and move towards what is meaningful. We acquire self-knowledge, shaping the dynamic process of becoming ourselves. To do this, puella faces the challenge of accepting the entire arc of life, from youth to the later stages.

The personality of puella is often characterised by fears of ageing, by vulnerability, superficiality and avoidance of reality. These attitudes preclude finding the beauty in all of life's stages. We see this evidenced in the prevalence of social media and its predominantly ego- and persona-idealised images. These images can be a form of narcissism, singularity and exclusion like those often adopted by puella. A superficial guise signifies blocks to inward communication and relational connections invariably halting deeper psychological processes. A woman said, 'I don't know who I am. There is a peculiar feeling of unreality. I feel like a facsimile, although I cannot say why. I was hoping to break through the sense of living behind a mask'. This describes the personality of puella and the various regions of the psyche remaining elusive and beyond her grasp.

A thick layer of impenetrability indicates a failure to be present. Puella resides behind the protection of translucent, not transparent barriers. 'Self-consciousness emerges as a kind of knowing that is at once a mode of becoming; it is suffered, dramatized, enacted' (Butler, 1987, p. 28). This is the self and its consciousness, which puella can miss when floating in unreality, restlessness and an inability to settle. It is also, at the same time, what ignites the creative verve, the spark and the light.

Puella can live in disarray. A solid-enough identity to cope with the disquieting feelings of inner fragmentation and worthlessness is missing. A persistent lack of vitality and emptiness can lead to psychic deadness, or 'feeling like a zombie' in

DOI: 10.4324/9781003449447-12

the popular vernacular. This familiar reaction is experienced by many. Butler noted, 'Desire is intentional in that it is always desire of or for a given object or Other, but it is also reflexive in the sense that desire is a modality in which the subject is both discovered and enhanced' (1987, p. 25). It is this desire puella in her unreality cannot hold or develop, and her energy becomes lost, diverted and scattered. This is accompanied by the conviction that nothing is worth it, and then all is dropped.

For puella, fantasy allows her to escape what seems like an overwhelming reality. American relational psychoanalyst Michael Eigen noted, 'More people than in the past seek help for feeling dead. Although feeling dead is a central complaint of many individuals, it is not clear where this deadness comes from, or what can be done about it' (Connelly, 2013, p. 640). This kind of deadness can sever access to selfhood.

The deadness loudly speaks the voice of psychic pain and the vanished self. There is loss of investment in the body, leading to disembodiment or depersonalisation in which there is an alteration in the perception or experience of the self, a not feeling real to oneself (Connelly, 2013, p. 639). Reality is too painful when the bottom line of self-talk is that I am not lovable and will be rejected for who I am. When puella forces herself into a rigid ideal or obsessive need for achievement, she lacks the nourishment of relatedness or self-agency. Puella is rarely content, always running or dreaming about the marvellous past or future but not in physical embodiment because that means living in the present.

The worshipping of illusions is fostered by the overarching image of what life should be but is not. As Jung said, 'To the extent that she first completely identified herself with her role, she was altogether unconscious of her real self' (Jung, 1966a, CW 7, para. 248). This attitude also causes deadness, lack of connection, helplessness, defeat and despair. The flattening of affects and nullifying subjectivity can obscure the imaginal, obstruct the symbolic functioning and limit psychological insight.

Out of body

The loss of desire results in the disappearance of self, of not being received or seen. As Janine said,

> I do not know what it feels like to be centred. I am usually not in my body and am in my head. I do not know why I resort to playing that game on my computer. I tell myself it does not take so long but then I keep on playing and the hours go by. However, I also do not know what I am doing in my life or if there is any meaning. I rarely try to figure it out because I never have. After several therapies and years of this, can anything help?

Her negation of emotional self-reflection is striking. At issue is intimacy with self and others because she has not known it. Janine describes feeling wooden; affectionate sharing and people being too close make her uncomfortable. She dreams *vaguely in generalities about having to pay attention to the needs of others, but not knowing why. There are voices in the next room speaking to this effect.* She has no idea what she feels; she just knows to attend to them as the other dream figures expect her attention. Janine gets no notice, is invisible emotionally, expects to get nothing and is silent, polite, quiet. She feels the world's catastrophes but not her own. She learned from mother to not bother, from stepfather that other people were insufficient and from the actual father to be ignored. He was self-serving, demanded focus but gave little care. She learned from all these primary relationships she should not ask for anything as this would only irritate or anger them. Her hurt did not count, so her emotions shut down, and for the longest time she lived alone in her mind. She has ignored the need to turn inwards emotionally for so long that the natural instincts and impetus to share, have needs and exist was almost gone.

She questions the reality of her life. Janine hardly feels; she thought she did not have to care about herself and could get away with ignoring self-treatment. After all, nothing bad had happened to her yet. In her 60s now, however, her body is reacting and breaking down, just a bit, not severely, but in increments she cannot ignore. She dreams *about a former past infatuation with a rather flighty sounding and uncommitted person. In the dream, the person is there and then gone without noticing her.* She is left with many feelings but nowhere to put them. This has been a theme since she was a young person with many feelings, but no one asked or noticed them, so she learned to eliminate how she felt through masking. Relationships became based on fact, not emotion, and now her whole being is reacting to the accumulated deadness.

Janine struggles to find the words. They slowly sputter forth. She has not gone here before in her mind, much less with someone else. She says she does not know and has rarely been living within herself. She just did what she was supposed to do, took care of life tasks, listened to the needs of others. Janine now questions why she is here; she cannot find herself or what gets in the way. She never thought she had much choice one way or another and did what others suggested. Now she often cannot decide what to eat or how to enact basic care. She is in a muddle and, although psychologically curious, uncertain how to proceed. Her mind is blank: She does not know how to be aware or value her reality; she just puts in time. She worries about her health but does little to care for her body. But now the problems are multiplying. In 'On the Psychology of the Unconscious', Jung wrote about the intersection of psyche and body:

> A wrong functioning of the psyche can do much to injure the body, just as conversely a bodily illness can affect the psyche; for psyche and body are not separate entities but one and the same life. Thus there is seldom a bodily ailment that does not show psychic complications, even if it is not psychically caused.
>
> (1966a, CW 7, para. 194)

Janine is experiencing the void of the disappearing self. Recovery requires finding what got lost, stretching all the way back to a childhood based on having to exert strong control over her feelings (Wilkinson, 2017, p. 532). The history, or recalled anamnesis of early life, illustrates why Janine's psychological masks initially developed. Her personality and its expression became hidden, and the carapace of image hardened. The result was a depersonalisation or derealisation, and the psyche and body became both fused and disconnected.

The lack of intimacy, the isolation from others and the discomfort of being real, have created the defences of withdrawing, compartmentalising, segregating one part of the mind from another. Left with shame and expecting indifference, Janine has assumed she was too much. Disintegrating into shambles within, she doubts whether she is capable of being loved. To restore what has been out of balance, she must connect spirit and body. Messages come from both areas, but can she listen and respond?

Italian psychoanalyst Antonino Ferro called this *mental anorexia* meaning a 'primal experience of having inadequate space in the Other's mind and a need to make oneself smaller and smaller' (2006, p. 213). This occurs by splitting off parts of the self that are felt to be upsetting or burdensome to others. Like puella, Janine anticipates being devoured by the void experienced with others. This is where the cognition of emotions has become twisted, disjointed from her possession.

Painful events in the family story emerge: She does not express grief, as she says she had worked this out previously. Now it is off limits. She hides the residue of sorrows. Being ashamed of her thoughts, any feelings and fantasies that show vulnerability are difficult to tolerate, much less to share. Emotions have a corporeal as well as intellectual nature. These realities are inseparable, and the raw elements have remained.

For Janine, like the puella type, the nameless dread of trauma, this indistinct but real feeling creeps over her, always lingering somewhere in her body. It affects her 'ability to think and feel about the unbearable unthinkable trauma, to transform this into communicable, shareable, symbolic thoughts as can occur in analysis' (Colman, 2022, p. 932). She has tried to deny and repress, fearing it would subsume her.

The trauma or wounding is now enacted by ignoring herself. Because the wounds had to be formerly damped down, it was as if she forgot – or nearly forgot – the former experiences. The wounds lodged within her inner world remain unavailable to process adequately (Wilkinson, 2017, p. 537). Her intellectual and professional work is an effort to escape from feeling any of the upsetting material.

The guise is that her world looks fine from the outside. She functions, causes no problems, says nothing. All has been packed inside with no noticeable complaints from her and nothing to crack the image built to satisfy first her parents and then adapted to the world. Janine silenced the inner voices so she could not hear their cries, nor could she cry. The absence of thought blocks access to the inner space necessary to think, fantasise or find meaning.

Being visible

What is visibility? Themes of looking, seeing and being seen might include the transgressive gaze. The parental vacuum of intimacy and imagery frustrate, agonise and absorb the child. The mixed messages to obey and remain compliant seep in. This becomes the 'inertia of libido, which will relinquish no object of the past, but would like to hold it fast forever ... a passive state where the libido is arrested in the objects of childhood' (Jung, 1966a, CW 7, para. 253). Throughout life the emotional recapitulations, physical abandonments and absence lead to a state of entrapment, a mire of suffering, loss and unreality. When sufficient parental care was unknown, a child feels unloved, and this attitude brings alienation from the body and the instincts and can escalate into a hatred of life and self-destructive behaviours.

An inauthentic pose and accommodation to outer demands protect a terrified and precarious self that feels fragile in the world. An 'as-if' self takes over, resulting from a loss of natural instincts, while the real self remains walled off and silent. It will require descent into the depths of the shadow to abandon the façade and access the real. The personal shadow is not identified with what is repressed but includes contents no longer, or not yet, accepted by consciousness (Jung, 1968b, CW 9ii, paras. 422 & 423). The encounter with oneself effectively requires an encounter with one's shadow, in which a '[woman] stands forth as [she] really is and shows what was hidden under the mask of conventional adaptation' (Jung, 1966b, CW 16, para. 452). As Jung noted, this 'encounter with the "naked truth" was positive, because the dark side is also part of the whole psyche. Nonetheless, the descent to the unconscious is a narrow door' whose constriction is painful (Jung 1968a, CW 9i, para. 45). For puella it is not easy to take off the mask and enter this seemingly dangerous terrain.

I dream about *Janine and myself in her home. She was nervous, perspiring. I was really seeing her up close. She looked different and a bit heavier*. I take the dream to indicate her fragility and how hard the process of inner work and being revealed is for her. She was sweating, and the dream indicates the need to get close in order to understand and assist in her self's development. This information helps move the process forwards and establish sensitive connections in the analytical work. The dream heightens awareness and reveals the tender aspects of her personality.

To articulate the larger emotional truths transcending time and space we have to find the voices of the invisible, undeveloped and unexplored. Much attention is required to put back together that which has been broken apart and scattered.

> The black hole is a signifier for an indescribable nothing that, paradoxically, is both the origin and the font of creativity and freedom. In this psychological space the entity is so densely packed at center and is a metaphor for troubling psychic states.
>
> (Hinton, 2007, p. 434)

Descending into the black hole brings forth images of claustrophobia and death, dramatically signifying the unknown others that threaten. The black hole forms from the original loss of the object, the caregiver, the parental holding, and the person is left with what feels like a gap inside that was caused from the outside

(Hinton, 2007, p. 438). Through analytical work the sense of loss and grief may open the psychological and interior space for new elements and an enriched presence in the world.

Transcendent function for self-emergence

The lack of emotional openness and how puella deals with and responds to the analyst and vice versa is affected by the mask hiding the real. In analysis this is encountered through the transcendent function involving the psychic process of assimilation and integration of unconscious elements (Jung, 1969a, CW 8, para. 257). Analysis brings the patient into direct contact with the transcendent function, which arises from the analytical relationship and brings conscious and unconscious into contact. The personality grows as the ego finds relationship to the overarching self. The unconscious material comes forth to compensate and enriches formerly one-sided conscious attitudes.

The transcendent function is composed, not of new, but unknown contents; it reveals the counter position in the unconscious and includes the acknowledgement of the risk of dissociation from unconscious contents. Analysis can bring these to awareness and free the psyche through the readjustment and reunification of the psychological contents.

Jungian analytical therapy is a process of exploring subjectivity and imagination. Not knowing precipitates transformation when the patient faces the gaps and abysses of life and is at the heart of analytic work (Hinton, 2007, p. 444). The transcendent function brings forth fantasy, imagination and makes new levels of reflection and symbolisation possible. It is an ongoing process of experiencing suspension between the formerly adopted deadness and possible aliveness.

Internally, a person might have no room for other thoughts or space for interpretations. All might seem noisy and intrusive, and a puella cannot think, perhaps feeling overrun by the therapist, as experienced in the family. Rather than this being an impediment, it exposes what has receded into the unconscious and formed into the dissociated elements living in the psyche. Puella often does not realise how much these elements control freedom of expression, confidence and ease in being. Here are the uncomfortable gaps between self and others, the idealisations, need for defence, all emerging in the therapeutic relationship.

These are the communications, oscillating in the analysis, to dialogue with and expose the relational wounds. The varied positions in the unconscious bring the psyche forwards, out of polarisation and oppositional states, enabling the process of individuation (Solomon, 1998, p. 232). Each psychological phenomenon contains within itself the means for interpretation and understanding. The psychological life is complex, as even in therapy puella fights desires and repressed dependency needs, including grief and mourning. Deprived of the alchemy of engagement long ago, she drew a magic circle around herself to be self-sufficient. The old way protected, and therefore, much as we may want them, new attitudes are not so easy to manage or accept.

Depression

Faced with something unknown, and everything has something unknown in it, we fill in our experience with fantasies, assumptions, anticipations and fears. Some of this is based on memory, the vestiges of past experiences good and bad. Some of it is based on possibility, the potentials within our personality that are not yet but could be.

There is an intention in depression to bring us downwards. It may be the direction we need to go, especially as culturally we are told to rise above it all. Depression is an expression notifying us of missed vitality, a consequence of becoming separated from the self. The path of learning from the depression, but not quickly getting rid of it, reflects the Jungian perspective. Culturally, the vacuity and absence of depth denies the shadow in a frantic search to fill what feels essentially empty. Yet few see the pain of puella underneath as her cover-up is well staged and refined.

The experience of meaning, even when it comes through the channel of depression, is a healing experience and can open opportunities for growth. Therefore, it is a way of approaching and understanding the malaise, the drag of energy and the pull inwards. We often begin analysis from suffering, displeasure, discomfort, both inner and outer, a life crisis, numbness, all of these pushing the desire for change. Analysis is about the meaning we make as we look at life from our specific background and cultural traditions. We must be vulnerable to the desolations, the things going awry to make the repair.

Ultimately, we must all wrestle with our own darkness and sense of unreality. As Jung said in 'The Philosophical Tree', 'One does not become conscious by imagining figures of light, but by making the darkness conscious' (1968d, CW 13, para. 335). This means not falling into a passive and defeated attitude as the goal is the movement of libido or psychic energy.

However, many puella types learn to distrust their emotional perceptions and reactions. The self was put in doubt early in life. Beginning with deficient parental interactions and emotional wounds creates a confusing series of mixed messages. The inconsistency of love and attention numbs the joy of existence. The ability to use personal truth for psychic nourishment and development becomes compromised. No matter how it looks to the contrary, puella did not trust or gain guidance in her truth. Her outer behaviour hides and protects, a survival technique needed in a discomfiting and untrusting world where one feels alien and alienated. Often puellas describe themselves as going through the motions, but not living. They come to analysis looking for what is missing. Isolated and without zest, the deadness is an absent space into which nothing else penetrates. By exploring this inner deadness, they find what can be replenished and regenerative to emerge into life.

Janine experienced a life nausea and existential dread that demonstrated needs for security. She took something over the counter for years for the nausea but did not figure there was an emotional component. As Jung commented in 'The Tavistock Lectures', however,

Whatever has an intense feeling tone is difficult to handle because such contents are associated with physiological reactions, with the processes of the heart, the tonus of the blood vessels, the condition of the intestines, the breathing and innervation of the skin.

(1954, CW 18, para. 148)

Insight and depth are revealed through symbols, conveying understanding of the psyche, and are fundamental to the Jungian approach. For Janine to become real was to risk being overwhelmed by intense feelings of anguish over the early loss of bonding and subsequent lack of mirroring. This set up a disconnect from the body. The idea is thus to bring body phenomena out of the shadows and situate body and psyche more consciously at the heart of the analysis. In the consulting room are not only two souls but also two bodies. Healing is possible if these two realms, soul and body, form a constant reciprocal interaction and exchange. In seeking to understand communications from the unconscious, do not dismiss the body.

Yet, Janine previously could not afford to feel as how she felt was unknown. She does not know her value. She keeps trying to fix partners but cannot. Who is she trying to repair and make better? She worries she will burden others, so she does not verbalise her needs or depressions. She says mother was like a queen, but cold, removed, no emotion. Janine's excellent and quick mind developed but not her emotions. She is not used to being reacted to. Who is she really? She knows being ignored, bewildered by relationships, and for years could not see how disappointing the family was to her. Like many, she blames herself. In fact, 'the unknown exercises a fascinating attraction that threatens to become the more overpowering the further [s]he penetrates into it' (Jung, 1968c, CW 12, para. 439).

Janine *dreams of a woman looking out at the water. There is a small girl in a red dress who comes back and forth to her. There is an abandoned red boat.* In this brief dream the association is to her mother who seems unconcerned and usually has her back to her. *This is the position of the women in dream after dream.* Janine thinks nothing of the mother/woman not watching out for the girl. Where is the care? She is ashamed the dream woman is so empty of feelings, thinking it is herself, but she recalls her mother's eyes were vacant, without soul or depth. Is this what she integrates about herself? It is a question, brought forth by the dream, that we can ponder.

In the presence of the therapist, puella actually comes to express herself a different way (Perelberg & Kohon, 2017, p. 130). Therapy helps re-negotiate the wounded places, dismantle the defensive strategies and, in the process, also reveals the psychic panic. The unmasking of reality opens the hidden, tender vulnerabilities in the patient's heartbroken world. The therapist must be willing to manage the 'real existential anguish, doubt, not knowing and the risk it takes for them to reveal emotions and real feelings' (Solomon, 2004, p. 643). The therapist is attuned to the gaps, silences and reversals in each session, listening to what is absent and what might be an invisible presence.

The therapeutic space includes encountering the vulnerability, the fantasies and tragedies. Within this is the tender, fragile and shy parts of the self. Affective emotional engagement in therapy enables emotional learning to occur and that learning may bring profound change in the inner patterning that determines the way the patient is able to relate (Wilkinson, 2017, p. 539).

Puella needs an opening of doors for psychological understanding. The 'act of self-recollection, a gathering together of what is scattered' indicates 'the integration and humanization of the self' (Jung, 1969b, CW 11, para. 400). The psyche is fluid, multidimensional, alive and capable of creative development. Jung paradoxically said, 'The secret is that only that which can destroy itself is truly alive' (Jung, 1968c, CW 12, para. 93). To retrieve her life, this requires puella to recognise the lost objects of desire, the parental lacks and losses, the emotional wounds. Transformation, not the erasure of memories, brings the submerged energy into conscious awareness.

Puella learns to live, not deny feelings, while developing her own cannon of being. It also means realising the history that haunts and shapes her, influencing the therapeutic experience. As André Green paradoxically noted, the representation of an absence of representation also suggests it contains what could not yet be represented (Kohon, 1999, p. 276). Herein lies the possibility of symbolic creation and imagery within the personality to repair the painful absence and come alive through the relational space of therapy. The re-creation of representation evolves in the dialogue of therapy, verbal and nonverbal, conscious and unconscious.

Janine *dreams she had turned the sweater inside out. It had defined seams, thick, and she liked the pattern. She cut out the labels and decided to wear it this way. She said it was now really hers. The seams were thick, the design interesting as was the purple/blue colour. The sweater was warm, and she felt good in it and claimed it as hers.*

The psychological journey involves finding what is called in Jungian analytical psychology the 'treasure hard to attain' or the knowledge residing in the unconscious and brought to conscious life. The therapeutic relationship and dreamwork are processes honouring the body, mind and soul. The therapeutic discourse gives additional meaning to past, present and future events, enabling puella to take possession of her abandoned or undeveloped potentials. She discovers the meaning in her personal drama as a step towards separating from restrictive attitudes. This comes with the transcendent function through the symbols arising from the union of the opposing tendencies for new perspectives emerging. The discovery of the self occurs through the minutely reflective and relational process integrating both the chaos and order of the psyche.

> The therapeutic situation is the only place explicitly provided for in the social contract in which we are allowed to talk about the wounds we have suffered and to search for possible new identities and new ways of talking about ourselves.
> (Kristeva, 1987, p. 6)

To accept the reality of lack and absence opens the doors to new experiences, ideals and relationships. The work of the inner life is a path of meaning in an act of self-surrender to open the unconscious and connect to conscious life. This also means choosing the individual trail, not the crowded avenues or highways. The way is long. The work is hard. The reward is remarkable but intangible, especially at the beginning when there is only a slim vantage point, and we are unable to envision little of the rich resources available for new awareness and creation.

References

Butler, J. (1987). *Subjects of desire: Hegelian reflections in twentieth-century France*. Columbia University Press.

Colman, W. (2022). Thinking the unthinkable: Trauma, defence and early states of mind in the work of Alessandra Cavalli. *Journal of Analytical Psychology, 67*(4), 919–938.

Connelly, A. (2013). Out of the body. *Journal of Analytical Psychology, 58*(5), 636–656.

Ferro, A. (2006). *Mind works: Technique and creativity in psychoanalysis*. Routledge.

Hinton, L. (2007). Black holes, uncanny spaces and radical shifts in awareness. *Journal of Analytical Psychology, 52*(4), 443–447.

Jung, C. G. (1954). *The collected works of C. G. Jung: Vol. 18. The symbolic life*. Pantheon Books.

Jung, C. G. (1966a). *The collected works of C. G. Jung: Vol. 7. Two essays in analytical psychology*. Princeton University Press.

Jung, C. G. (1966b). *The collected works of C. G. Jung: Vol. 16. The practice of psychotherapy*. Princeton University Press.

Jung, C. G. (1968a). *The collected works of C. G. Jung: Vol. 9i. The archetypes and the collective unconscious*. Pantheon Books.

Jung, C. G. (1968b). *The collected works of C. G. Jung: Vol. 9ii. Aion*. Princeton University Press.

Jung, C. G. (1968c). *The collected works of C. G. Jung: Vol. 12. Psychology and alchemy*. Princeton University Press.

Jung, C. G. (1968d). *The collected works of C. G. Jung: Vol. 13. Alchemical studies*. Princeton University Press.

Jung, C. G. (1969a). *The collected works of C. G. Jung: Vol. 8. The structure & dynamics of the psyche*. Princeton University Press.

Jung, C. G. (1969b). *The collected works of C. G. Jung: Vol. 11. Psychology and religion: East and West*. Princeton University Press.

Kohon, G. (1999). *The dead mother: The work of André Green*. Routledge.

Kristeva, J. (1987). *Tales of love*. Columbia University Press.

Perelberg, R., & Kohon, G. (2017). *The greening of psychoanalysis: André Green's new paradigm in contemporary theory and practice*. Karnac Books

Proust, M. (2022). *Swann's way: Remembrance of things past, vol. 1* (C. K. S. Moncrieff, Trans.). Henry Holt & Co. https://www.gutenberg.org/cache/epub/7178/pg7178-images.html

Solomon, H. M. (1998). The self in transformation: The passage from a two- to a three-dimensional internal world. *Journal of Analytical Psychology, 43*(2), 225–238.

Solomon, H. M. (2004). Self-creation and the limitless void of dissociation: The 'as if' personality. *Journal of Analytical Psychology, 49*(5), 635–656.

Wilkinson, M. (2017). Mind, brain, body. *Journal of Analytical Psychology, 62*(4), 526–543. https://doi.org/10.1111/1468-5922.12335

Chapter 13

Into the void – loss of the symbolic

Puella has a difficult time going beyond surface appearances and interactions. Her ethereal nature tends to skim rather than delve. She acts out of insecurity and fear of the unknown, anticipating she cannot do it or it will make no difference. However, her drive and need to know more pushes her into the process of individuation, which entails encountering the void. This is difficult for puella as she is not used to accessing her ability to symbolise and fears the psychological depths.

Defensively competitive and threatened, she asks, 'Who is this other? What does the other have that I don't have? What do I want? What do I lack?' André Green described this:

> The early emotional lacks form psychic holes, not the loss of something once had, but the absence of love objects that never existed … setting up internal world attack, time frozen, investment in self dismantled and void occupying the mind.
>
> (1986, p. 153)

Unearthed by emotional wounds, an emptiness plunges the puella into longing for eros, relatedness and relationship. This otherness is a meeting with what is unknown about the other and herself. She is entangled in both desire and lack, and this initiates a skirmish for recognition and gaining consciousness.

Puella lives one-dimensionally, contour-less, without inner substance, her body feelings numb. She exists at the edge of non-living. All feels flat and partial, the world two-dimensional. She does not trust deeply. Ronald Britton, British psychoanalyst, presented the idea of 'trauma precipitated by an internal, subjective event, and the aversion of these patients for their own subjectivity. In such cases the persons dislodge themselves from an internal space to distance themselves from their traumatized core and externalize their minds' (Mizen & Morris, 2008, p. 101). These people rely on others to get by, waiting for answers from them rather than accessing their own.

What fills the absence within? Despair, defeat, depression, joy, pleasure, new ways of being? Absence is an area to explore, to understand, to gain release and to become oneself.

The Self seems threatened with annihilation, which may be more to do with a rupturing of the ego-Self axis. In the first case the fear is of disintegration, whereas in the second the experience is one of the living dead, as though the individual is cut off from the life source.

(Ashton, 2007, p. 1)

There is a melancholia about puella, indicating a void, a loss of centre and an unstable self. The puella may be unable to contain and reflect upon affective experiences from not having internalised a process for containment or affect expression. 'Such patients can experience some of their affect but cannot form a representation. There is no ability to symbolize and develop meaning' (Willemsen, 2014, p. 699). For puella the lack of healthy relating experiences adversely affects self-security and compromises spontaneity and enthusiasm.

In Jungian analytical psychology the reflections in images, dreams and symbolic messages from the unconscious help restore the personality. 'Applied consciousness ... facilitates reflection which attends upon effective realization of the self' (Shorter, 1986, p. 174). It means emerging from the ashes to the creative, recognising the pain and feeling the places that are unrepaired or missing. By doing so self-expression emerges alongside the individuation process. 'Individual self-reflection, return of the individual to the ground of human nature, to his own deepest being with its individual and social destiny here is the beginning of a cure for that blindness which reigns at the present hour' (Jung, 1966a, CW 7, p. 5). In relation to this Jung described 'a process by which a new content forces itself upon consciousness either from without (through the senses) or from within (from the unconscious) and, as it were, compels attention and enforces apprehension' (1971, CW 6, para. 683).

Intrusion of others

For many puellas the self is insecure and fragile. There is emptiness, isolation, alienation and rootlessness. Jung said, however, 'In the intensity of the emotional disturbance itself lies the value, the energy which he should have at his disposal in order to remedy the state of reduced adaptation' (1969, CW 8, para. 166). The feeling of void can seem impossible to negotiate. This can show up as idealisation of others, projections and denials of the collective and personal shadow. In the psychological treatment transferences reveal the complexes.

Stella is a composite example of many. She has a repetitive image, dream or feeling, she does not know which, but *in it she is dangling from a cliff by a rope. She has somehow dropped down and is just there, hanging by a thread. She has no thoughts of getting help yet feels helpless*. Her recounting of this dream memory occurred when she felt more than the usual despair and defeat. She describes too much being stacked against her due to social class, inadequate early-life support, not enough money, debt and feeling the burden and unfairness of it all. She was raised in a working-class family, and to her this meant the weight of never getting out, and it now feels even more limiting.

She feels caught in quicksand. She looks in the mirror and is dismayed. She feels ugly, heavy with a few extra pounds. Does the mirror tell the truth? She is ageing; she has not done what she wanted and feels it is too late. All these thoughts and feelings combine into a sense of defeat. She sees little future and fears she will be stuck and will just die. This loneliness radically cuts her off from human connection with self and others. After this session, she wants to go home, which means being alone, collapsing on the bed, not being with anyone and without pressure. She sees nothing meaningful and, as portrayed by the helplessness of her dream, does not find anything symbolic of hope. She is sad when sitting down to write in her journal and the pages remain blank. Stella is lonely, is unable to get through the mire and feels deserted.

She is literal and concrete, unable to believe she is valued. She wonders if the woundedness occurred too early and the aloneness is too profound. As a complex emotional experience of loss, the self represents a lack of 'the capacity to value one's own uniqueness as a separate person, different from, albeit intimately connected with others' (Colman, 1991, p. 356).

My dream after she called for a longer session was of her calling three times and my reaction of worry that I will not be enough. The dream is an obvious image of the transference. It also reveals a questioning about our fitness for each other, overlaid with uneasy apprehension. Stella's despair takes her from life, and in the analytic process her desire for perfection in order to make up for past wounds is unrealistic. Her image of hanging from a rope is a signal of the dependency and trust needed to extricate herself, not alone, but accompanied, responded to and saved. The question in this short vignette is whether she can take the chance and whether I can respond and be there. My dream reaction reflects the hesitancy about whether it can happen.

Stella lacks emotional openness, and it makes analysis more difficult as she has for so long lived behind the mask that everything is fine. The masks were part of why her relationships did not fully take with herself or others. They were part of the despair and misery, her personality hidden and unrevealed, her emotional expression and ability to symbolise hampered. These factors block communication, affect transference connections and halt the deeper analytical work. What seems missing is a way to access the meaning-making that could arise from a symbolic attitude and penetrate the avoidance perpetuating in the analytic field. The intimacy necessary to develop both within and beyond the analytic encounter also remains masked, causing loneliness and preventing the psychological connection so desired.

In Jungian psychology the symbolism of the process of becoming oneself parallels alchemy, with its symbolic approach revealing the way inwards for transformation. The self is discovered through the feelings of void and nothingness and leads to burning away the old. In alchemical terms this is a stage called the *mortification*. Alchemy is an existential, symbolic and poetic process illustrating psychological life pushing into and through the void to gain consciousness. At the same time, the 'refusal or inability to respond to the depth or symbolic dimension leads to a loss of reality' (Collins & Molchanov, 2022, p. 173).

Current emotional wounding replicates the impact of past experiences, bringing back the lack, loss and sense of not belonging. It can be felt as or more powerful in memory than the actual experiences themselves. Stella assumes she will be wronged, overlooked and misunderstood. Or, perhaps she would feel more pain and dependency, and she does not know or trust there could be healing. The residue for Stella has been diminished self-feeling. The self is felt as fragile and vulnerable, empty and dead, as if nothing is there (Modell, 1996, p. 151). The inner darkness, the shadow, potential and energy lie secreted beneath a surface that seems brittle, a façade of deflection. Stella is masterful at self-deception and hiding. She engages in flights from reality as it has been so distressing.

Jungian analysis

To overcome the conflict of opposites Jung described the concept of the transcendent function and its healing action activated in analytical treatment. This is associated with the symbolic dimension, so essential for change and growth, bringing the psyche out of polarised states and enabling the individuation process to proceed. Jung commented, 'Every psychological expression is a symbol if we assume that it states or signifies something more and other than itself which eludes our present knowledge' (Jung, 1971, CW 6, para. 817). The old breaks down before the new can be erected through movement, oscillation and its dynamic process. Yet, for people like Stella, this can be terrifying because she must encounter the unknown. Warren Colman said, 'The symbols exist in the gap between what is and what is not ... the not-yet' (2006, p. 37).

The analytical process intensely involves both people in the mystery of what will evolve. Analysis fosters the individuation process through the relationship between patient and analyst, making room for the possibility of new experiences and transformation of self. 'The self is relatedness ... The self only exists inasmuch as you appear' (Jung, 1998, p. 73). Individuation can be understood as the drive of the self towards consciousness, expanding the constriction in the personality with its evolution dependent on relationships with others.

> In analysis we discover how the self can be safely opened to the reality and existence of another so that authentic relating is possible, and it means going from two-dimensional existence in which others are ignored to the three dimensional in which the other is related to.
>
> (Solomon, 2007, p. 241)

The puella type often presents as able, confident, yet her core is shaky. Her emptiness, longing and needs are re-enacted through the therapeutic relationship. Human beings are born naturally passionate, according to Jung, but the 'blocking of libido' (1967, CW 5, para. 249), as he called it, can lead to feeling life has lost its zest and enjoyment. Such a person sadly and dejectedly negates the value of the arc of life. This type of loneliness is a kind of desertion from human companionship and can be felt quite sharply, especially in the company of others. This appears in analysis as the various and disparate personality parts vie for attention and inclusion. Jungian analytical treatment allows for a place to dissolve the falsity, the reliance on persona and the gradual emergence of the more complete personality.

Symbolism

Analytical psychology accesses the imaginal and creative. The ego learns to trust the fantasies emerging from the unconscious so they can develop. This fosters images, bringing them to life, strengthening the belief that the fantasies are useful, meaningful, the acceptance of the imaginal world as different from the physical world (Colman, 2006, p. 28).

The symbolic process is an experience of images, as Jung discovered in his descent into the unconscious described in *The Red Book*. Jung defines *image* as

> a condensed expression of the psychic situation as a whole ... an expression of the unconscious as well as the conscious situation of the moment. The interpretation of its meaning, therefore, can start neither from the conscious alone nor from the unconscious alone but only from their reciprocal relationship. The symbol is the best possible formulation of a relatively unknown thing, which for that reason cannot be more clearly or characteristically represented.
> (Jung, 1971, CW 6, para. 743)

Theory grounded in image brings forth the lived experience and engagement with the unconscious, transporting healing contents into consciousness. The images can be visual, auditory, kinaesthetic and reveal a symbolic representation that cannot be formulated in any other or better way (1966b, CW 15, para. 105).

The purpose of the symbol is to bring something new to consciousness, shifting previously held psychological positions. Becoming aware of these images dominating our lives, as sources, distortions and inadequacies, brings to consciousness the formerly undisclosed contents (Shorter, 1987, p. 81). The symbols are alive and acquire meaning and their creative function derives from the fact they are embedded in and cross refer to a network of other symbols (Connolly, 2003). The emergence of meaning through analogy and metaphor restores to the psyche its healing powers.

The imaginary is also used to defend against the intolerable, to deny painful feelings of absence and loss. Yet, paradoxically, without the sense of absence a crucial aspect of reality is missing. Reality depends on the capacity to bring together absence and presence in a symbolic form (Colman, 2006, p. 22). In addition, symbols link together inner and outer experiences.

> The Jungian symbol anticipates that which the culture will explicate only in the course of time and in times and in ways that are impossible to determine a priori ...

Thus, the Jungian symbol has a dimension that is not only individual and subjective but collective and cultural.

(Connolly, 2003, p. 365)

The void state

Many puella feel their lives are senseless and that barriers exist between them and others, exacerbating feelings of apathy and lack of connection. They construct a false image to which they cling to ward off not feeling numb and disembodied. An irresolvable impasse can lead to a state of despair. There is precariousness to their defences, panic and fear, and they often exclude others to protect the vulnerable self.

A shutdown of the attachment system has become a recourse for survival. Relationships feel unsafe because they risk activating feelings, desires and emotional needs. For instance, Stella felt too alone, raised without parents who could be fully present. Early on she had to develop what Michael Fordham described as the primitive defences of the self. This concept refers to the barriers between the baby self and the environment set up to ward off what feels inimical to survival (Colman, 1991, p. 365).

However, for Stella, the defences remained and became increasingly rigid. The early emotional deprivation and trauma caused by aloneness left Stella with an apprehension that grief would overwhelm her, and she would never emerge. She could not find joy. She lived 'kind of', wishing, never present, always disappointed and unsatisfied.

In childhood her parents were inundated by children and work. Although they provided the basics, they were undemonstrative and did not provide the necessary emotional attention. Stella needed more than they could give. She was left alone with a terror she was too young to process on her own. Subsequently she admitted no others into her private world. 'The early and primitive defenses reveal the fears of authentic relating' (Solomon, 2007, p. 241). There is an externally created void, a feeling of being alone in this universe that then becomes the internalised experience. Stella could not understand why things were the way they were. She felt she was always getting less than others, especially as she was good.

After many months in analysis, she brings up the emptiness inside and questions whether she can be fully herself. She wonders why the process needs a relationship. Dependency is difficult when one's learned responses were to maintain the illusion of needing no one. However, in the analysis, Stella suffers and is obsessed by the thought of what is lacking between us. In that moment she is 'bombarded with otherness to the point it fractures our secure little world we have made for ourselves' (Mills, 2004, p. 478). This occurs when there was too little experience of solid and supportive relatedness. For Stella the world is held distant; she is separated from others, barricaded against anyone seeing what she considers weakness – her needs.

Stella expresses existential isolation, helplessness and a threat of disintegration (Colman, 1991, p. 366). She was met with too much negation, bullied when young and left to feel unacceptable without sufficient recognition of her internal strivings. The external world seemed to destroy her subjectivity and call it something different, so she retreated to an imaginary world, and the bad world was then magically gone. This imaginary state leaves no real connection to the world, however, because she is trying to force subjective illusions onto reality (Colman, 2006, p. 27).

Feeling negated when so young and without the love she needed at home has manifested as anxiety about her appearance and whether she is interesting enough to others. Usually, Stella feels unappealing, too heavy, too unaccomplished, too little equipped for the world. She is embarrassed and ashamed by these issues. She remains with a 'sense of void or facing a vast emptiness, an absence devoid of resources to nourish and sustain the self' (Solomon, 2004, p. 636).

Whole parts of her were projected, unacknowledged, abject. The self was not only desired but also deprecated. British psychoanalyst John Steiner described these psychic states as retreats. He portrayed 'an avoidance of contact with reality. The retreat then serves as an area of the mind where reality does not have to be faced, where phantasy and omnipotence can exist unchecked and where anything is permitted' (1993, p. 3). Psychic retreats or systems of defence are the places into which the patient withdraws to avoid contact both with herself and with the analyst. Any other realities are foreclosed. For example, in analysis, Stella often cannot take in new information, keeps many of her words and thoughts inside, organising them before each therapy session so as to not make a mistake and to be right, allowing little accompaniment from anyone, myself included.

Illusions and pretending are ineffective, however. The fragmentation of the personality and lost parts of the self are kept within these psychic retreats while the point of individuation is to acknowledge and reintegrate them. Failure to expose the psychic retreats and get through the impasse impedes life and analysis until understood. The retreat is from reality, so the puella does not have face it as she feels impotent to cope. The creation of these alternative worlds prevents access to the interior for the means of self-preservation (Modell, 1996, p. 77).

Lacking inner nourishment, estranged from their true selves, a person comes to a place where they can no longer deny the haunting sense of living in a void and are now facing the emptiness (Solomon, 2004, p. 636). The puella experiences torturing dependence, fixation on the incomplete self, lack of identity. All this must be hidden due to fears of abandonment, and it is such a tender area. The impoverishment of personality occurs when undesirable feelings become split off, causing depression. It feels like living in an empty house. Something is needed to combat the deadness and emptiness, and a façade is erected to cover the distress.

What seems like self-absorption is a defence against anyone getting close. Interior reflection may be shut down. The intolerance of criticism as well as admiration seeking and arrogance is mixed with a tendency to depreciate others. A falsely inflated self-esteem is contrary to her vulnerability, hypersensitivity and withdrawal. An individual like Stella experiences frustration in getting their basic needs met because she is constantly seeking after approval and success. Nothing fills what feels like the dark hole inside, and no one is to know it is there.

Absence and presence

Void here refers to the presence of absence. It is experienced as a closed, retracted, painful state, like a pocket with a hole, and it is not just empty space. The capacity to be alone implies the capacity to bear the absence and then fill it. However, puella appropriates aspects of others to fill the otherwise empty void because she lacks access to those resources nourishing the self (Solomon, 2007, p. 197). Puella compensates through omnipotence, omniscience and by not allowing others to see her limitations.

An answer to the presence of absence is to mourn, but this is difficult when the imaginary world is constructed to prevent feeling the pain of absence and loss – or exposing it. The world is apprehended as an infinite absence, and she is filled with the inability to tolerate this vastness. The gap between ego and self feels too intolerable and defences are erected to protect against the various and expected disappointments. The bridge between inner and outer becomes short-circuited. Puella turns away from others in fear of annihilation, erecting evermore defences. This sets up a quest to imagine a world that excludes terror of the gap or black hole, the void of non-existence into which she can so easily fall.

Stella *dreams of being out in space without a tether, or it is broken. Or the cell phone does not work, the connection drops, 911 has no response. No one realises, knows, or comes to her aid, and there is no way to be heard as she is too far away.* The search to incorporate the negation and develop the symbolic, grounds the puella in the creative reality of imagination. When the void is constellated in these individuals it is often defended against and 'what seems to be necessary is to help them find structure and meaning in their lives, i.e. non-void attributes' (Ashton, 2007, pp. 1–2).

To add to this concept and difficult feeling is André Green's conceptualisation of the deleterious result of internalised conflict as absence, or the failure to represent the missed object. This is the province of absence or the realm of the 'Dead Mother/Father' as detailed in his famous paper (Green, 1986). According to him, the psychic universe is no longer filled with presences, but also with 'absences, the spaces between meaning and no meaning, since it is through the relation to objects that meaning is created' (Reed & Baudry, 2017, p. 132). Instead of the object/person representations there is a hole in the psyche.

Green wrote about parental absence and the emotional deadness unconsciously transferred onto children. The absence remains a presence and a representation within the psyche. Yet, even when the experience has been lacking, a representation of presence can be created. This requires staying conscious of the hurt, cynicism, denial or avoidance to make it through the void space. 'The psychic abandonment affects access to the self' (Green, 1986, p. 153). Awareness of this absence enables us to imagine the potential space formed by a good-enough relationship with another person. However, people who live in the void cannot imagine two differentiated individuals. They experience from within their fragmentary, unindividuated, non-symbolising perspective no relationship of passion or eventual feeling (Reed & Baudry, 2017, p. 148).

The void indicates this absence and what feels like catastrophic annihilation, the fear of being taken over or intruded upon by what has been experienced as malignant, omnipotent objects able to destroy. Although all this occurred very early, it nevertheless is present in multi-layered form in the psyche, both disguised and obscured. Jung commented, 'Images of the unconscious place a great responsibility on a man. Failure to understand them, or a shirking of ethical responsibility deprives him of his wholeness and imposes a painful fragmentariness on his life' (1989, p. 193). Yet, a puella like Stella holds onto the representation as the loss. The sign of its hidden presence makes up the symptoms and appears in images, symbols and dreams.

Into the depression

In-depth psychological work constellates self and other, patient and analyst, depicting together the movement of the psyche. The analyst's challenge is to assist the patient in finding her unknown aspects and escape the limits she has instituted. 'In the final analysis, the therapist must always strive to constellate the healing factor in the patient' (Guggenbühl-Craig, 1999, p. 92). The therapist provides a mirror for the patient to perceive what she could not previously due to the arrested images of a starved psyche. The process is facilitated by dreams, the therapeutic relationship and other life events.

The emotional and motivational energy moving us again is part of the hidden intention in depression. It forces us downwards and is a result of becoming cut off from something essential within ourselves, some aspect of our vital and vitalising wholeness. Depression, I could say, is an expression of missing vitality.

The path of learning from one's depression, not merely getting rid of it, is a pathway for restoring meaning. We can be met with others who can think and feel in tune with our self. In this the analyst is used to make up for missed mirror experiences (Wilkinson, 2017, p. 533). Analysis is then a healing experience and an opportunity for growth and understanding from wrestling with one's own darkness. As Jung said, 'One does not become conscious by imagining figures of light, but by making the darkness conscious' (Jung, 1968b, CW 13, para. 335). This means making sense of falling into a passive, defeated attitude to be able to emerge.

Early mis-attachments absorb the psyche and become preserved in a melancholic and invisible interior space. Abandonment heightens awareness of these places for the work of analysis. The longing to which they are connected comes forth in the therapeutic process for recovering what has thus far been un-mourned (Perelberg, 2018, p. 44). This is where the transferences help bring the person to more development than they can imagine alone.

By entering the problems in a real way and accepting and untangling projections common to all relationships, analysis helps a person feel the right and safety to exist. Analysis and therapy are containers in which one can grow beyond the unseen and create new possibilities from the relationship. Hope can be activated in analytical space as a bridge to connect and transition between what was not existent previously to what can now emerge. These experiences increase the capacity to manage as analyst and patient stand together in the space between what seemed unimaginable and now becomes possible – to be one's real self.

Therapy is a process to reconstruct and reassemble the personality fragments by comprehending and making sense of them from another perspective. It provides the experiences needed to explore one's subjectivity and imagination. 'The main therapeutic problem is ... how to integrate the dissociation ... it possesses the quality of psychic autonomy ... an attempt to reintegrate the autonomous complex ... by living the traumatic situation over again, once or repeatedly' (Jung, 1966c, CW 16, paras. 266, 268).

These are natural processes deriving from a matrix based on the earliest relationships. In some ways, analysis re-creates the original injuries damaging the ego and distorting relationships to self and others. This includes connection or not to one's physicality of being, which also needs to be addressed in the analytical relationship. Jung said,

> Symbols of the self arise in the depths of the body and they express its materiality every bit as much as the structure of the perceiving consciousness. The symbol is thus a living body, corpus et anima, hence the "child" is an apt formula for the symbol.
>
> (Jung, 1968a, CW 9i, para. 29)

Filling the gap

The process often begins with feeling a gap, dissociation, threat, the world in shambles, coming apart, a void. A puella does not realise how much these elements control freedom of expression, confidence and ease in being. The unconscious influences are important intrusions happening daily; these are the communications oscillating in unspoken ways to dialogue with the exposed relational wounds.

Jungian analysis can bring these to awareness and free the psyche in a readjustment of the psychological contents. This theory presents a unique view of the psyche, encouraging us to change orientation and regard the problems as having purpose. From the language arising from the psyche, the personal and collective images embody the problems, prospective aspects and treatment direction.

The process includes regression to previous times, experiences, memories. We become ourselves through the process of individuation, supported by the creative and symbolic resources of the unconscious.

> We are led by desire for wider perspectives, to know the other as well as ourselves through the emerging insights into psychic development. To deal with the collective unconscious demands a solid ego consciousness and an adequate adaptation to reality.
>
> (Wolff, 1956, p. 12)

This comes by expanding beyond the stereotypes and the limits to dynamic interplay and personal synthesis.

The symbolical and imaginal aims towards psychological development through contemplation and reflection, abilities often acquired in Jungian analytical treatment. Jung said, 'The symbolical represents an attempt to elucidate through what still belongs entirely to the domain of the unknown or something that is still to be' (1966a, CW 7, paras. 493–495).

References

Ashton, P. W. (2007). *From the brink: Experiences of the void from a depth psychology perspective*. Karnac.

Collins, A. & Molchanov, E. (Eds.). (2022). Seeing and not seeing the symbol: Greta Thunberg the Indian demon devotee, and Jung's Virgin Sophia. In M. Stein (Ed.), *Jung's Red Book for our time*. Chiron Publications.

Colman, W. (1991). Envy, self-esteem and the fear of separateness. *British Journal of Psychotherapy, 7*(4), 356–367.

Colman, W. (2006). Imagination and the imaginary. *Journal of Analytical Psychology, 5*(1), 21–41.

Connolly, A. (2003). To speak in tongues: Language, diversity and psychoanalysis. *Journal of Analytical Psychology, 47*(3), 359–382. https://doi.org/10.1111/1465-5922.00325

Green, A. (1986). *On private madness*. Hogarth Press.

Guggenbühl-Craig, A. (1999). *Power in the helping professions*. Spring Publications.

Jung, C. G. (1966a). Preface (1918). *The collected works of C. G. Jung: Vol. 7. Two essays in analytical psychology*. Princeton University Press.

Jung, C. G. (1966b). *The collected works of C. G. Jung: Vol. 15. The spirit of art in man, art, and literature*. Princeton University Press.

Jung, C. G. (1966c). *The collected works of C. G. Jung: Vol. 16. The practice of psychotherapy*. Princeton University Press.

Jung, C. G. (1967). *The collected works of C. G. Jung: Vol. 5. The symbols of transformation*. Princeton University Press.

Jung, C. G. (1968a). *The collected works of C. G. Jung: Vol. 9i. The archetypes and the collective unconscious*. Pantheon Books.

Jung, C. G. (1968b). *The collected works of C. G. Jung: Vol. 13. Alchemical studies*. Princeton University Press.

Jung, C. G. (1969). *The collected works of C. G. Jung: Vol. 8. The structure & dynamics of the psyche*. Princeton University Press.

Jung, C. G. (1971) *The collected works of C. G. Jung: Vol. 6. Psychological types*. Princeton University Press.

Jung, C. G. (1989). *Memories, dreams, reflections*. Vintage Books.

Jung, C. G. (1998). *The Zarathustra Seminars*. Pantheon Books.

Mills, J. (2004). Countertransference revisited. *Psychoanalytic Quarterly, 91*(4), 467–515.

Mizen, R., & Morris, M. (2008). On aggression and violence: An analytic perspective. *British Journal of Psychotherapy, 24*(1), 98–103. http://dx.doi.org/10.1111/j.1752-0118.2007.00067_1.x

Modell, A. (1996). *The private self*. Harvard University Press.

Perelberg, R. (Ed.). (2018). *The psychic bisexuality: A British-French dialogue*. Routledge.

Reed, G. S., & Baudry, F. D. (2017). Conflict, structure, and absence. *Psychoanalytic Quarterly, LXXIV*(1), 121–155.

Shorter, B. (1986). The concealed body language of anorexia nervosa. In A. Samuels (Ed.), *The father: Contemporary Jungian perspectives* (pp. 171–186). New York University Press.

Shorter, B. (1987). *An image darkly forming*. Routledge.

Solomon, H. (2004). Self-creation and the limitless void of dissociation: The 'as-if' personality. *Journal of Analytical Psychology, 49*(5), 635–656. https://doi.org/10.1111/j.0021-8774.2004.00493.x

Solomon, H. (2007). *The self in transformation*. Routledge.

Steiner, J. (1993). *Psychic retreats: Pathological organizations in psychotic, neurotic and borderline patients*. Routledge.

Wilkinson, M. (2017). Mind, brain, body. *Journal of Analytical Psychology, 62*(4), 526–543. https://doi.org/10.1111/1468-5922.12335

Willemsen, H. (2014). Early trauma and affect: the importance of the body for the development of the capacity to symbolize. *Journal of Analytical Psychology, 59*(5), 695–712.

Wolff, T. (1956). *Structural forms of the feminine psyche*. Jung Institut.

Chapter 14
A fascist state of mind – the complex

The personality is multifaceted; we come to ourselves through others. The *fascist state of mind* is a phrase taken from an essay by Italian Jungian analyst Francesco Bisagni (2022). The fascist state of mind refers to a complex that rules the culture, family and personality. For example, a woman dreamt, *I am about to be married to Putin. He is tricky and fast. He tells me he is going to St. Petersburg but will not say why. I tell him with a joke to watch his cell phone – he is the one bugging the cell of the prime minister of England.* I do not take this seriously until I wake up. What was I doing married to Putin?! I was not shocked in the dream. It came to me when I awoke, but not immediately. Did my delayed reaction show I was this unconscious? Was it worse than I thought?

She seemed taken aback by the realisation of this complex defined by a dictatorial, rigid and authoritarian figure. How did it coalesce inside her in its powerful past and present and how would it affect her future? All these factors represented the tenacity of this complex. It was composed of the male/father/fascist state of mind to which she was married, according to the dream (Bisagni, 2022, p. 434). In the dream she portrayed the young, innocent puella who is susceptible to being under the aegis of this personality aspect. The dream pointed out the necessity of dealing with a psychological situation that had become this dire because it had been unconscious. The complexity within the complex, especially one so dictatorial and therefore limiting, needs to be known. The point is to become aware of the fascist state of mind and find a relationship to the complex, so it does not continue to operate unconsciously, under the surface, creating restrictions and strict rules of conduct, lessening freedom of expression.

This woman commented on the dream, surprised at the existence and strength of this complex within her system that was described as her partner. In its negative form this part held her hostage, diminishing her talents and abilities for living. Although aware of it, she did not realise how much she was wedded to it. As Jung described, 'The complex as autonomous groups of associations with a tendency to move by themselves, to live their own lives apart from our conscious intentions … the unconscious consists of an infinite, because unknown, number of complexes or fragmentary personalities' (1935/1977, CW 18, para. 151). This outlines the Jungian perspective on psychic dissociability as presupposing the underlying tendency towards uniting into an integral psyche. 'The proximity of otherness within the self ... both constitutive of the self and at the same time destabilizes any self-certainty, self-sameness, and self-unity' (Oliver, 2015, p. 42). In other words, the self falls apart in a kind of regression, not as a defence, but because of some deficiency and the need to rearrange the personality. The regression in Jung's view was not the illness; instead, it was connected to an inherent impulse towards a unitary psyche. Because of this impulse, a pathologically disintegrated psyche spontaneously attempts to reintegrate. Regression activates the impulse towards reintegration in a dynamic interplay of psychological elements.

> The dissociation allows certain parts of the psychic structure to be singled out so that, by concentration of the will, they can be trained and brought to their maximum development ... This produces an unbalanced state similar to that caused by a dominant complex – a change of personality.
>
> (Jung, 1969, CW 8, p. 122)

This woman spent much emotional time and energy responding to the anticipated needs of others, thereby hiding her personal insecurities and vulnerability. From a young age she was preoccupied with satisfying her father, making him feel happy, creating no problems, wanting to be special to him. In effect, paralysis of the self prevented its own unfolding. This situation limited her capacity for personality integration and individuation, her development suffered, and she could make little commitment to her life. As the dream stated, she was married to the fascist state of mind. Perhaps the dream was meant to wake her up.

When identity is negated, we begin to question where and how we belong. 'The alien sense of identity becomes installed in the child's psyche and is experienced as an alien self' (Knox, 2007, p. 556). Parental demands can inhibit natural growth. In the woman's case the early sense of unfairness and the power of the instability left her no way to confront the persecuting parent who wielded power, authority, discipline (Steiner, 1993, p. 102). As a child, she learnt she must not have a mind of her own, including her own thoughts, needs, emotions and desires. These seemed so unwanted by the parents that her own emerging independent sense of identity had to be eliminated, and she must be in tune with their desires over her own. It is the individuation process itself which such parents experience as threatening and which they can destroy with conscious and unconscious intercessions on a child's self-agency.

Precarious identity

From childhood we create complexes, ongoing narratives shaped by words, body language, emotions, images, rituals and interactions articulating life. A precarious identity creates no end of emotional confusion, lack of internal connection and a self out of kilter with the rest of the personality. Randi, a woman in her 30s, has encountered relationships with those unable to commit, or they betrayed her or were unable to satisfy her emotionally. She was repeatedly disappointed, and the pattern has continued. Being an adult has not led her to the life she wanted of children, solidity and security; she is caught in a complex, idealising partners, betraying herself and accepting the deceptions of others over listening to herself.

Complexes highlight what needs integration in the personality. As Jung said,

> to have complexes ... only means that something discordant, unassimilated and antagonistic exists, perhaps as an obstacle, but also as an incentive to greater effort, and so, perhaps, to new possibilities of achievement. ... complexes are focal points or nodal points of psychic life which we would not wish to do without; for otherwise psychic activity would come to a fatal standstill.
> (Jung, 1971, CW 6, para. 925)

Analysis provides a bridge from self to other, to inner and outer. It is a relentless sifting through the creative possibilities of anxieties, doubts and self-torments. Analysis helps break down restrictions, persona façades and complexes stifling language and imprisoning understanding.

Randi is questioning who she authentically is. She has felt flawed, lacking, uncertain, split into multiple roles. The answers arise in the analysis, as we build a bridge between new and old attitudes for rescuing her beleaguered self. 'We find our truth in the face of others in the dynamics of absence/presence, existence/non-existence' (Levy, Huang & Bonanno, 2018, p. 47). Images arise from the ancient and deeply personal centre of her personality, exposing the tensions felt from inner and outer issues. Within these experiences are the elements that offer the possibility of transforming her into all she can be.

Randi is experiencing despair in finding anyone able to meet her, to understand, to feel comfort. There is always something wrong. The reality of being together means acknowledging separateness while also feeling deep connection. Self and other are fused and confused with idealisations and hopes. Her pattern has been psychic retreat and insulation, resulting in only short-term relationships that end not only with painful emotions but also with relief. Randi is uncertain she can show up and knows vulnerability is difficult.

Randi wants romance and intimacy; at the same time, she is uneasy with relationships. With little constructive or loving modelling from her parents, she is naïve. Things do not easily flow for her, and a watchful discomfort keeps her at least one step removed from feelings. Being real seems anathema. Randi is descriptive of puella run by a fascist state of mind, making her stiff, self-conscious and defended but no closer to herself. Jung contended that 'the durability of a complex is guaranteed by its continually active feeling tone. If the feeling tone is extinguished, then the complex is extinguished with it' (Jung, 1960, CW 3, para. 90). In fact, she is awkward. Her habitual singularity and aloneness must be relinquished to be with someone. She hides from her partner her fears of the world and insecurity in crowds; she is so scared she needs to be right. She can often not rest or be free except when alone and quiet. She holds back and does not expose her feelings. Uneasy in the other's gaze, she tries to avoid exposing her anxieties and being seen up close. Yet she desperately wants notice, approval and security.

At the core of her internal conflicts are feelings of failure and incapacity, an inability to hate or love, to enjoy or think (Green, 1986, p. 154). Love is frozen and she remains numb. This happens from within and is experienced with others. Although she desires otherwise, she cannot handle too much of anything – love, pleasure or enjoyment. These all disturb the order she needs to project to the world, yet underneath is the nakedness of despair. In this state she suffers narcissistic depletion, emptiness and depression, repeatedly re-occurring because of the emotional wounds (Green, 1986, p. 155).

Randi wants to believe differently and trust but cannot allow the dependency this would entail. In a relationship she tries to be good and avoid conflict, emotion or what she considers wild or angry feelings. The male images in her dreams are of betrayers who are dishonest in one way or another. In a dream *she keeps repeating a phrase about ill children over and over*. What does this mean? Do the ill children point to her lack of connection, emotion, caring, to undifferentiated and undeveloped aspects of the personality?

In the analytical work, she expects disapproval from me and yet wants adulation for being good, interesting, able, hard working. Quite paradoxically, I am interpreted by her as inflicting more pain, creating more shame. She suffers from many of my interpretations, feeling robbed of her own thoughts, although she wants the interaction and attention. Affronted and trapped in what she cannot endure and cannot escape from, she expects the voice of the other to be critical and harsh. Nothing seems to make any difference or change the complex, as Randi is sure she will be slighted. Where does this come from? She keeps insisting she has forgiven the past and it was resolved, but was it?

She recalls a session of hypnosis earlier in her life in which she screamed although she realised there was nothing threatening. She was shocked and did not know the reason for the scream. Something just burst forth. Now she is uneasy in the wider world, holds back and is often depleted of energy. As Jung said,

> Whatever has an intense feeling tone is difficult to handle because such contents are associated with physiological reactions, with the processes of the heart, the tonus of the blood vessels, the condition of the intestines, the breathing and innervation of the skin.
>
> (1976, CW 18, para. 148)

Randi often has little impetus for self-care, and if anything goes awry physically, she immediately slides into catastrophic fears of dire effects and the belief that she will be unable to save herself.

She views herself as young, somewhat helpless, cannot make up her mind, loses focus, becomes overstimulated easily and then goes off one course onto another. To regain balance things must be just so and in her control. She takes hours to get ready for the world; however, she is never ready enough although she spends much time on hair and clothes.

Randi dreams *she is looking for a bathroom in a hotel that previously appeared in several dreams. In every dream she has to go all over to find a clean and private bathroom. Then she encounters a large figure, heavy, dark colour and androgenous. Suddenly, a silver bullet hit her in the vagina and a pulsating penis emerged. She is not frightened but intrigued. She feels the figure, although in many ways grotesque, is an omen of the unexpected.*

The strangeness of the dream accentuates her desire for some radical change and transformation. We could interpret this as a symbol indicating the approach of the opposites, the shock of penetration and the arrival of an unexpected new element. It indicates a new development within her, arising alongside the analytical work. The dream presents an active confrontation between conscious and unconscious, resulting in the emergence of new symbolic forms. The symbols serve to transcend the internal conflicts, leading to increased psychic awareness. The process indicates what is called in Jungian psychology the *transcendent function* as a bridge to the more complete self. The metaphor transfers meaning between domains of experience, creating a novel route for their re-combination (Winborn, 2022, p. 3).

Randi has another dream bringing forth a different figure in male garb: I am at a bar-like place. The two guys I am to meet are there. Neither approaches me. A woman comes and I explain nothing is happening. One guy leaves. The guy I like remains, but he is preoccupied. There are no connections made. I do not approach him. I feel badly but as I awake, I realise this is the wrong male energy and he no longer wants me. He is a one-night stand, seductive, attractive, aloof but going nowhere. I wonder if one of the guys is the destruction inside myself, I so often feel, and the other is my father who never paid enough emotional attention to me. I was relieved the dream showed release from my old attraction to those not paying attention, putting me down. They do not let me achieve or be creative. This is the masculine and rapacious energy Randi knows only too well. This is the man who just takes, lures with false promises, attempting to vanquish, creating insecurity and erasing strength of being.

The fascist state of mind is an aggressive aspect 'killing off the loving dependent self and identifying themselves almost entirely with the destructive narcissistic parts of the self which provides them with a sense of superiority and self-admiration' (Bollas, 1992, p. 198). When the sense of self becomes disturbed by a powerful complex, a person like Randi, typical of the puella types, suffers the failure of linkage between body, affect and mind. Integration is difficult for a person run by such a complex, creating fear and distrust of the other. Fantasy replaces any delight in reality. It removes her from self, blocks love and creates dissociation between body and psyche (Green, 1986, p. 152).

The emotional and physical losses combined with the need for belonging can feel so intolerable the puella tries to deny it all, although paradoxically the pain can take her to the core of who she is. Jung described such states as 'complexes, autonomous "splinter psyches", fragments, which have split off because of traumatic experience' (Jung, 1969, CW 8, para. 253). These events form a living reality of ideas, beliefs, memories, feelings and images. Indelible traces, traumatic blanks and distortions in the individual and collective unconscious are passed from generation to generation in an unending spiral.

Randi recounts a lonely childhood at home. She was caught in a parental gap, lacking correct attention from both mother and father. The loss of attention and interest in this child left her with premature disillusionment; her parents were emotionally dead and inaccessible (Green, 1986, p. 150). Because no one saw her, she is uncomfortable being seen. There is no balm for the internal diatribe, no comfort from the other. Her memory returned to the alcoholic mother who screamed for no reason, grounded her in a rage and the next day hardly recalled these events. Randi could say nothing. It was her fault, and mother's lack of memory made no difference. There was no retribution, no recognition of her hurt and pain. This made her acutely sensitive to the world, striving to not make any errors and avoid conflict; it also separated her from joy or ease with others.

At school she had friends, but the home atmosphere felt leaden, heavy with lack of something she could not name. She could not understand and tried to make her parents happy. She recalls retreating to her room as child. It was like a sanctuary separated from parental influence. It was there she could put down the distress, listen to music, write in her journals. Her child's need for quiet is the same today as it has always been – it may even be greater – for the quiet is an essential part of gaining awareness. In quiet Randi can dwell in thoughts and stories of her own. Now she realises she holds stress in her body and what has endured is the dulled psychic pain. Randi presents as 'lifeless at times, and it seems there is a dissociation between the subjective self and the body, which is experienced as something cold, frozen or even dead' (Connolly, 2013, p. 646).

'There is an inner displacement in the self due to a dramatic change in the interplay between inner and outer worlds that profoundly alters the previous organization between the ego-complex and other autonomous complexes' (Luci, 2020, p. 269). Over time, sometimes after a long time, we become increasingly conscious of the burdens we carry psychologically from our socio-historical experiences, including those not addressed by previous generations. Unable to get close enough or feel securely accepted, Randi did not know how to parent herself, how to sooth or comfort herself. She also did not value herself and it was difficult to devote time to herself. Many feelings were stored in her body and psyche as unassimilated material. They were compensated by focusing on the need to prove herself and satisfy others through her achievements and intellect.

Self-fictions and cultural conflicts

The notion of complexes provides a container for understanding the nature of an intrapsychic and interpersonal conflict that can be stronger than realised. A university professor, Zhi was constantly drawn to assist and put others first. She explained it was due to her Asian background of hard work, family first, with personal sacrifice expected. Did her individual desires count? She was raised in the United States in a culture of personal striving that clashed with her Asian background that expected devotion to family. Generational values and family attitudes haunted her, yet they were part of her unique personality. Her understanding this by exploring it in analysis helped navigate the conflictual pull between cultures, which tugged at her consciously and unconsciously. As we explored in analysis either one could be perceived as reinforcing the fascist state of mind. Zhi wondered what she wanted, how to develop self-assertion and not just automatically succumb to the demands of others.

This was becoming more difficult to juggle as her professional advancement lagged and lacked focus, and partnerships were continually fractured and unsupportive. In relationships she found one self-centred person after another to whom she gave but was incompletely met. Zhi was raised to believe service to others took precedence over herself, to the point she was becoming exhausted. The reality of herself was becoming more elusive, and she seemed not to count. How easily fictions and true stories can trade places, how quickly the assumed verities of life can become confused and keep one from what is desired. Zhi was beginning to face the deficit she experienced in the relational domain, her unmet career goals and the alterations of her self-image due to ageing. It was not easy as the process was wrenching her from who she thought she was supposed to be to who she actually was.

A complex hardens when tendencies interfere with natural desires and impulses. The psychological fallout from a negative complex appears through various symptoms of depression, depersonalisation, dissociation, despair, anxiety, all representing the disturbed connection to self and others.

How could Zhi feel love when she did not fully exist in her own eyes? She fought against the negative self-assessment, feeling inadequate, unable to choose her own advancement. Too often love meant being controlled by the other, whether family, partner, children, friends. She was facing this difficult and ingrained knowledge, and the release from the complex was giving her the ability to learn from new experiences. Otherwise, 'there is failure to modify ... and the complex remains encapsulated and split off from the rest of the psyche' (Knox, 1999, p. 528).

Much of what tears us apart can be understood as the manifestation of autonomous processes in the collective and individual psyche that organise themselves as cultural complexes (Singer & Kimbles, 2004, p. 2). For Zhi, family history was a powerful influencer and emotionally entangled within her psyche. She existed in the pull of expectations to follow the Asian way. Having been raised in the US, she could not completely follow the Asian way, yet she could not discard it. The cultural complex had taken on a life of its own within Zhi, creating a disturbance. This psychological state of mind can manifest in various forms, making it difficult to love or care for oneself. Conscious experience must be manipulated while its distortion is based on the need to remain within old patterns, concrete thinking and narrow perceptions tied to limitations.

People can fall into states where they avoid embracing life, sacrificing so they remain within the complex. Complexes cause the necessary disconnection and disequilibrium; the ego becomes alienated, and the psyche seeks balance. The natural instincts for movement become thwarted, holding a person prisoner in the concrete and narrow. Zhi's career, assertion in the world and intimate relationships were all subject to the weight of the fascist state of mind manifested in the cultural battles from the outside, their impact registering within her personality.

However, this opened the analytical discussion as we sought areas of uniqueness and differences. Zhi expressed distress about being taken advantage of due to the projections and assumptions put on her as an Asian woman. She spoke about frustration and wanting to meet the demands of family pressures while needing her own time and space. We addressed the mixed cultural conflicts, the stereotypes each culture held of the other and how to negotiate to her truth.

'The analysand may resort to hiding or disavowing the importance of their class-related concerns in order to maintain a sense of belonging' (Kiehl, 2016, p. 476). The impact of differences in culture and social class has implications on the psychological transference and countertransference relationship. These include feelings often unaddressed concerning class roots and social hierarchy. Class, like cultural background, is absorbed into the psyche 'affecting sense of self, sense of self-worth and belonging, arousing shame, envy, and many misperceptions' (Kiehl, 2016, p. 468). There are also the wounds from being born into a different class and feeling lack of equality and privilege based on money and status.

The hidden injuries of class come from a person's primary identification with a social class of people who have suffered power discrepancies, assaults to their dignity, lack of opportunity or a compromised sense of positive possibilities (Sennett & Cobb, 1972, p.11). Zhi expressed class-related anxieties in her work and relationships. These were stereotypes made up of the deepest, most shame-sensitive vulnerabilities regarding belonging, wanting and worries about being found lacking (Corpt, 2013, p. 8).

Here is the complex, the state of mind dictating lack, unprotected, judged, less than, imperfect (Cambray, 2022, pp. 82–83). The dyadic relationship with its many channels of communication creates the emergence of the third and new element to appear symbolically, like in a dream. The changes in the states of consciousness allow the relationship to transcend the now and move into the not-yet. The effects are transformative, mind altering, about insight and reconciling basic existence for changes in consciousness and personality (Wirtz, 2022, p. 230).

In a dream *Zhi and her current dating partner who was a white American male were driving over a bridge. He was the driver, and she did not know where they were going. The dream repeated.* Although brief, the dream itself was a bridge, but it was unclear where it was coming from or where it was going. Symbolically the bridge anticipated meeting the unknown, the personal and cultural influences and shadows, and the past, present and future. It implies differences explored for deepening mutuality rather than dividing the psyche into disconnected complexes. The dream symbolically enacted traversing the bridge of Zhi's own lived experience within the mixture of cultures as a minority, as a woman, and the forces that are personal, collective and unconscious propelling her. Through analysis she began to move beyond the conflictual voices clashing loudly from her mixed background.

The varied positions in the unconscious bring the psyche forwards, out of polarisation and oppositional states, and this enables the process of individuation (Solomon, 1998, p. 232). The Jungian therapeutic process promotes a kind of psychic activity that requires a tolerance for contradiction and holding the energy that pulls in many directions. Jungian psychology is 'of the personality which does not pathologize spontaneous and autonomous expressions' (Astor, 2002, p. 600). The paradoxes and the back and forth, the psyche with its principle of synthesis and balance bring forth the submerged parts of the personality. Therapy explores loss and wounding of all kinds, internal and external, acute and cumulative, personal and collective.

Zhi was encountering the traumatic dissociation of aspects of the feminine inherited from her parents' Asian perspective (Ghate, 2018, p. 150), made stronger owing to their cultural displacement from their homeland to the USA. Zhi rejected the traditional Chinese woman's role of submission to the family and was keen to embrace her modern Western identity. Yet she continually faced questions regarding the emotional truth of her identity. She felt two ways about many things. Although this occurred on a conscious plane, unconsciously she felt cultural ties she could neither negate nor leave. It takes much effort to make sense of painful formative and transgenerational experiences, exposing us to a complex world at visceral and raw levels.

The developing self is driven by the sense of something needing to be addressed. Pain and resistance accompany breaking from the old even though the steps forwards are desired and taken towards movement and change. From this emotionally interactive, dynamic conscious and unconscious process, the transcendent function forms a bridge uniting all aspects but resulting in something else. The capacity to gather the personal and collective threads for the co-construction of belonging occurs through the transcendent function in Jungian psychological treatment. 'From the activity of the unconscious there now emerges a new content, constellated by thesis and antithesis in equal measure and standing in complementary relation to both' (Jung, 1971, CW 6, para. 825).

As we look at dreams, we find the presence of connection as the mediator or bridge between the ego and the self as an archetype of wholeness. Energies are present in the body and psyche and can usher us even deeper, opening psyche's terrain. The dream figures are the characters of which we are composed and 'deliver us to the power of a partner who seems compounded of all the qualities we have failed to realize in ourselves' (Jung, 1966, CW 16, para. 534). As opposites, the yin and yang, in the *Chinese Book of Wisdom* called the *I Ching*, are not translatable as male and female but include qualities as passive, active, receptive, creative forces in nature. Although they co-exist, they provide other points of view the ego must address and form a conversation to configure different relational dynamics.

The 'transformative significance of the anima/animus in the development of an individual … evidences the value of the contrasexual as a bridge to symbolic thought'

(Astor, 2000, p. 564). The experience of alterity disrupts former coherence. We can never return to how it was prior to a particular interaction with anyone or anything different from ourselves. As a result, we change fundamentally and irreversibly from interactions with others. What is significant is the relationship and the dialogue occurring in a back-and-forth dynamic. This only happens if we are open to the voices asking who or what is this other coming from within. If we listen, the inner conversation can become a living dialogue in which identity is discovered.

Jungian psychology attends to the cross-cultural aspects of the personality through the recognition of the collective unconscious, the symbolic, imagistic, archetypal and psychological layers where we can understand each other. Cultural complexes are psychological realities within the integral structure of the personality (Singer & Kimbles, 2004, p. 7). The forces at work are energies that are more than personal and include collective phenomena, spurring ongoing tensions, activity and eventual growth. There we often face divides wider than realised where the nature of the psyche includes the known and the stranger. Jung believed 'the durability of a complex is guaranteed by its continually active feeling tone. If the feeling tone is extinguished, then the complex is extinguished with it' (Jung, 1960, CW 3, para. 90).

Feelings of impotence

The dissociated parts of the psyche are disjointed from the self, creating a place of dis-ease (Brewster, 2022, p. 76). This is where the autonomous nature of the complex distracts and separates from the centre of the personality and the psychic disturbance affects ego functioning. This can translate to loss of meaning and intensified feelings of emptiness mixed with experiences of being unseen and unacknowledged as an individual.

Self-consciousness can become so acute it takes over. Zhi has felt embarrassment, shame, humiliation and often misunderstood by many in her world, especially at work and in relationships. The complex develops rigidity from being held in the unconscious, and the fascist state of mind replicates 'the dragging movement of regression and the fascinating power of fixation' (Green, 2003, pp. 2–3). This sense of helplessness, without status or power, social class seemingly not good enough, all can create a feeling of being looked down on by analyst. Being seen means the gaze from the other feels threatening, especially in analysis (Steiner, 1993, p. 10). In many instances the complex of inferiority and being less than can combine with the envy of an analyst who might seem to have it all. This attitude, when unexplored, can prevent a patient from taking in any good, can arouse powerlessness and intensify defences. It fosters projections and detracts from the personality when unexplored.

However, in the analysis Zhi and I were able to examine many of the areas in which she felt misunderstood, and this helped open Zhi's psyche and she gained confidence to establish some pathway through the cultural conflicts. 'The facets of experience, behaviour and ways of relating ... manifest in the transference-countertransference so the traumatic complex can be detoxified and the individual freed to fully embrace and constructively express and develop themselves and their relationships' (West, 2013, p. 74). Despite the fear and anxiety aroused through the clinical work the unconscious became a container in which she could grow. The ego gained the capacity to manage distress and fostered hope. As analyst and patient, we stood together in the space between realities where what seemed unimaginable became possible. The emphasis is on the co-creation of meaning in the interpersonal space.

From the perspective of Jungian analytical psychology, the self seeks union of the disparate aspects of unconscious to conscious, personal to cultural and vice versa. The Jungian process of individuation is a coming to oneself as personality transformation occurs, fulfilling the basic longing for inclusive acceptance. The rejected, uncomfortable material retains its pressure and, if not integrated, consciously manifests in various symptoms as the psyche seeks to be known and to establish equilibrium. This fills the longing for connection, a sense of belonging and identity.

Zhi began to negotiate the internal conflicts by focusing on her individual work and refusing to be drawn into relationships that sucked her energy. She was contemplating a career move with more advancement and opportunity to publish her work. The world seemed to be opening and she was discovering her value and fine reputation. Engagement with others was giving voice to her many selves for expression, increased consciousness and inclusion. She was released from the complex and able to breathe easier. Engagement with the others within was bringing about recognition of the self, giving her a sense of personal and collective belonging and pride in her identity. This integration resulted in communication between self and others, the complex and the unification of the personality. As the fascist state of mind loosens its grip, the self gains freedom. 'What we see is determined by how we look, which is in turn determined by where we stand' (Hillman, 2005, p. 347).

References

Astor, J. (2002). Analytical psychology and its relation to psychoanalysis: A personal view. *Journal of Analytical Psychology, 47*(4), 599–612.

Bisagni, F. (2022). Digressions on the fascist state of mind: Psychoanalytic perspectives on narcissism and 'social-ism'. *Journal of Analytical Psychology, 67*(2), 434–444.

Bollas, C. (1992). *Being a character: Psychoanalysis and self experience*. Hill & Wang.

Brewster, F. (2022). The racial complex: Disassociation and the search for unification with the self. In S. Carpani (Ed.), *Anthology of contemporary clinical classics: The new ancestors* (pp. 71–79). Routledge.

Cambray, J. (2022). Moments of complexity and enigmatic action: A Jungian view of the therapeutic field. In S. Carpani (Ed.), *Anthology of contemporary clinical classics: The new ancestors* (pp. 80–94). Routledge.

Connolly, A. (2013). Out of the body: Embodiment and its vicissitudes. *Journal of Analytical Psychology, 58*(5), 636–656.

Corpt, E. A. (2013). Peasant in the analyst's chair: Reflections, personal and otherwise, on class and the forming of an analytic identity. *International Journal of Psychoanalytic Self-Psychology, 8*(1), 52–67.

Ghate, A. (2018). Traumatic disassociation of aspects of the feminine: An Asian cultural complex. *Journal of Analytical Psychology, 53*(2), 150–165.

Green, A. (1986). *On private madness.* Karnac.

Green, A. (2003). *Diachrony in psychoanalysis.* Free Association Books.

Hillman, J. (2005). *Senex and puer: Uniform edition of the writings of James Hillman Vol. 3.* Spring Publications.

Jung, C. G. (1960). *The collected works of C. G. Jung: Vol. 3. The psychogenesis of mental disease.* Princeton University Press.

Jung, C. G. (1966). *The collected works of C. G. Jung: Vol. 16. The practice of psychotherapy.* Princeton University Press.

Jung, C. G. (1969). *The collected works of C. G. Jung: Vol. 8. The structure and dynamics of the psyche.* Princeton University Press.

Jung, C. G. (1971) *The collected works of C. G. Jung: Vol. 6. Psychological types.* Princeton University Press.

Jung, C. G. (1976). *The collected works of C. G. Jung: Vol. 18. The symbolic life.* Princeton University Press.

Kiehl, E. (2016). '*You were not born here, so you are classless, you are free!*' Social class and cultural complex in analysis. *Journal of Analytical Psychology, 61*(4), 465–480.

Knox, J. (1999). The relevance of attachment theory to the contemporary Jungian view of the internal world: Internal working models, implicit memory, internal objects. *Journal of Analytical Psychology, 44*(4), 511–530.

Knox, J. (2007). The fear of love: The denial of self in relationship. *Journal of Analytical Psychology, 52*(5), 543–563.

Levy, I., Huang, S., & Bonanno, G. (2018). Trajectories of resilience and dysfunction following potential trauma: A review and statistical evaluation. *Clinical Psychology Review, 63*(July), 41–55.

Luci, M. (2020). Displacement as trauma and trauma as displacement in the experience of refugees. *Journal of Analytical Psychology, 65*(2), 260–280.

Oliver, K. (2015). Psychoanalysis and deconstruction. *Journal of French and Francophone Philosophy, 23*(2), 35–44.

Sennett, R., & Cobb, J. (1972). *The hidden injuries of class.* Knopf.

Singer, T., & Kimbles, S. (2004). *The cultural complex: Contemporary Jungian perspectives on psyche and society.* Routledge.

Solomon, H. M. (1998). The self in transformation: The passage from a two- to a three-dimensional internal world. *Journal of Analytical Psychology, 43*(2), 225–238.

Steiner, J. (1993). *Psychic retreats: Pathological organizations in psychotic, neurotic and borderline patients.* Routledge.

West, M. (2013). Trauma and the transference-countertransference: Working with the bad object and the wounded self. *Journal of Analytical Psychology, 58*(1), 73–98.

Winborn, M. (2022). Whispering at the edges: engaging ephemeral phenomena. *Journal of Analytical Psychology, 67*(1), 363–374.

Wirtz, U. (2022). Traumatic experiences and transformation of consciousness. In S. Carpani (Ed.), *Anthology of contemporary clinical classics: The new ancestors* (pp. 221–236). Routledge.

Chapter 15

End notes – gaining joy

The puella aspect of the personality evolves over time through listening and gathering the pieces into an authentic personality. This includes an emphasis on the body as part of soul work, deepening into the layers of her psychological complexity. Puella expresses the restlessness of the psyche seeking more than the complacency of the here and now. At issue is not to solve or completely understand but to learn about and use these aspects consciously. Although many of the examples here are feminine, they apply to the psychological life of all people. From learning to live with loss, lack and being imperfect, puella can emerge into love for herself and others. The puella life-force, when embodied and intentional, is aimed towards conscious awareness and integration. As we uncover the psyche, her mystery opens and connects to an intensity and desire for a vibrant and rewarding life. As spoken by Sojourner Truth, in 'And a'n't I a woman?'

> And raising herself to her full height, and her voice to a pitch like rolling thunders, she asked 'And a'n't I a woman? Look at me! Look at me! Look at my arm! (and she bared her right arm to the shoulder, showing her tremendous muscular power). I have ploughed, and planted, and gathered into barns, and no man could head me!
> (Mabee & Newhouse, 1995, p. x)

Well-being links us to others through the processes of emotional and social connection. The intersecting of Jungian thought with other analytical and philosophical perspectives expands this exploration. After all, the psyche has many mirrors. We need our body, mind and soul to do the mirroring to create within ourselves and in society a thoughtful, contemplative and reflective state.

The search unveils all that unsettles. It requires attention to the process, attunement to what is needed, acknowledging the importance of inner work. Opening to the puella is an invitation and opportunity to open the psyche to elements at the periphery of our minds. It's exhilarating some days and exhausting other days. It means uncovering and re-examining the recent and ancestral past. A puella type said,

> External forces are tough enough to wrestle with, forces of epic proportions to battle against. Cluelessly fumbling through life where truth gets less obvious.

> In the back of my mind is this fear of being a burden ... is that a common fear? I feel substantially less wise but there is a new sense of calm and stability. It is more regulated but also less bridled. Small but big shifts are happening. Little earthquakes? Is this to be expected? Common? I have an infinite amount to still unlearn and learn ... even with so much unknown, a very tragic family on both sides ... a miracle we've made it this far ...

Life is a series of deaths and rebirths. We all outgrow patterns, people, goals. If frightened, defensive and without a flexible personality, the puella struggles to live. There is melancholy behind this pose; putting on a false front to the world makes her feel less real and more disconnected from others. These contradictory feelings stress her body and soul, giving rise to the need to find herself. Her unfolding involves revealing her heart and communicating it with vulnerability.

'The presence of internal absence, although harmful, implies a space to be filled, a lack to be given attention. It is a call for the potential of the positive to emerge ... it allows for new thought and fresh experience' (Kohon, 1999, pp. 114–115). Wounds resulting from the holes in the personality, the undeveloped areas, once understood and integrated gradually offer the hope of development. Puella is filling a space that is key to understanding female development, not by using the male model as the rule, but by understanding and appreciating the differences and different contributions all orientations offer. As Jung said,

> This is how you must live – without reservation, whether in giving or withholding, according to what the circumstances requires. Then you will get through. After all, if you should still get stuck, there is always the enantiodromia from the unconscious, which opens new avenues.
>
> (Jung, 1987, p. 156)

Anxiety is a response to fear of the unknown along with the responsibility to be oneself. It is insufficient to retreat into avoidance, grandiosity and various forms of withdrawal; instead, moving forward requires meeting head on the challenges to old structures and monuments. Remaining lost in the self-consciousness, self-aggrandisement or self-exaltation of unconscious reactions will not suffice. Hope arises, not through illusion or self-delusion, nor from retreat into isolated bubbles. We need to know how we got here and where we came from to get through the inevitable moments of breakdown to emerge into recovery. With each time, moment and cycle, there is opportunity for greater knowledge and wisdom.

The inner life takes a path of meaning. It tends towards self-surrender, chooses the individual trail, not the crowded roads. The way is long, hard. The reward is intangible. Faced with the unknown we tend to fantasy, assumptions, anticipations and fears. Some of this is based on memory, the vestiges of past experiences good and bad. Some of it is based on possibility, the potentials within our personality – that which is not yet but could be.

Puella, a previously ignored aspect of the psyche, is of course not fully developed. She is becoming, ever growing and ever young, filled with promise. The many issues denoted here are not easily accessible, but from facing them we gain knowledge of the intricacies of the puella aspects of the personality. She is not simple; she exists in places we might have missed. When understood, the sorrows and losses become meaningful and emerge into creativity. Her journey is through melancholia and into accessing and manifesting the spark of the unusual.

A dreamer with many puella aspects to her personality walked on a path, passing a priest carving a cross out of stone. She did not stop but passed on. Then she saw a small shovel and began to dig and hit something. She then used her hands and found a stone made of a string of moons on one side and string of suns on the other. The face was indistinct but round in shape. She was going to take this stone, even though a piece was missing. The dreamer was raised in a religion but had long ago parted from it, like in the dream. She had no idea of the medieval alchemical references in the image but recognised it signified a process of becoming and creating balance. She wondered how she would find the missing piece and what she would do with herself. The self was calling, and even though the past was vacant with emotionally absent parents and a family that could not match her intensity, she had contended with all this as she aimed to develop an individual self. She needed to shake the narrative to see where it would take her. There was apprehension and excitement of the unknown. The question is who am I? What is the centre of myself?

The journey of puella is to extricate herself from the psychological retreats of obsessions, food and substance addictions and the numerous other mechanisms of internal distancing to the healing and joyful layers of the psyche. The energy becomes amassed by breaking patterns that no longer fit, peeling off the dross and being real. The psyche looks to complete itself, fill in the lack and unify. Its quest for truth and fulfilment is an organic, developmental and relational process. Rediscovery of the puella, the honouring of vigour and fortitude, the creative edge and her authenticity make sense of her losses, yearnings, needs, anxieties. From this process of evolving and becoming she becomes more defined, secure and stable. The conscious life, fed by the layers of the unconscious with its personal and collective impact, is enriched from valuing and knowing the puella.

Accessing joy means an openness and appreciation of oneself and honouring one's place in the world. As Swiss Jungian analyst Verena Kast noted (2003, p. 38),

> Emotion is an expression of the self ... If we decide we no longer want to hide behind empty shells, then we will have to allow certain emotions more room. We will have to let ourselves laugh louder, cry louder, and shout for joy.

References

Jung, C. G. (1987). *C. G. Jung speaking: Interviews and encounters.* Princeton University Press.
Kast, V. (2003). *Joy, inspiration, and hope.* Texas A&M University Press.
Kohon, G. (Ed). (1999). *The dead mother, the work of André Green.* Routledge
Mabee, C., & Newhouse, S. M. (1995). *Sojourner truth: Slave, prophet, legend.* New York University Press.

Index

abjection 33
Aciman, A.: *Homo Irrealis* 50
adolescent 107–108
affective emotional engagement, in therapy 123
alchemy 120, 127
Anima (Hillman) 84–85, 96–97, 110–111
anima archetype 7; *see also* archetype
animus 84–85, 92, 96–97, 104, 110–111, 145
archetypal girl/woman 4–8; etymology of puella 11; modern 11–12; mythology of puella 8–11; plurality of psyche 12–15
archetype 3, 6–8, 13, 22, 40, 46, 63, 84, 95, 106, 108, 111, 113, 145; core 99–103; girl/woman *see* archetypal girl/woman
Artemis 8–10
'as-if' personality 50, 51, 57, 58, 107; therapist and 54–56; *see also* personality
Austen, J.: *Pride and Prejudice* 60
authenticity 24, 78, 85–86, 151
authentic personality 149; *see also* personality

beauty 9, 17, 69–72, 79–80, 115; and body in analysis 73–74; cultural influences 76–77; facing inwards 77–79; melancholia 72–73; screaming 74–76
Benjamin, J. 53
Bisagni, F. 137
The Bloody Chamber (Carter) 101
bluebeard fairy tale 94–96, 104; animus questioned 96–97; archetypal core 99–103; demon lover 97–99; heroine challenges 103
body: beauty and 73–74; effect on 112–113; mother's body 33–34; out of 116–118; and psyche 145; unlinked to 83–84
bond of puella 47–48
bones of the father 39–41; disappointment and doubt 41–44; gaze 45–46; loss 45; puella-father bond/bondage 47–48; redefining fathers 48
Britton, R. 125
Bronte, E.: *Withering Heights* 100
Butler, J. 3, 82, 86, 92, 116; *Gender Trouble* 82, 89, 91

Carter, A.: *The Bloody Chamber* 101
catastrophic annihilation 133
Catullus 11
Chinese Book of Wisdom 145
Cixous, H. 33, 71
Colman, W. 15, 128
complex 2, 3, 12, 13, 19, 29, 31, 32, 35, 37, 40, 43–45, 47, 51, 55, 56, 70, 72, 82, 84, 86, 89, 92, 97–103, 112, 120, 127, 137–138; *Electra complex* 88; feelings of impotence 146–147; negative father complex 39, 43; notion of 142; precarious identity 138–142; self-fictions and cultural conflicts 142–146; traumatic complex 146
compulsive negative thoughts and behaviours 71, 77, 78
countertransference 51, 54, 55, 61, 144, 146
cross-disciplinary approach 3
culture: conflicts 142–146; framework 87, 89; ideals of beauty 76–77

Damasio, A. 52
deadness 34–36, 90, 115, 116
De Beauvoir, S. 89; *The Second Sex* 13
demon lovers 97–99, 101–103
depression 1, 11, 19, 23, 32, 35, 73–77, 83, 85, 90, 101, 108, 121–125, 131, 133–134, 140, 143
De Saussure, F. 60

diachrony, of dreams 60–62; inspiration 64–67; meaning of time 62–64; *see also* dreams
Dionysus 105
docta puella 11
dreams 7, 11, 12, 17, 19, 20, 23, 29–32, 34, 39, 43, 44, 46, 50–53, 83, 84, 86, 95, 99, 106, 107, 109, 111, 112, 116, 117, 119, 122, 123, 126, 127, 132, 133; destiny dreams 87; *diachrony* of *see diachrony*, of dreams; and symbols 2; unrealistic dreams 22

ego consciousness 53, 90, 134
Egyptian mythology 106; *see also* myth/mythology
Eigen, M. 116
Electra complex 88; *see also* complex
emotions 58, 151; deadness 34–36; learning 52; and motivational energy 133
engagement 2, 41, 52, 77, 106, 107, 111, 120, 123, 129, 147
eros (feminine principle) 12, 19, 84, 86, 96, 97, 101, 102, 105, 125
etymology, of puella 4, 11

fairy tale 69; bluebeard fairy tale *see* bluebeard fairy tale
fascist state of mind 137–138; feelings of impotence 146–147; precarious identity 138–142; self-fictions and cultural conflicts 142–146
father 4, 5, 9–11, 34, 56–58, 87, 88, 95–97, 102, 105; bones of *see* bones of the father
feminine 5, 7; puella and treatment of 10
Ferro, A.: *mental anorexia* 118
fixities 86–88
flexible psyche 82; *see also* psyche/psychic
Fordham, M. 51, 130
foundationalist models of identity 82
Freud, S. 8, 44
furor poeticus 65

Gander, F. 28–29
gender 84, 88–91; ground-breaking theory of 89; identity 18, 92; roles 103; stereotypes 5, 8
Gender Trouble (Butler) 82, 89, 91
girl/woman, archetype 4–8; etymology of puella 11; modern 11–12; mythology of puella 8–11; plurality of psyche 12–15; *see also* mother

Greek myths 8, 105; *see also* myth/mythology
Green, A. 3, 27–28, 32, 34, 45, 51, 56, 78, 123, 125, 132
ground-breaking theory of gender 89

heroine, challenges of 103
Herzog, J.: *father hunger* 45
Hillman, J. 7, 20, 109; *Anima* 84–85, 96–97, 110–111; betrayal 99; *The Puer Papers* 1

impotence, feelings of 146–147
individual expression 82
individuation process 5, 83, 91, 128, 138, 145, 147
inspiration 64–67
intrapsychic personality 37

Jewish mythology 60; *see also* myth/mythology
Joplin, J. 75
joy 149–151
Jung, C. G. 5, 7, 8, 33, 71, 100, 105, 115, 119, 126, 133–135, 140, 141, 150; analysis process 67, 128–129, 134; analytical psychology 1, 63, 123, 126, 129, 147; analytical treatment 120, 129, 135; 'blocking of libido' 55; conception of the complex 92; description of the archetypes 6; *Essays on a Science of Mythology* 30; 'Essays on Contemporary Events' 18; 'The "eternal child"' 1; 'General Aspects of Dream Psychology' 6; ideas 96; imagination 66; individuation process 5, 83, 91, 128, 138, 145, 147; *Integration of the Personality* 111; 'The Meaning of Psychology for Modern Man' 50; *Memories, Dreams, Reflections* 2, 25, 66; 'On Psychic Energy' 20; 'On the Psychology of the Unconscious' 117; perspective 121, 137; 'The Philosophical Tree' 121; 'Psychological Aspects of the Mother Archetype' 17–18; psychological treatment 145; 'A Psychological View of Conscience' 67; psychology 5, 127, 141, 145, 146; 'The Psychology of the Child Archetype' 1, 6; 'The Psychology of the Unconscious' 62; *Red Book* 2, 19, 51, 66, 129; self-regulating system 65; symbol 129–130; 'The Tavistock Lectures'

121; Terry Lectures 15; therapeutic process 145; transcendent function 53, 128; 'Transformation Symbolism in the Mass' 21; *unconscious* 66
Jung, E. 104

Kafka, F.: *Letter to My Father* 48
Kast, V. 58, 64, 151
Kerényi, K.: *Essays on a Science of Mythology* 30
Kristeva, J. 3, 33, 84, 90

libido movement 19, 29, 78, 106, 119, 121
linguistic structure 89
logos (masculine principle) 84
loss of symbolic 125–126; absence and presence 132–133; into depression 133–134; feeling a gap 134–135; intrusion of others 126–128; Jungian analysis 128–129; symbolism 129–130; void state 130–131
love 46, 107, 140, 143; ability to 111–112; emotions of 113; four ways of 12

masochistic 46, 86
meaning, of time 62–64
melancholia 72–73, 126
modern girl/woman 11–12
Morrison, T. 14
mortification 127
mother 27–28, 41, 42, 47, 56, 73, 75, 87, 94, 95, 97–99, 101, 117, 122, 142; The analysis 36–37; body 33–34; deadness 34–36; male experiencing the blank mother 28–30; The trap 30–31; *see also* girl/woman, archetype
mourning 90–91
myth/mythology: of beauty 77; of Demeter 8, 30; Egyptian mythology 106; fairy tales and 95; Greek myths 8, 105; Jewish mythology 60; of Persephone (Kore) 8, 30; of puella 8–11; Sumerian mythology 105

narcissism 15, 69, 113, 115
narcissistic defence 74
negative father complex 39, 43, 44, 47; *see also* complex
normative heterosexuality 89
notion of complexes 142; *see also* complex

Ovid: *Metamorphoses* 105

performance 88–91
performativity 82–83; actions 91–92; *anima* and *animus* 84–85; authenticity 85–86; fixities 86–87; mourning 90–91; performance 88–89; unlinked to the body 83–84
Perrault, C. 95, 99
Persephone (Kore) 8–11, 30, 86
persona 109–110
persona-idealised images 115
personality 1, 10, 84, 120–121; 'as-if' personality 50, 51, 54–58; authentic personality 149; changes in consciousness and 144; concept and 5; cross-cultural aspects of 146; and culture 3; development of 4, 60; exploration and integration 21; feminine growth in 9; and femininity 4; fragmentation of 131; impoverishment of 131; integral structure of 146; integration in 139; intrapsychic personality 37; modern personality 12; and psychic disturbance 146; psychic personality 113; puella aspect of 2, 12, 14, 18, 69, 82, 95, 115, 137, 149, 151; *puer* 18, 107; *puer aeternus* 105
Philips, A. 44
Pizarnik, A. 69–71, 77–79; 'Clock' 75; 'Drawing' 73; 'Nemo' 72; 'Sex, Night' 80
pluralism 12
plurality, of psyche 12–15; *see also* psyche/psychic
precarious identity 138–142
Pride and Prejudice (Austen) 60
Proust, M.: *Within a Budding Grove* 4; *Swann's Way: Remembrance of Things Past* 115
psyche/psychic 8, 45, 54, 122, 151; African woman 10; body and 145; and body, intersection of 117; deadness 115; disturbance 146; energy 111, 121; flexible psyche 82; function 52; love and attention 106; mobility 34, 37; nourishment 121; plurality of 12–15; process 120; reality 34, 41, 63; retreats/systems of defence 131; seeking 149; self-discovery process in 15; symbolisation of 85; tenderness of 113; void 41
psychology/psychological: behaviour 65; development 7, 13, 99, 102, 135;

dissociation 113; process 39, 57, 67, 115; trauma 42; wounds 45, 77
psychotherapy 44, 90
puella 1–5, 7, 12–15, 28–44, 46, 60, 62, 63, 85–87, 90, 91, 95, 97–98, 100–102, 105, 116, 118, 119–123, 125, 126, 130–134, 137, 139, 141, 150; aspect of personality 149, 151; beauty *see* beauty; bond of 47–48; curiosity 100; *docta puella* 11; etymology of 11; journey of 151; life-force 149; mythology of 8–11; personality of 115; presence of absence 132–133; psychological understanding 123; puella's shadow 17–25; puer and 105; self-agency of 41; shadow 17–22, 24–25; as symbolic and psychological figure 2; task 82; *threshold experiences* 22; types 84; women and 2
Puella aeterna 11
puer 18, 20; archetypal spectrum 108; disembodiment and psychological distancing in 108; emotional and relational wounds 106; and puella 105; puer quandary *see* puer quandary; shadow 108–109; task of 108
puer aeternus 20, 105
puer quandary 105–107; ability to love 111–112; adolescent 107–108; animus and anima 110–111; effect on body 112–113; persona 109–110; shadow 108–109; *see also* puer

Red Book (Jung) 2, 19, 51, 66, 129
regression 35, 134, 138, 146
repression 5, 18, 29, 35, 64, 66, 74, 85, 101
Rose, J. 77

Samuels, A. 12, 51
The Second Sex (de Beauvoir) 13
self-absorption 71, 78, 131
self-consciousness 115, 146, 150
self-emergence, transcendent function for 120
self-encapsulated system 45
self-fictions 142–146
self-perpetuating negative cycle 47
shadow 5, 6, 12, 14, 15, 41, 43–46, 73, 76, 84, 86, 90, 95, 100, 106, 112, 113, 119, 121, 122, 126, 128, 144; puella's shadow 17–25; puer's shadow 108–109
Solomon, H. 54–55

somatic function 52
Steiner, J. 131
Stein, M. 4, 54
Sumerian mythology 105; *see also* myth/mythology
Swann's Way: Remembrance of Things Past (Proust) 115
symbolic 1, 2, 8, 20, 21, 51–53, 60, 61, 63, 85, 89, 95, 116, 118, 123; loss of *see* loss of symbolic; process 129
symbolisation, of psyche 85; *see also* psyche/psychic
symbolism 50, 51, 70, 129–130
symbol of the empty chair 51–53
symbolon 63
syzygy 84

therapist 51, 61, 120, 122, 133; and 'as-if' personality 54–56
time 108; and ideology 6; meaning of 62–64; movement in 7
traditional psychoanalytic theory 41
transcendent function 52, 53, 123, 128, 141, 145; for self-emergence 120
transference 51, 53–55, 60, 61, 126, 127, 133, 144, 146
traumatic complex 55, 146; *see also* complex
triple goddess cycle 8
Truth, S.: 'And a'n't I a woman?' 149

unconscious process 57, 111; creative and symbolic resources of 134
unconscious psyche 62, 64, 85
unitary psyche 138; *see also* psyche/psychic

Varo, R.: *Woman Leaving the Psychoanalyst* 39
virginity 9
vocation 85
void state 125–126, 130–131; absence and presence 132–133; into depression 133–134; filling the gap 134–135; intrusion of others 126–128; Jungian analysis 128–129; symbolism 129–130
Von Franz, M. L. 20, 98, 110

Waldron, S. 57
Western cultures: beauty in 71; heritage 9
Wheatley, P.: "On Imagination" 17
Wilde, O.: *The Picture of Dorian Grey* 101

Winnicott, D. 31; puer 106
Withering Heights (Bronte) 100
Within a Budding Grove (Proust) 4
Wolff, T. 4, 22
woman, archetype 4–8; etymology of puella 11; modern 11–12; mythology of puella 8–11; plurality of psyche 12–15; *see also* archetype
Woman Leaving the Psychoanalyst (Varo) 39
Wordsworth, W.: "My Heart Leaps Up" 25

Milton Keynes UK
Ingram Content Group UK Ltd.
UKHW021142281124
451785UK00006B/62